ACCOUNTS PAYABLE
WORK EXPERIENCE
USING QUICKBOOKS ONLINE

Step by step practical guide

STERLING LIBS FCCA, FCPA

PRACTICAL WORK EXPERIENCE IN ACCOUNTANCY – ACCOUNTS PAYABLE.

The role of the Accounts Payable clerk involves providing financial, administrative and clerical support to the organisation. Their role is to complete payments and control expenses by receiving payments, plus processing, verifying and reconciling invoices. A typical Accounts Payable job description also highlights the day-to-day management of all payment cycle activities in a timely and efficient manner.

Professionals who work in this business function are responsible for keeping business operations funded. They receive invoices from company suppliers and other costs of goods sources and account for them individually.

For an Accounts Payable role, an understanding of basic bookkeeping and accounting skills is required. Whilst a degree is not mandatory for this role, a degree in the following subjects would be beneficial for an Accounts Payable career:

- Finance or Economics
- Business Studies
- Accounting

Having an AAT qualification (level 2-4) and ACCA Foundation stage will also be very beneficial for a career as an accounts payable clerk.

Attention to detail and data entry skills are important requirements for an Accounts Payable job description. In this role, you will be interacting with employers and suppliers/vendors on a daily basis, so it is imperative that you are able to interact on a professional manner at all times.

If you are looking for an Accounts Payable role, this book will give you a good head start and help build your confidence and competence.

On page 1 of this book, you will find detailed job description of an Accounts Payable clerk and do also have a look at the table of contents of this book for the details of what is covered.

Your role in a nutshell

Your role as an Accounts Payable/Purchase Ledger Clerk is to provide a professional and efficient service to the finance function, monitoring how much is owed at all times and providing accurate financial information to the Finance Director or manager as needed.

Table of Contents

NOTE TO THE READER

This step by step guide is designed to provide practical information on how to work as an Accounts payable clerk using QuickBooks Online accounting software.

Every effort has been made to make this book as complete and accurate as possible. However, no assurance is given that the information is comprehensive in its coverage or that it is suitable for dealing with your particular situation. Accordingly, the information provided should not be relied upon as a substitute for independent research. It is sold with the understanding that the publisher and author are not engaged in rendering any accounting, legal, or other professional advice nor do they have any responsibility for updating or revising any information presented herein.

No representation or warranty (express or implied) is given as to the accuracy or completeness of the information contained in this book, and, to the extent permitted by law, the Author/publisher, its members, employees and agents do not accept or assume any liability, responsibility or duty of care for any consequences of you or anyone else acting, or refraining to act, in reliance on the information contained in this book or for any decision based on it.
 If legal or other expert assistance is required, the services of a competent professional should be sought.

The author and publisher cannot warrant that the material contained herein will continue to be accurate nor that it is completely free of errors when published. Readers should verify statements before relying on them.

Purpose

This book is information only and has been prepared for general guidance for those who are interested in learning how to work as an Accounts payable clerk/purchase ledger clerk as described in the job description of an Accounts payable clerk/purchase ledger clerk in page 1 of this book and is current at the time of publication.

About this book

This book a step by step guide designed to provide practical information on how to work as an Accounts Payable/Purchase Ledger Clerk using QuickBooks Online accounting software.

WORKING AS AN ACCOUNTS PAYABLE CLERK

If you choose to work as an Accounts Payable/Purchase Ledger Clerk, what are you most likely to be doing?

Job profile summary:

As an Accounts payable clerk, you will be fully accountable for the whole purchase ledger process, from purchase orders through to invoices and supplier statement reconciliation.

Your main duties will include matching and coding invoices, preparing and running BACS payments, reconciling supplier statements and working out VAT payments. You will generally work as part of the finance team; however, you may work independently in a smaller organisation.

In a nutshell, your role as an Accounts Payable Clerk is to provide a professional and efficient service to the finance function, monitoring how much is owed at all times and providing accurate financial information to the Finance Director or manager as needed.

Working hours:

Typical work hours are 9:00 am – 5:00 pm Monday to Friday.

Key responsibilities:

Your responsibilities will depend on the size of the company you work for, and they can include any or all of the following duties and responsibilities:
,
- *Matching, checking and coding invoices*
- *Working out VAT payments*
- *Making payments via BACS and cheques*
- *Processing staff expenses*
- *Setting up of new supplier accounts and maintaining existing account details*
- *Reconciliation of supplier statements*
- *Filing invoices*
- *Managing petty cash*
- *Data entry*
- *Reviewing systems and processes and making improvements where necessary*
- *Raising purchase orders*
- Processing supplier invoices
- *Check and reconcile supplier statements*
- *Prepare payment runs to pay suppliers*
- *Deal with purchase enquiries*
- *File invoices and statements*
- *Process staff expenses*
- Posting standing orders and direct debits
- Doing other ad hoc administrative duties as and when needed.

Testing your practical accounting knowledge (17 Questions & Answers)

Question 1: Under what legal entities can businesses operate in the UK?

Answer: *Sole Trader, Partnership, Company Limited by Shares (LTD), Company Limited by guarantee (Charity), Community Interest Company (CIC), Limited Liability Partnership (LLP) Designated Activity Company, Public Listed Company (PLC)*

Question 2: What is a tax year and what is a financial year?

Answer: *A tax year in the UK is from the 6th of April the current year to the following 5th April next year.*
A financial year is a 12-month period commencing from the date the business starts trading or gets registered with Companies House (UK)

Question 3: What are the three key stages of the accounting cycle?

Answer: *Analysis stage, Recording stage and Reporting stage*

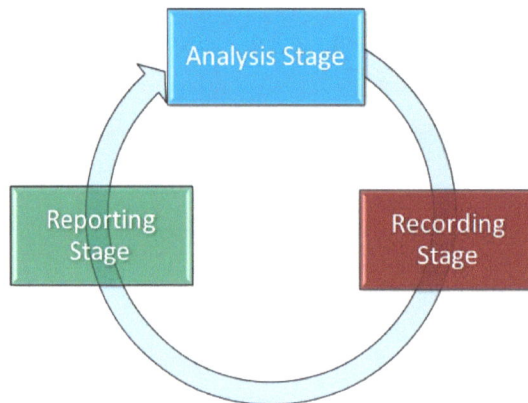

Question 4: Briefly describe what you should do at each of the three stages listed above.

Answer:
a. *Analysis Stage*
  - *Classification of financial documents*
  - *Checking that the correct values are reflected in the financial documents*
  - *Making sure that the documents are within the financial year date to which they relate to.*

b. *Recording stage*
  - *It is mostly about data entry*
  - *Using double-entry bookkeeping principles*

c. *Reporting stage*
  - *Checking for any errors in the nominal accounts*
  - *Making yearend/period end adjustments*
  - *Producing yearend/period end reports and statements for filing with government agencies (Companies House & HMRC in the UK)*

Question 5: What are the key steps in the sales ledger (Accounts Receivable process)

Answer:

Accounting process for Sales (Accounts Receivable)

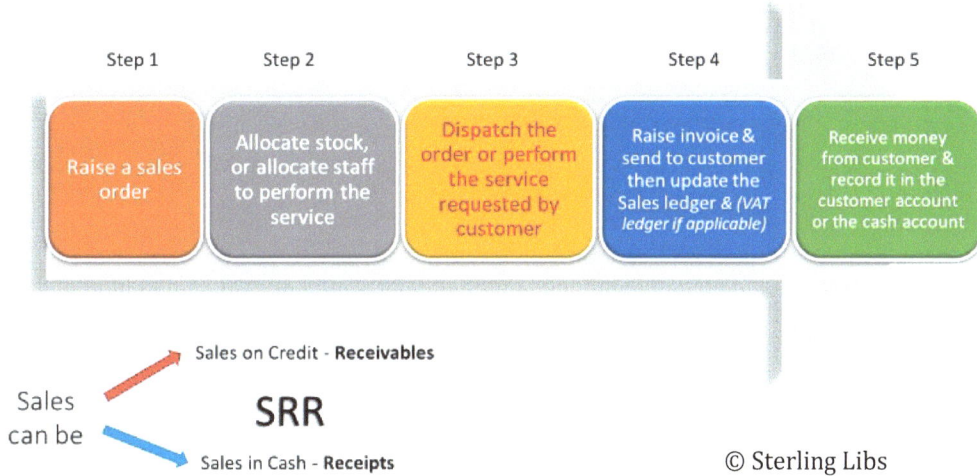

Step 1	Step 2	Step 3	Step 4	Step 5
Raise a sales order	Allocate stock, or allocate staff to perform the service	Dispatch the order or perform the service requested by customer	Raise invoice & send to customer then update the Sales ledger & (VAT ledger if applicable)	Receive money from customer & record it in the customer account or the cash account

Sales can be:
- Sales on Credit - **Receivables**
- Sales in Cash - **Receipts**

SRR

© Sterling Libs

Question 6: What are the key steps in the purchase ledger (Accounts payable) process

Answer:

Accounting process for Purchases (Accounts payable)

Step 1	Step 2	Step 3	Step 4	Step 5	Monthly
Raise a new purchase order	Send the purchase order to the preferred supplier	Receive delivery from the supplier	Update the ledgers with invoice from supplier	Pay supplier as per agreed days	Reconcile supplier statements periodically

Purchases can be:
- Purchases on Credit - **Payables**
- Purchases in Cash - **Payments**

PPP

© Sterling Libs

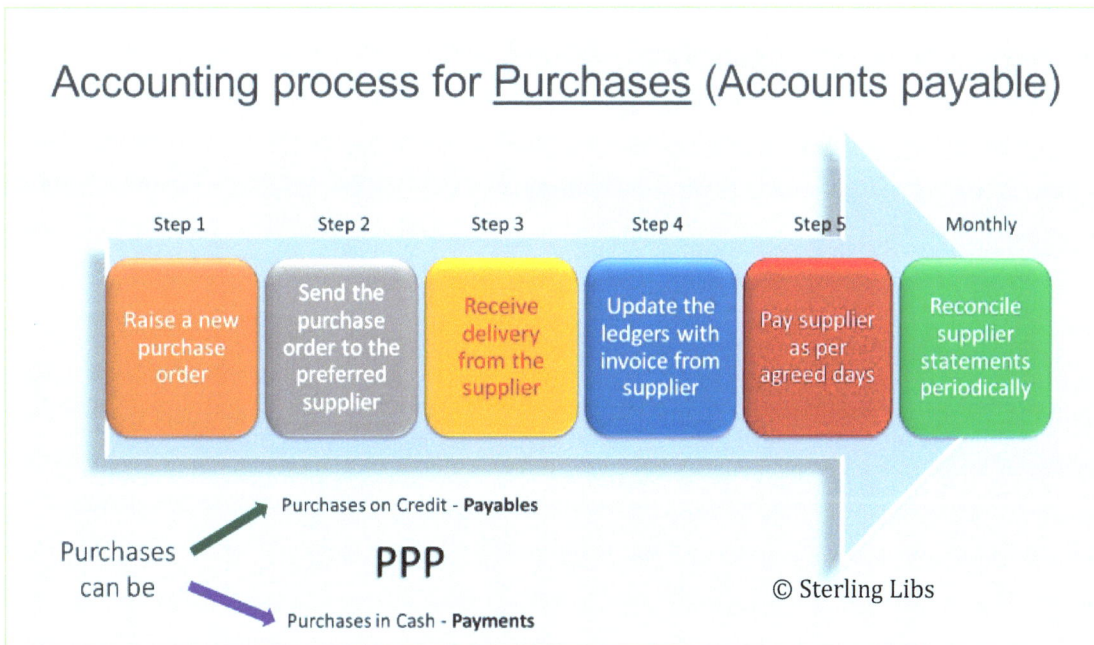

Question 7: When does a business need to register for PAYE in the UK?

Answer: *When it starts employing people or becomes an employer*

Question 8: When does a business have to register for VAT?
Answer: *Compulsory **registration**. You must **register for VAT** if: your **VAT** taxable turnover is more than £85,000 (the 'threshold') in a 12-month period or if you expect to go over the threshold in a single 30-day period.*

Question 9: What is the current standard rate of VAT in the UK
Answer: *20%*

Question 10: What is the current rate of corporation tax in the UK?
Answer: *19% for tax year 2017/2018*

Question 11: What is normally done at the month end close process
Answer: *Three key steps are usually performed to manage the end-of-the-month accounting process successfully. They are:*

Description of the key steps	What to do at each stage (the tasks)
Key step 1: Checking the general ledger accounts for errors & making the necessary corrections	• *Correct the general ledger account errors including mispostings and inaccuracies.*
Key step 2: Doing Adjustments and Reconciliations	• *Financial adjustments, e.g. interest payments adjustments, prepayments, accruals and depreciation* • *Control account reconciliations: Debtors' control account, Creditors' control account, VAT control account, Bank account, Wages account etc.* • *Balance sheet reconciliation (Reconciliation of the Assets, Liabilities, Equity & Reserves)* • *Calculations of closing balances of the accounts after adjustments & reconciliations*
Key step 3: Reporting to senior management	• *Producing a profit & Loss statement and other various management reports if necessary.*

Question 12: Why is it important to do bank reconciliation?

Answer:
A bank reconciliation is used to compare your records to those of your bank, to see if there are any differences between these two sets of records for your cash transactions. The ending balance of your version of the cash records is known as the book balance, while the bank's version is called the bank balance. It is extremely common for there to be differences between the two balances, which you should track down and adjust in your own records. If you were to ignore these differences, there would eventually be substantial variances between the amount of cash that you think you have and the amount the bank says you actually have in an account. The result could be an overdrawn bank account, bounced checks, and overdraft fees. In some cases, the bank may even elect to shut down your bank account.

It is also useful to complete a bank reconciliation to see if any customer checks have bounced, or if any checks you issued were altered or even stolen and cashed without your knowledge. Thus, fraud detection is a key reason for completing a bank reconciliation. When there is an ongoing search for fraudulent transactions, it may be necessary to reconcile a bank account on a daily basis, in order to obtain early warning of a problem.

Question 13: Which government agencies do businesses in the UK need to submit accounts and returns to?

Answer:
Her Majesty's Revenue and Customs (HMRC) and Companies House.

Question 14: Which reports usually are submitted to the government agencies you have stated above?

Answer:
  a) HMRC – *Tax returns, VAT Returns,*
  b) Companies House - *Statutory annual accounts and annual returns*

Question 15: And who is legally responsible for submitting the reports you've stated above?

Answer: *The Director(s) of the company*

Question 16: What key competencies will help you work effectively as an accountant?

Answer:
a. Attention to detail
b. Analytical skills
c. Numerical skills
d. Communication skills and teamwork
e. Accounting software skills
f. Speed and accuracy

Question 17: What code of ethics are accountants expected to abide by?

Answer:
a. Integrity
b. Objectivity
c. Confidentiality
d. Professional competence and due care
e. Adopting professional behaviour

The professional code of ethics you are required to abide by as an accountant.

Under the Code of Professional Ethics, as an accountant, you must follow these five principles:

1. **Integrity.**

You must be straightforward and honest in all professional and business relationships.

2. **Objectivity.**

You must not compromise professional or business judgment because of bias, conflict of interest or the undue influence of others.

3. **Professional competence and due care.**

You must maintain professional knowledge and skill (in practice, legislation and techniques) to ensure that a client or employer receives competent professional service.

4. **Confidentiality.**

You must not disclose confidential professional or business information or use it to your advantage unless you have explicit permission to disclose it, or a legal or professional right or duty to disclose it.

5. Professional behaviour.

You must comply with relevant laws and regulations and avoid any action that may bring disrepute to the profession.

Professional Ethics | AAT. (n.d.). Retrieved from https://www.aat.org.uk/about-aat/professional-ethics

The key skills that can help you get and keep an accounting job

Skilled people in any profession are very valuable. So let me take this opportunity to talk to you about some of the skills you should look to develop at the early formative years of your accounting career.

Identifying the skills that lead to success in accounting will not only increase your job satisfaction but also make it easier for you to build your long-term career goals.

No matter how big a company ever gets, the need for an accounts department persists. Perhaps that focus is on auditing, maybe management or tax and finance related. Chances are, you will start in one of two career paths – technical or commercial.

Accounting requires certain hard skills, such as mathematics and expertise with accounting software. Thorough knowledge of relevant laws and regulations is necessary for many positions, too.

However, accounting also requires some soft skills that you might not learn in school but will help you land and keep a job.

Staying current with technology is perhaps the most significant pressure you will continuously face in your accounting and finance career. As technology impacts on the way you do your job as an accountant, make sure you stay abreast of the changes and train and retrain to keep your skills up to date

Here is a list of six accounting skills that you should look to hone in your career as a professional accountant. Your CV/resume, cover letter, job application will be scrutinised for these skills and even during your job interviews – if you make it that far. It will serve you well to be in possession of these skills in increasing measure as you progress in your accounting career.

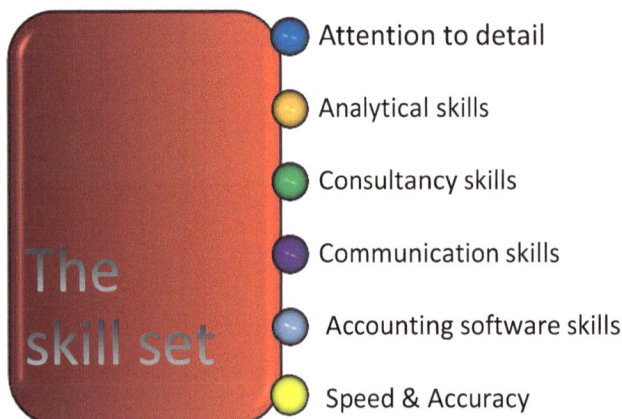

The skill set
- Attention to detail
- Analytical skills
- Consultancy skills
- Communication skills
- Accounting software skills
- Speed & Accuracy

Let me elaborate a bit more on each skill above.

Attention to detail

Attention to detail is an essential requirement for a successful accounting career. The ability to notice an error, inconsistency or discrepancy can often lead to discovering other inaccuracies. On the other hand, missing a small detail can affect the integrity of the organisation's financial records and may have dire consequences. It is therefore quite essential that you should have a detail-oriented approach to your work to ensure that financial records conform to standards, laws and regulations.

Analytical Skills

As an accountant, you must be analytical when examining documents and financial processes. The use of critical thinking skills to determine ways to make the organisation more financially efficient will be required of any good accountant. My experience in working with many businesses is that; the analytical skills help you develop ways to reduce costs, increase revenues, improve profits and eliminate waste.

You will also have to carefully evaluate financial performance and investigate financial investments at some point in your accountancy career as you keep growing and that my friend, will call for excellent analytical skills.

Hopefully, with the passage of time, you will be able to demonstrate this skill in greater measure.

Consultancy skills

The Accountant of the 21st century is more of a consultant than a person who merely deals with numbers. As a professional accountant of nowadays, you should also be a problem solver and possess sound judgement, and you shouldn't not jump to conclusions.

Good consultants study, consider the facts, ask questions, challenge the norm and then make a recommendation or a decision. They use their experience from previous assignments to solve new problems and challenges in your current assignment. They possess excellent written and oral communication skills as well as good listening skills. These are the kind of things you will be expected to do more of as the accountant of the 21st century because accounting software's are doing a lot more of what the traditional accountant of yesteryears used to do. So you need to evolve to what I would call – the Accounting consultant.

Communication skills

How are your written and verbal communication skills like?

You see, the accountant of the 21st century now interacts with a variety of people ranging from managers and directors to members of the accounting staff and various stakeholders in a business. You will meet people through the course of your work with a wide range of unique characteristics, not all of them pleasant or to your liking.
It is therefore important that train yourself to be able to clearly converse or correspond and to ask questions and discuss issues or discrepancies quite easily.
Also, accountants offer advice and make recommendations regarding the best financial business decisions. Therefore, being articulate and well presented will help a great deal here.

Accounting software skills

Gone are the days when accounting used to be done manually. Almost invariably, every business now uses some form of software to do their bookkeeping and accounts. From Excel to the more sophisticated ERP accounting software, accounting and financial analysis are now so much software based and the better you are in using any of these accounting software, the better you will be in your accounting career.

Accounting software all use the same basic principle of double entry, so if you are proficient in one, you will find it easy to learn any other accounting software relatively quickly.

I suggest therefore that you learn at least how to use one accounting software very well because that will act as a stepping stone for you learning other software should you change jobs and find that your new employer uses a different accounting software. At least know how to use one software proficiently.

Speed & Accuracy

You need to be conscious of the fact that accounting is a very dynamic profession and at times very highly pressured. If you are looking to be successful in your accounting career, you've got to develop a reputation for speed and dependability (producing accurate & trustworthy information).

Time is the currency of the 21st century. Business today is very, very dynamic. Employers are less and less patient with slow, incompetent employees because they recognise that customers will change suppliers overnight if someone else can serve them faster than the people they are currently dealing with.

So, your job, as you start developing your accountancy career is to develop a reputation for speed. Move fast on opportunities, move quickly when you see something that needs to be done. You've heard it said that whenever you want to get something done, give it to a busy man or woman.

Employees who have a reputation for moving quickly, attract more and more opportunities and possibilities to them and that is the kind of thing you want in the early years of your accountancy career development.

If you can combine your ability to determine your highest priority tasks with the commitment to getting it done quickly and accurately, you will find yourself progressing through your accounting career with flying colours and moving to the front/top of it. More and more doors and opportunities will open for you that you can't even imagine today.

One more thing – very, very important indeed.

Underlying all of the skills you will ever have is one very important and profound aspect of life you need to watch over. What am I talking about? Your attitude. That's right, has to do a lot with your quality of life and success in any career or profession.

Come to think it; you could be a genius as far as accounting is concerned and even have the most excellent and lofty practical experience there is to find. However, if you have a terrible attitude, you will realise soon or later that not many people would like to work with you or have dealings with you whatsoever. They would prefer keeping their distance from you. Is that good, you think, for your career? Not in the slightest if you ask me.

So, let me talk to you a little bit about attitude since it is such a crucial aspect of your job success as an accountant just as it is in any area of your life. Your attitude goes a long way in determining what company of people you will keep, what actions you will take, how successful you will be in your accounting career and above all, how much and how deep you will enjoy life. Something worth exploring, wouldn't you agree? Yes, of course.

Look, I can guarantee you that your current attitude is either helping you move forward or is making you lag behind in life. The good news though is this; your attitude is 100% under your control, and you can change it at any time to help support your career progression.

Your Life only gets better when you get better, and since there is no limit on how much better you can become, there is no limit on how much better your life can become. True? Well, judge for yourself.

Zig Ziglar once said; "*It's your attitude and not your aptitude that determines your altitude*".

Here then are some of the attitudes that I believe will help you make excellent progress in your accountancy career.

1. **Attitude of gratitude**

When you exude an attitude of gratitude at all times, you make people around you feel important. The truth is, everything you say or do that causes another person to feel better in any way also causes you to feel better to the same degree.

Haven't you realised that when you encourage, inspire, motivate someone else, you feel motivated, inspired and encouraged yourself?

And guess what...

The converse is true when you degrade, insult and abhor someone else, you feel the same too!

The need for appreciation is a deep subconscious desire of every individual you meet. When you satisfy this need, you will by all accounts become one of the most popular people in that person's world, and what is the key to expressing gratitude and appreciation? Simple, just say 'thank you' on every occasion and mean it.

You say thanks in a whole host of different ways: by giving compliments, admiration, giving encouragement, by unconditionally accepting people for who they are, by smiling, giving a hug, a pat on the back....., all these actions communicate one message ;-well done 'buddy' I am really proud of you'. If you become a finance manager, you should do more of this with your juniors.

In fact, the best way to ensure your happiness is to assist others to experience their own. "Those who bring Sunshine to others cannot keep it from themselves" James Banie
Be a professional, happy, gregarious and friendly accountant. It will do you good.

2.   A forgiving attitude
Jim Loehr & Tony Schwartz in their book; In the power of Full engagement, said: "*The richer and deeper the source of our emotional recovery, the more we refill our reserves and the more resilient we become.*"

You see, people are emotional beings. People decide emotionally then justify logically. Emotion comes first. So when we are hurt, our emotions immediately take over, and for some, this leads to prolonged periods of sulking and being grumpy, and they will justify it logically by saying that they are hurt. What they seem not to understand is that a lot of their emotional energy which could otherwise be expended in some other productive venture is being put to waste on destructive tendencies. So the faster they recover from any hurt through total and sincere forgiveness, the better for them.

I know it is not easy to forgive, but I also know that it is difficult to enjoy life in an accounting career if you are hurting from the inside.

So if there is anyone who has hurt you; whoever it is, or wherever it was, please forgive them. It could be your parent(s), your spouse, your close friend, your sibling, your pastor, teacher, work mate, it could be anyone and everyone really, whoever it is, find it in your heart to forgive and release them from the pain they have caused you. It's very noble, and it is an eternal act, which has both present and eternal rewards.

Forgiveness is a choice, and we all have to make that choice time and again if our relationships and careers are to be worth our time, effort and rewards thereof.
Be a forgiving accountant. Don't be a grumpy & bitter accountant.

3.   Courageous attitude
Courage is a very admirable quality. Your boldness will help you get as much as you need in life. The bold move makes you seem larger and more powerful than you are. More than that, the bold draw attention and what draws attention, draws power. We simply cannot keep our eyes off the audacious, can we? We can't wait to see their next bold move.
Everyone admires the bold; no one honours the timid, isn't that true?

Better still...

A courageous person is an upward and forward-looking person, he/she faces the future without fear but with determination, not with doubt but with faith. He/she is willing to take great chances and reach for new horizons and remake the world around them. They recognise that there is more to their life than the ordinary, they take the status quo and turn it around. It is simply magnetic and very inspiring to be around them. The good news is that you can be one of those very courageous ones as well.

The courageous individuals teach us to have our horizons limitless. Ultimately if we are to be true to our past, we also have to seize the future every day, and courage will help us make the most of our; time, abilities (effort), and opportunities that will ultimately help us make the most of our lives and accounting career.

And...

No matter how bitter the raw, how stony the accountancy road, courage enables us to persevere, not to falter or grow weary but to demand, strive and shape a better accountancy career for yourself!
Simply refuse to give up on the idea of the forward and upward move but ultimate triumph, despite the most extreme odds that you will sometimes face during your accountancy career. In some circumstances, you will need a lot of courage to do the right thing that the code of ethics demands of you.

4. A compassionate attitude

Compassion makes you believable, it magnetises and magnifies the power of your faith and undeniably makes you very welcoming and attractive in the sight and hearts of many people. Compassion moves the heavens on your behalf and bestows upon you the invisible power of influence and force of accomplishment.

Compassion naturally leads you to be a giver; it enhances the quality of benevolence – one of the hallmark characteristics of the truly superior person.

When you give freely and generously of yourself to others or for a cause, you feel more valuable and happier inside.
Here is a principle to remember when it comes to benevolence and compassion: "The more you give of yourself to others without expectation of return, the more good things there are that will come back to you from most unexpected sources."

You will also realise that, over time, you are becoming more patient and understanding, less judgmental or demanding of others. You will feel peaceful, confident and pleasant to be around. In a nutshell, you become a better and finer person and more importantly a compassionate accountant.

Isn't that wonderful?

5. Integrity

Your Character is the most important thing that you develop in your entire life, and one of the cornerstones of your character is your integrity.

You develop integrity, and become a completely honest person, by practising telling the truth to yourself and others in every situation.

It is imperative that your relationships and accountancy career are based on the foundation of truth, and this can be done by developing the habit of living in truth with yourself and with everyone around you. Of course, this does not mean that you will always be right 100% of the time, it, however, emphasises the fact that you endeavour to tell the truth, as you see or know it.

Others will learn to know that they can confidently rely on you and your word (and that is very important for an accountant). Though they may not like what you say on certain occasions, they will still know that you always speak the truth. This goes a very long way to earn you a great reputation in your accounting career and form a very solid foundation for your integrity. Listen to what Shakespeare once wrote, "*To thine own self be true, and then it must follow, as the night the day, thou canst not then be false to any man*".

In this day and age with the advancement of technology, CCTV and satellite, you cannot afford to be careless about how you conduct yourself or how you treat others or do business. To be successful nowadays is largely determined by the number of people who trust you and who are willing to work with you or give you credit if you are a borrower or help you during difficult times etc. Trust is essential, and trust is earned not given, and you earn trust by being a person of integrity.

You must guard your integrity as a sacred thing, as the most important statement about you as an accountant.
As Brian Tracy once said; "Whenever you are in doubt about a course of action, simply ask yourself, Is this the right thing to do?" And then behave accordingly.

"Weakness of attitude becomes weakness of Character" – A. Einstein

6. A loving attitude

As Apostle Paul said in 1Corinthians 13:2-3 *"And though I have the gift of prophecy, and understand all mysteries, and all knowledge; and though I have all faith so that I could remove mountains,.....And though I bestow all my goods to feed the poor, and though I give my body to be burned, and have not Love, I am nothing."*

Without genuine, heartfelt love for the people in your life and the things you do, your relationships and success in life are doomed to fail.

Jesus Christ emphasised this point of love so much that He gave a new commandment: *"...Thou shalt love the Lord thy God with all thy heart, and with all thy soul and with all thy mind........., Thou shalt love thy neighbour as thyself"* Matthew 22:37-3

To love is a decision you make and should form a core part of your attitude in life and especially in your accounting career. I think it is important to bear in mind what Jesus Christ said in the scripture above and also to embrace the Golden Rule: *"Do unto others what you would have them do unto you".*

In closing on this aspect of attitudes of success in accountancy, I would like to say that; the way to a super attitude and hence a great accountancy career at any time of the day and at any day of the week is to trust in God with all your heart and lean not on your own understanding.

I am not being religious here, but simply stating the obvious and plain truth. If you don't believe me, try it your way or any other way and see how far you can go being successful and happy at the same time.

I hope you will forever resolve to be a grateful, forgiving, courageous, compassionate, trustworthy and loving accountant. I really do hope so.

Okay. I am done with that bit. Let's get to work, shall we?

Integrity

You must guard your integrity as a sacred thing, as the most important statement about you as an accountant.

As Brian Tracy once said; "Whenever you are in doubt about a course of action, simply ask yourself, is this the right thing to do?" And then behave accordingly.

TASK 1: SETTING UP & GETTING STARTED

Introduction to QuickBooks Online

QuickBooks is an accounting software package developed and marketed by Intuit. QuickBooks products are geared mainly toward small and medium-sized businesses and offer on-premises accounting applications as well as cloud-based versions that accept business payments, manage and pay bills, and payroll functions.

There are three versions of QuickBooks Online. A plan can be chosen to suit the requirements of the business. Each offering provides features relevant to the selected plan. Further details on the features available under each product version can be found at https://quickbooks.intuit.com/pricing/

Task 1a: Setting up the business in QuickBooks Online

The details you have been given about the business to set up in QuickBooks Online are as follows:

- **Company/Business name:** *Horizon Tristar Ltd*
- **Business address:** *77 Lee Road, London, SE3 9DE*
- **Financial year:** *Set to the 1st November last year*
- **Home currency:** *Depending on where you are doing this work experience from (country), Use the currency of that country as the home currency in QuickBooks Online (We will be using the British Pound in this tutorial)*
- **VAT information:** *Registered for VAT on the standard VAT scheme and the registration number is 843277159*
- **Director/Manager:** *Mr Terry Smith*
- **Opening balances** to be entered in QuickBooks online as of 1st January this year.

Let's get started.

Look at the links below and depending on which part of the world you are in, use the appropriate link to get started.

If you are based in the **United Kingdom (UK),** use/click on - https://quickbooks.intuit.com/uk/

If you are based in the **United States (US)**, use/click on - https://quickbooks.intuit.com

If you are based in the **European Union (EU),** use/click on - https://quickbooks.intuit.com/eu/

If you are based in **Australia,** use/click on - https://quickbooks.intuit.com/au/

For all the **Rest of the World**, use/click on - https://quickbooks.intuit.com/global/

For this work experience, I have opted to use the UK site, https://quickbooks.intuit.com/uk/ because I live in the UK. However, the software functionally is the same regardless of which part of the world you are based in. So, follow through with me.

Once you visit any of the sites above, the landing pages are quite similar, and there will be an offer for a free 30 day trial in almost all the sites - See figures 1 & 2 below.

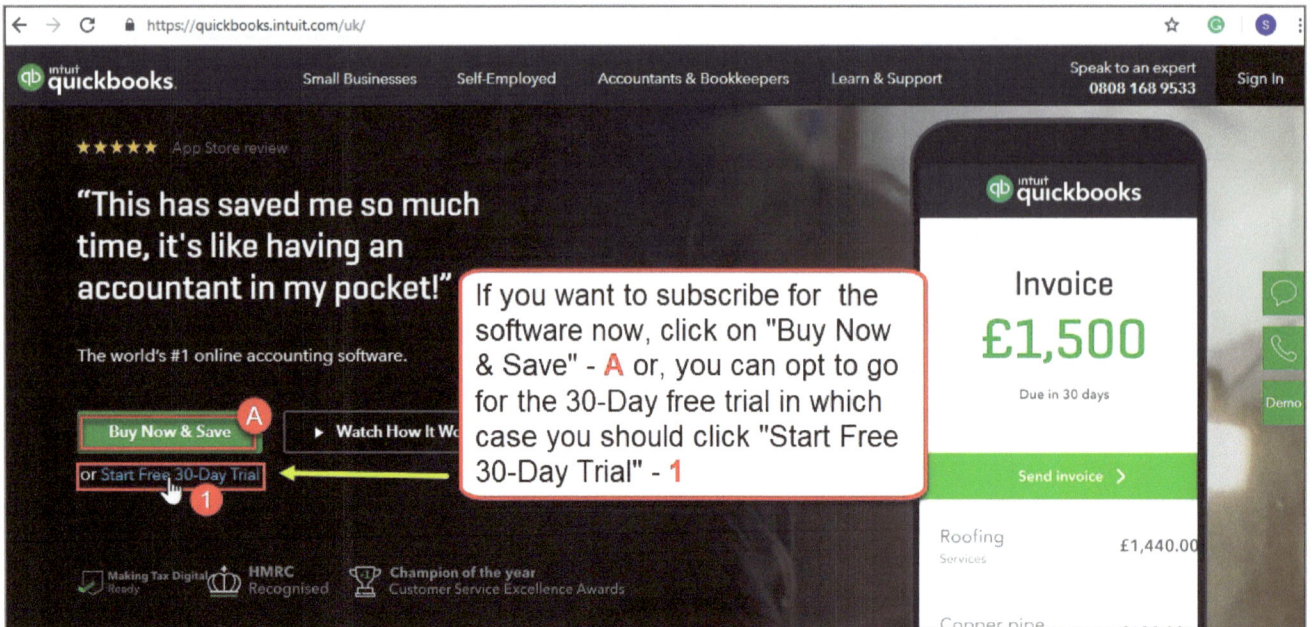

Fig. 1

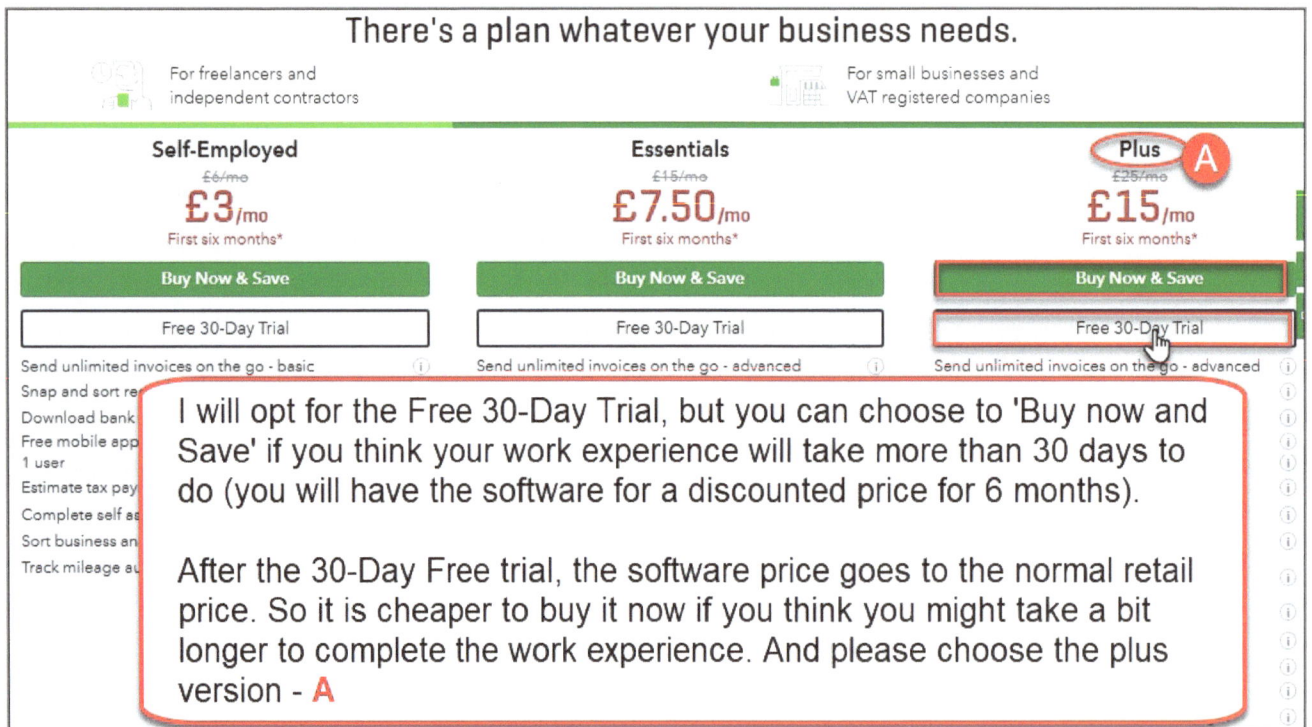

Fig. 2

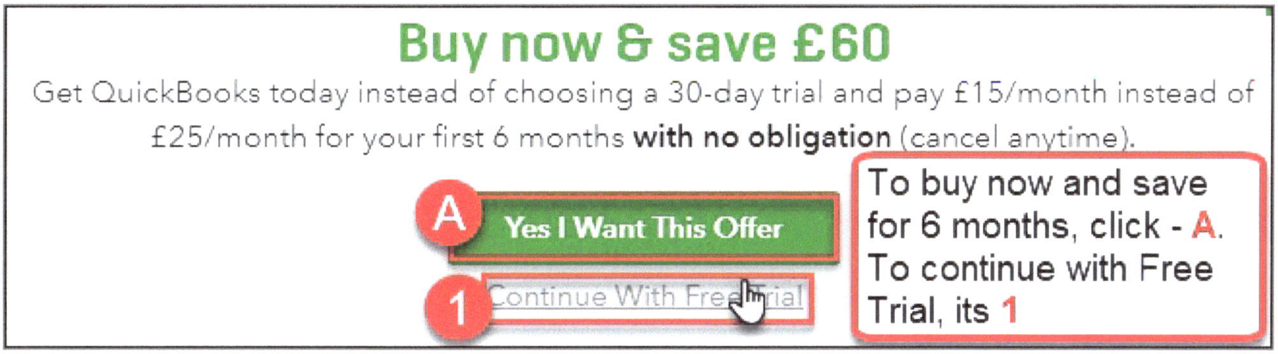

Buy now & save £60

Get QuickBooks today instead of choosing a 30-day trial and pay £15/month instead of £25/month for your first 6 months **with no obligation** (cancel anytime).

A Yes I Want This Offer

1 Continue With Free Trial

To buy now and save for 6 months, click - **A**. To continue with Free Trial, its **1**

Fig. 3

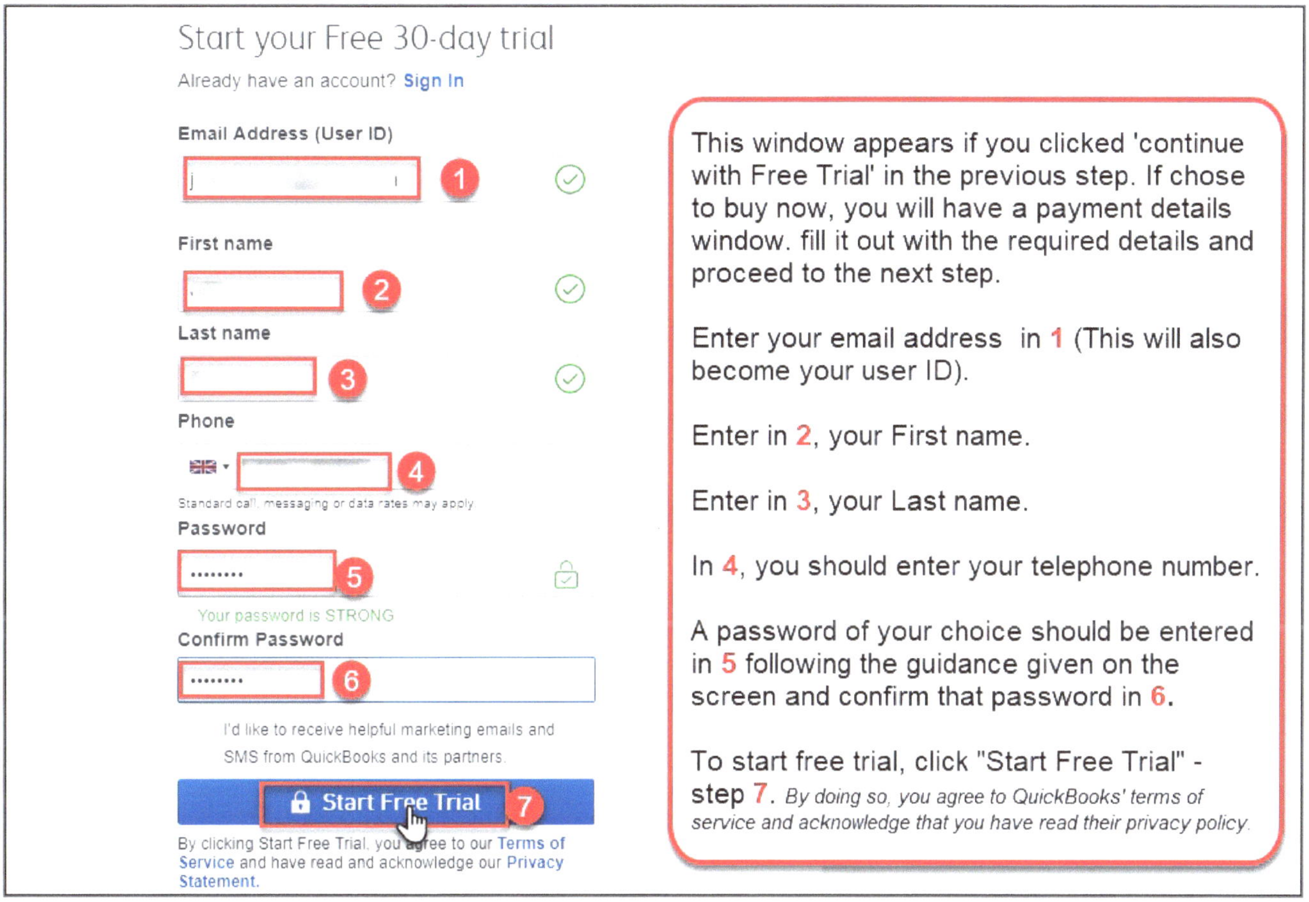

Start your Free 30-day trial

Already have an account? Sign In

Email Address (User ID)

1 ✓

First name

2 ✓

Last name

3 ✓

Phone

🇬🇧 ▾ **4**

Standard call, messaging or data rates may apply

Password

•••••••• **5** 🔒

Your password is STRONG

Confirm Password

•••••••• **6**

I'd like to receive helpful marketing emails and SMS from QuickBooks and its partners

🔒 **Start Free Trial** **7**

By clicking Start Free Trial, you agree to our Terms of Service and have read and acknowledge our Privacy Statement.

This window appears if you clicked 'continue with Free Trial' in the previous step. If chose to buy now, you will have a payment details window. fill it out with the required details and proceed to the next step.

Enter your email address in **1** (This will also become your user ID).

Enter in **2**, your First name.

Enter in **3**, your Last name.

In **4**, you should enter your telephone number.

A password of your choice should be entered in **5** following the guidance given on the screen and confirm that password in **6**.

To start free trial, click "Start Free Trial" - step **7**. *By doing so, you agree to QuickBooks' terms of service and acknowledge that you have read their privacy policy.*

Fig. 4

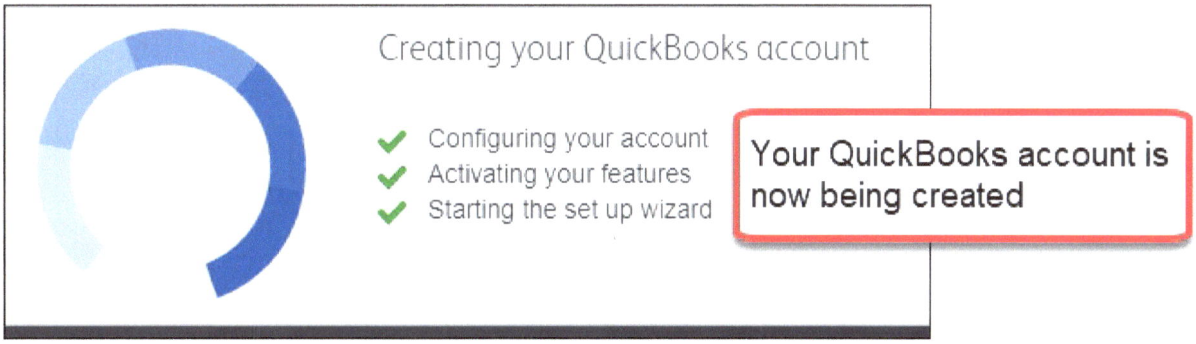

Creating your QuickBooks account

✓ Configuring your account
✓ Activating your features
✓ Starting the set up wizard

Your QuickBooks account is now being created

Fig. 5

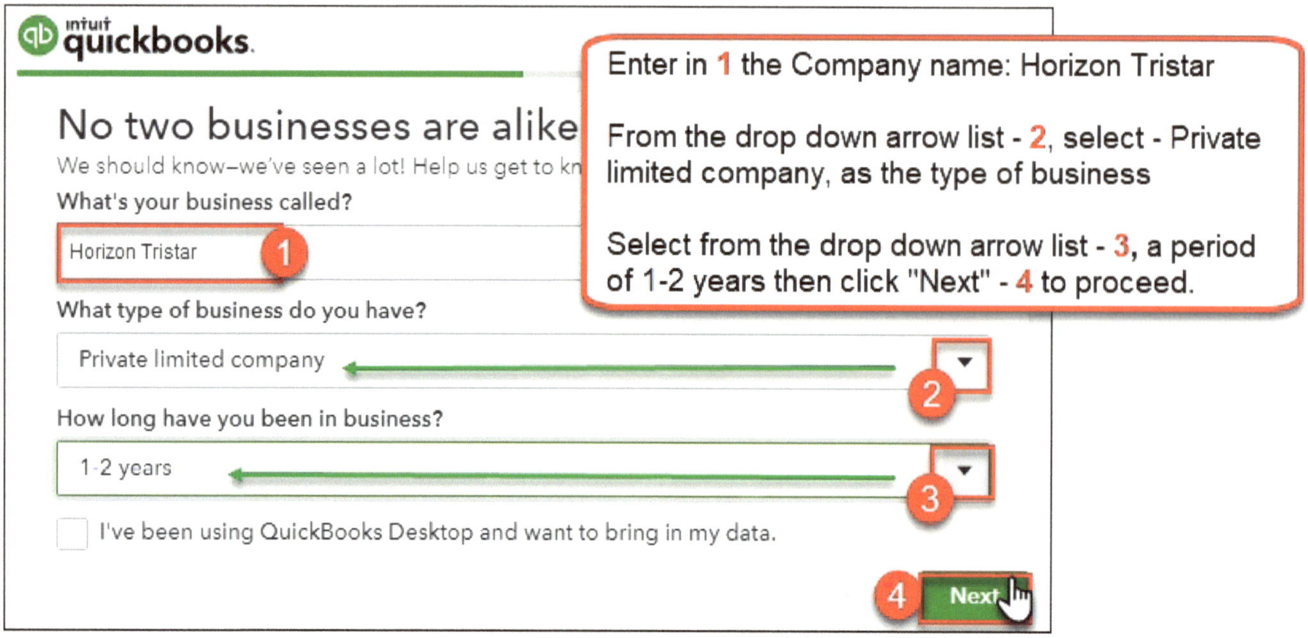

Fig. 6

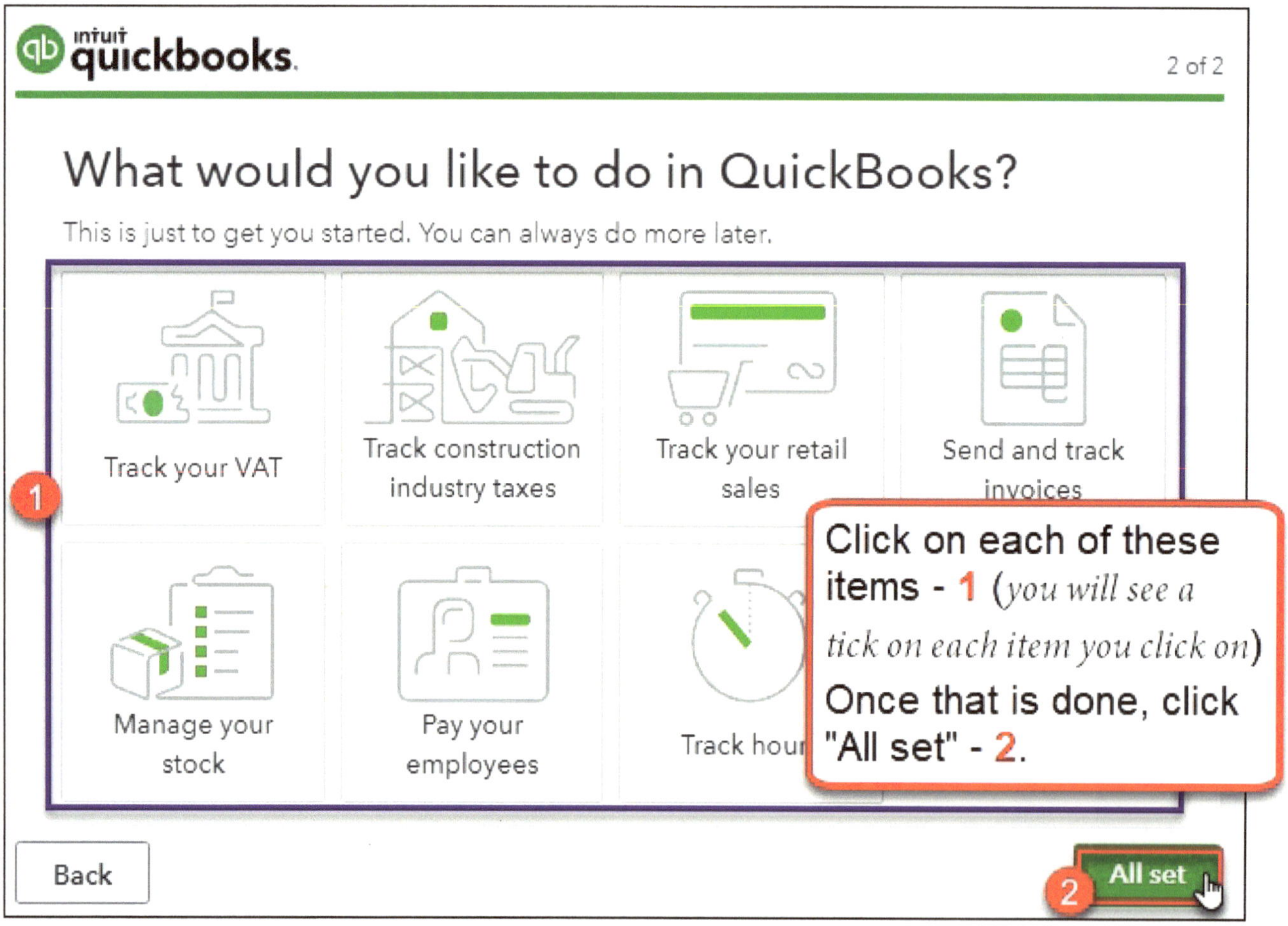

Fig. 7

After you click "All set" as illustrated in the figure above, the home page appears. The Home page displays a summary of key information. A new file set up would display as in figure 8 (on the next page) with no transactions.

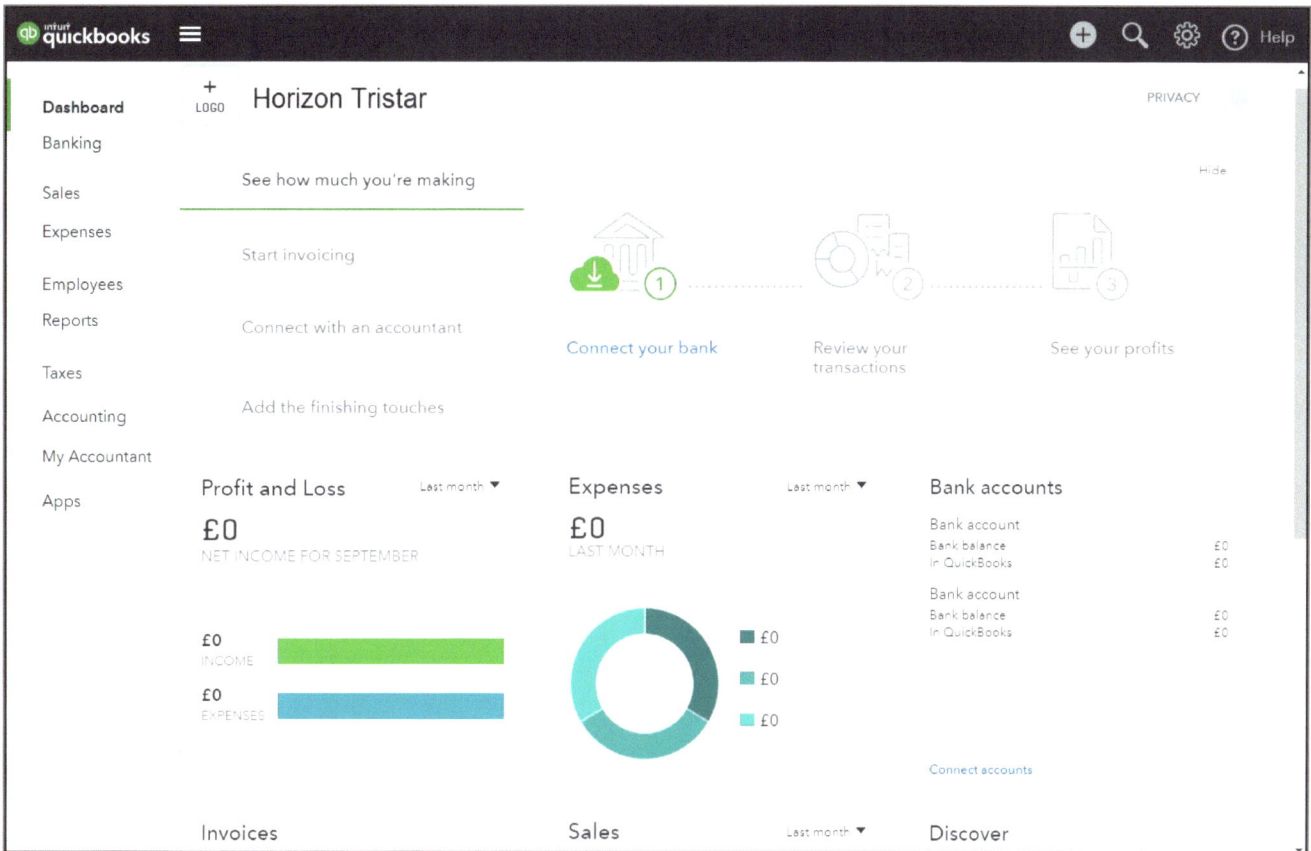

Fig. 8

To sign out of your QuickBooks online screen, see details on the figure below.

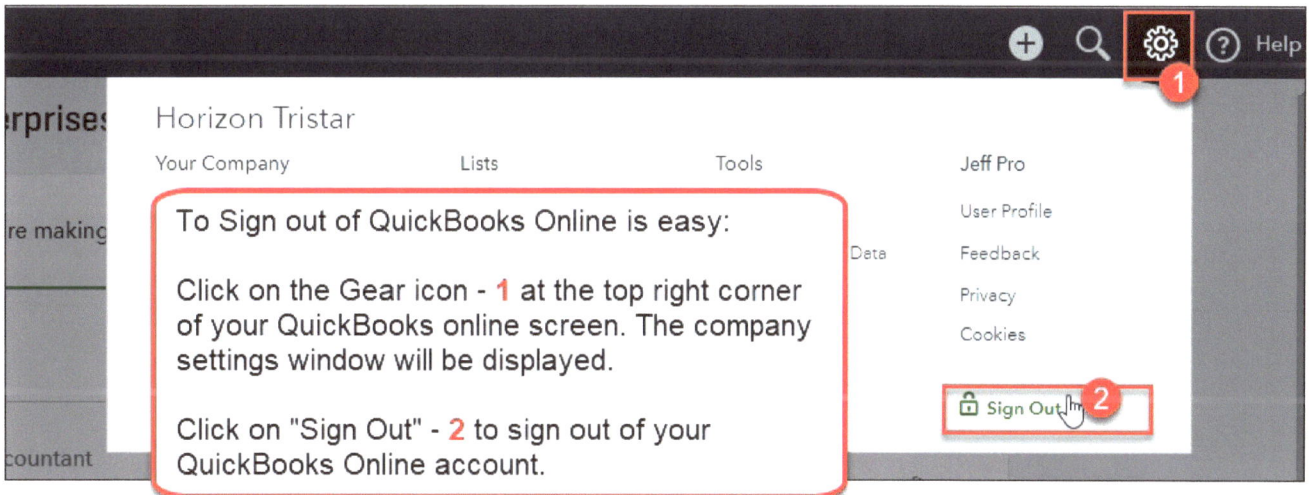

To Sign out of QuickBooks Online is easy:

Click on the Gear icon - 1 at the top right corner of your QuickBooks online screen. The company settings window will be displayed.

Click on "Sign Out" - 2 to sign out of your QuickBooks Online account.

Fig. 9

This space is for notes

To sign back into your QuickBooks online account, follow the steps as illustrated in the figure below.

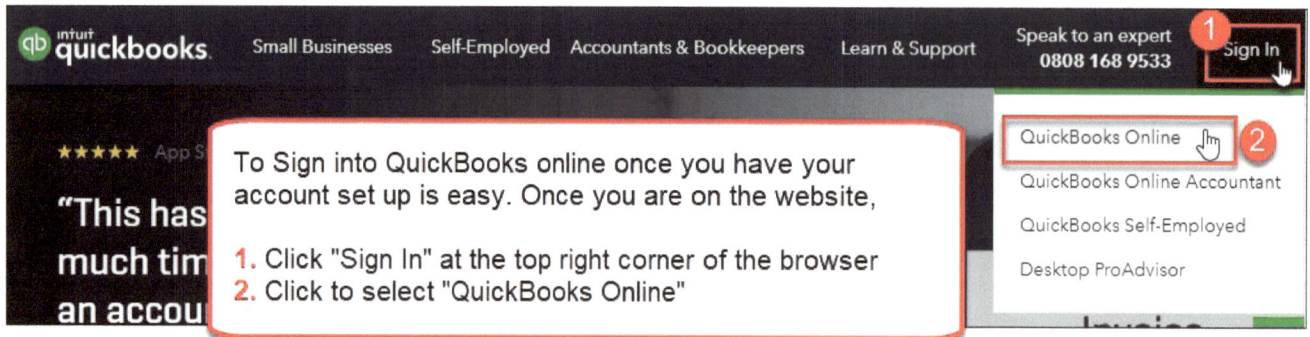

Fig. 10

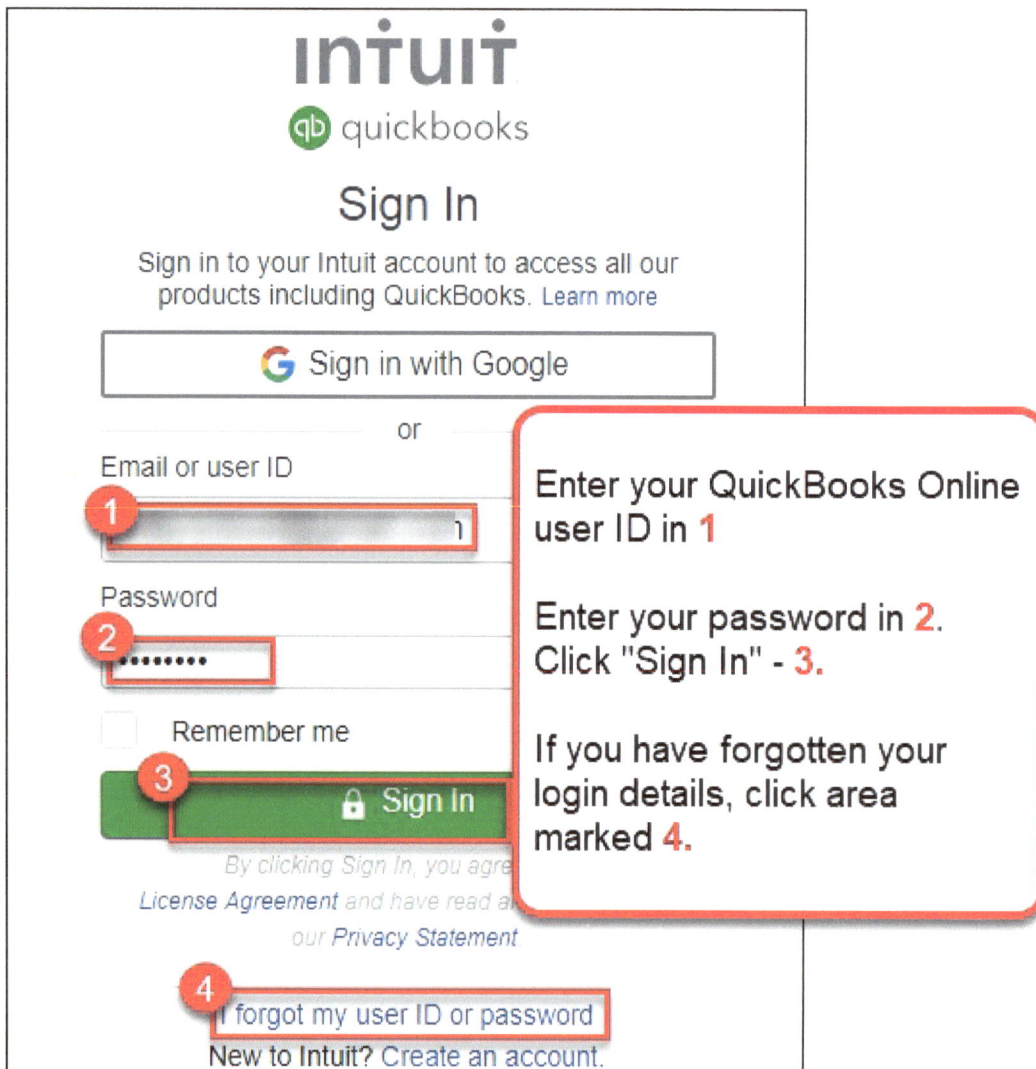

Fig. 11

Task 1a(i). Understanding the general layout of QuickBooks Online

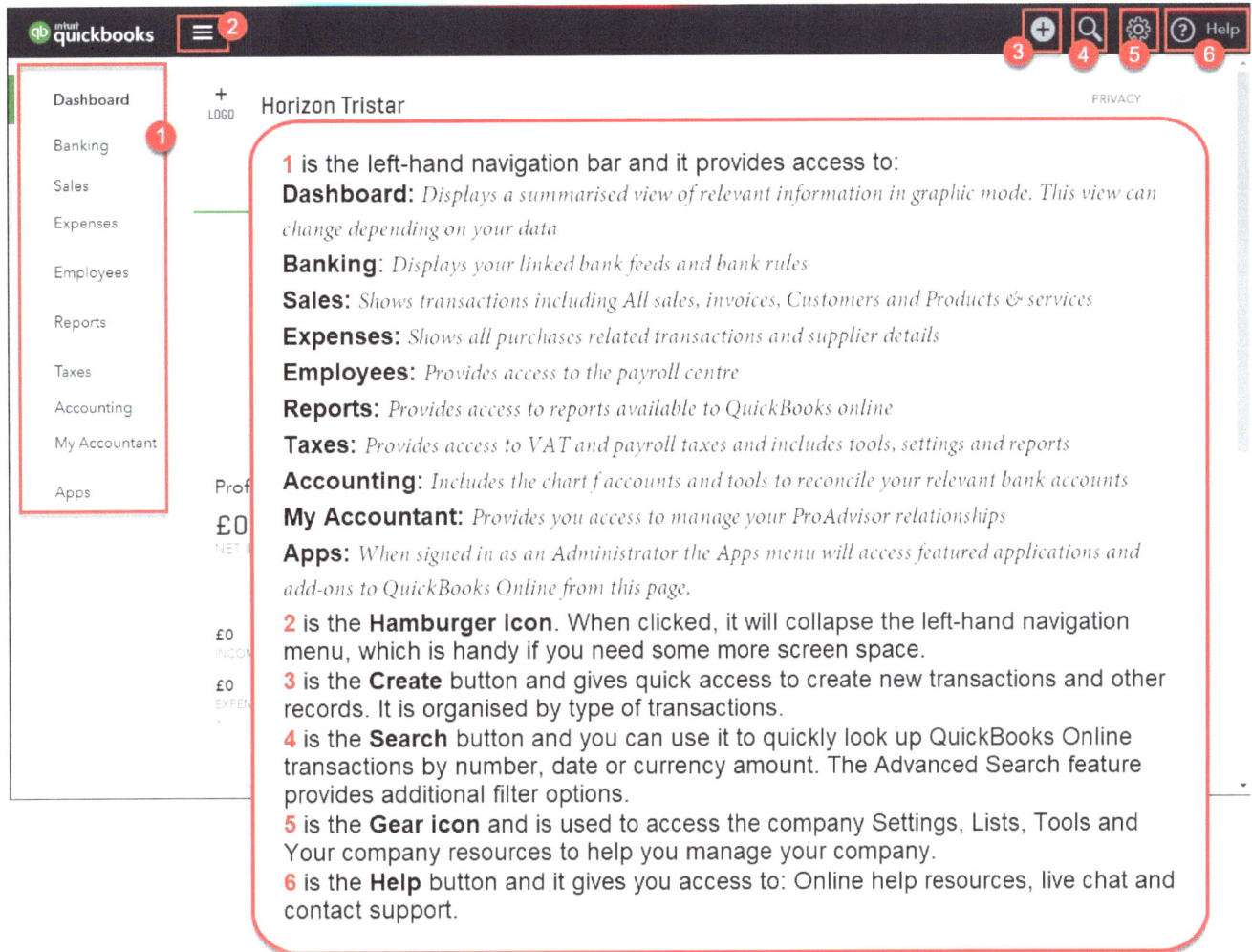

1 is the left-hand navigation bar and it provides access to:

Dashboard: *Displays a summarised view of relevant information in graphic mode. This view can change depending on your data*

Banking: *Displays your linked bank feeds and bank rules*

Sales: *Shows transactions including All sales, invoices, Customers and Products & services*

Expenses: *Shows all purchases related transactions and supplier details*

Employees: *Provides access to the payroll centre*

Reports: *Provides access to reports available to QuickBooks online*

Taxes: *Provides access to VAT and payroll taxes and includes tools, settings and reports*

Accounting: *Includes the chart f accounts and tools to reconcile your relevant bank accounts*

My Accountant: *Provides you access to manage your ProAdvisor relationships*

Apps: *When signed in as an Administrator the Apps menu will access featured applications and add-ons to QuickBooks Online from this page.*

2 is the **Hamburger icon**. When clicked, it will collapse the left-hand navigation menu, which is handy if you need some more screen space.

3 is the **Create** button and gives quick access to create new transactions and other records. It is organised by type of transactions.

4 is the **Search** button and you can use it to quickly look up QuickBooks Online transactions by number, date or currency amount. The Advanced Search feature provides additional filter options.

5 is the **Gear icon** and is used to access the company Settings, Lists, Tools and Your company resources to help you manage your company.

6 is the **Help** button and it gives you access to: Online help resources, live chat and contact support.

Fig. 12

Let's move on and set up the company's financial year date.

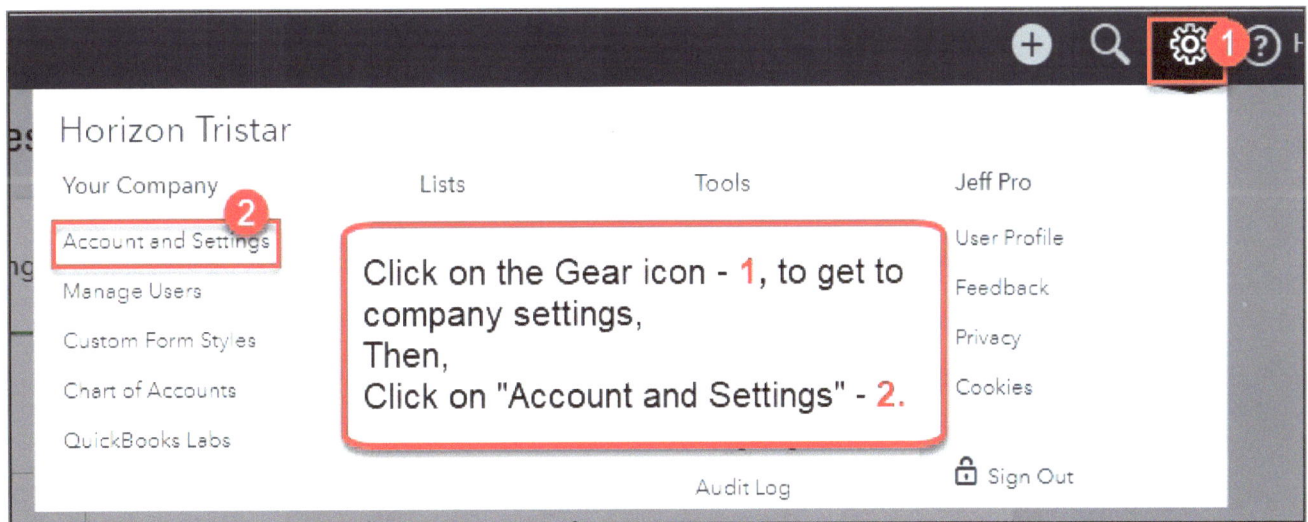

Click on the Gear icon - **1**, to get to company settings,
Then,
Click on "Account and Settings" - **2**.

Fig. 13

Fig. 14

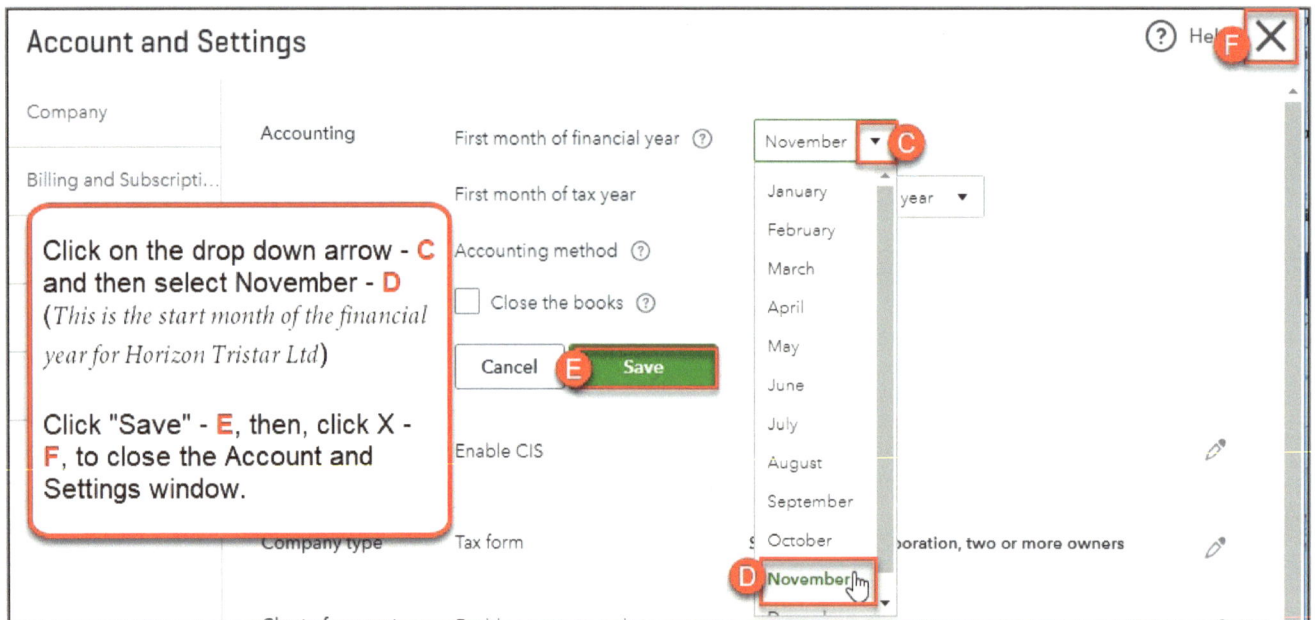

Fig. 15

Multicurrency

Trade nowadays is quite international, and that means having to deal with different currencies as a business buys and sells internationally. We are therefore going to set the multicurrency option in QuickBooks Online for Horizon Tristar Ltd.

To do so, we have to go to the company settings - see figure 16 on the next page.

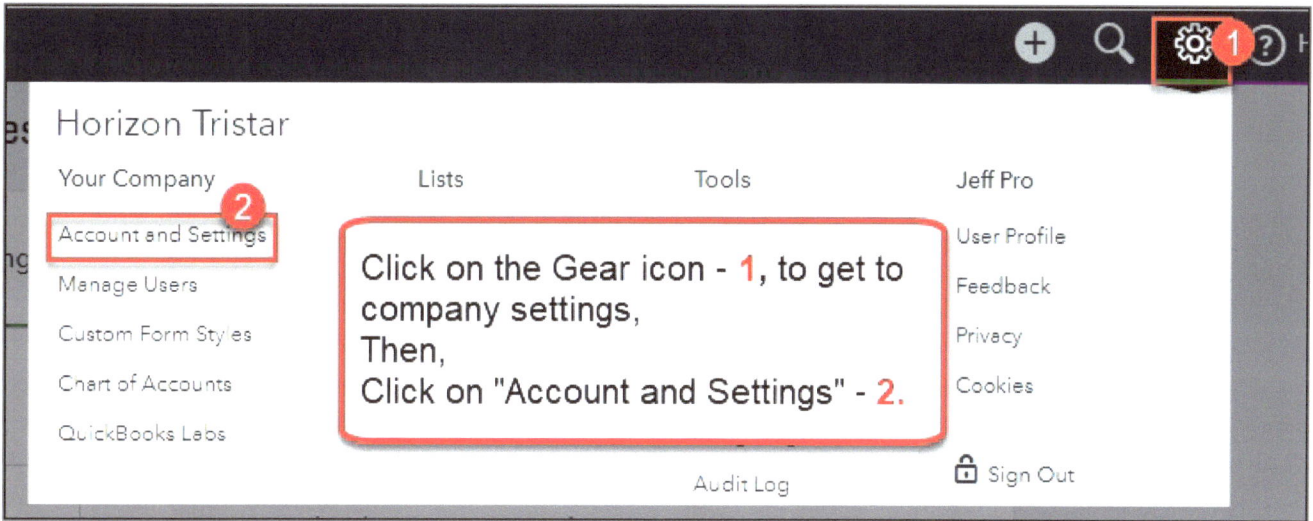

Fig. 16

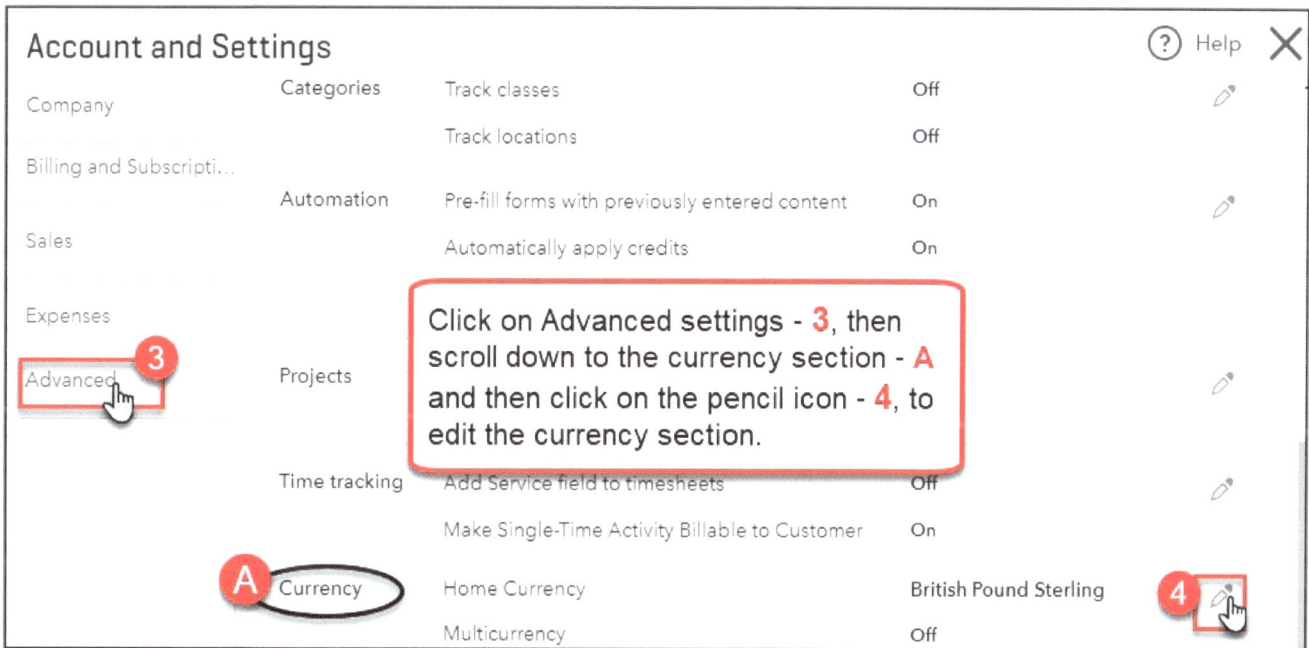

Fig. 17

This space is for notes

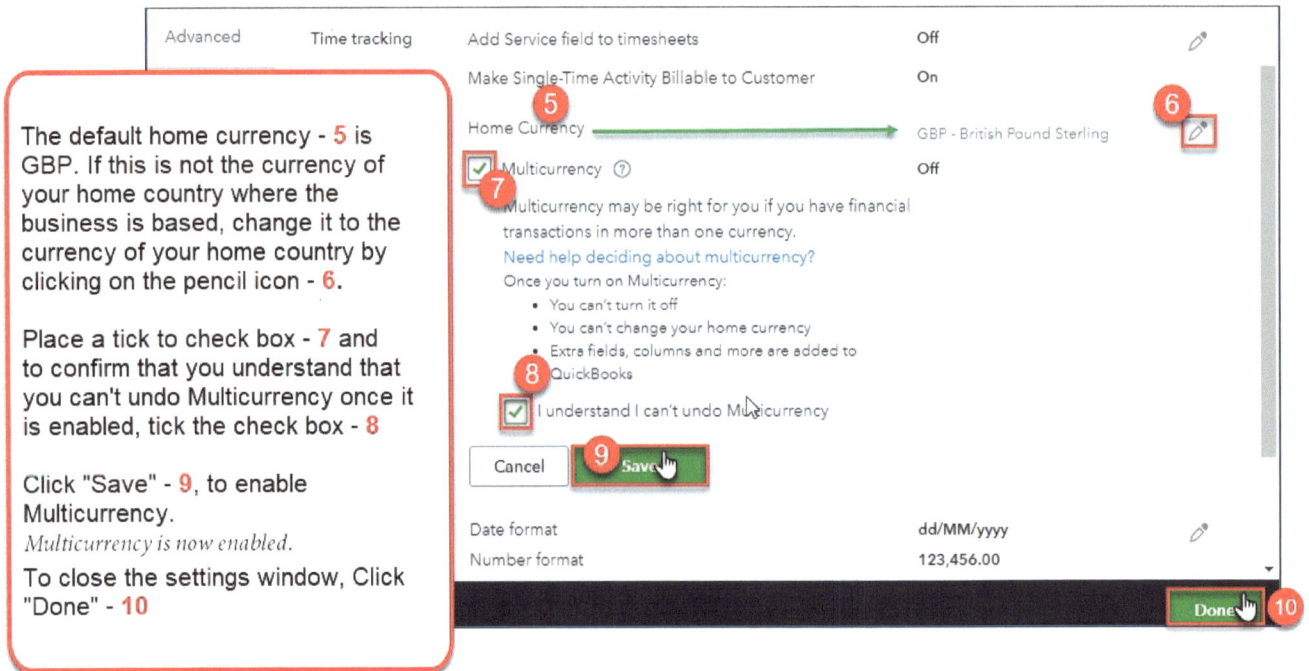

The default home currency - 5 is GBP. If this is not the currency of your home country where the business is based, change it to the currency of your home country by clicking on the pencil icon - 6.

Place a tick to check box - 7 and to confirm that you understand that you can't undo Multicurrency once it is enabled, tick the check box - 8

Click "Save" - 9, to enable Multicurrency.
Multicurrency is now enabled.
To close the settings window, Click "Done" - 10

Fig. 18

The Multicurrency section of the set up is now done. Let's move next to looking at the VAT codes in QuickBooks Online.

Task 1a(ii). Understanding QuickBooks Online VAT Codes

Horizon Tristar Ltd is registered for VAT and therefore has to charge VAT at the standard rate on all its taxable goods and services.

To understand more about VAT rates, visit HMRC website on http://www.hmrc.gov.uk/vat/start/ to find out what rate of VAT applies in any particular set of circumstances.

To understand the VAT codes in QuickBooks Online, we have to first set up VAT in QuickBooks.

To do so, **Click on Taxes on the left navigation bar > then click on Set up VAT**

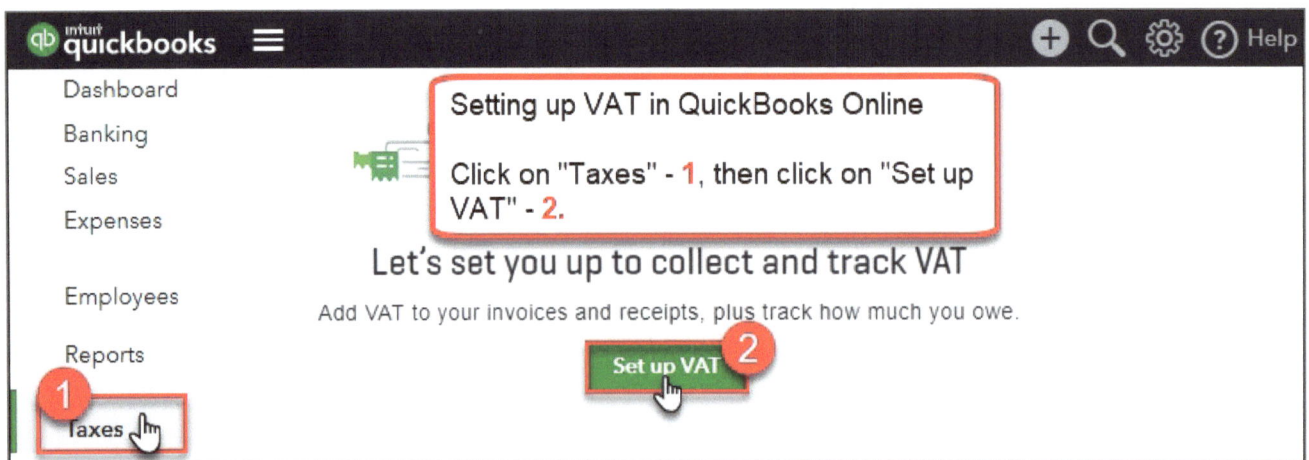

Setting up VAT in QuickBooks Online

Click on "Taxes" - 1, then click on "Set up VAT" - 2.

Let's set you up to collect and track VAT

Add VAT to your invoices and receipts, plus track how much you owe.

Fig. 19

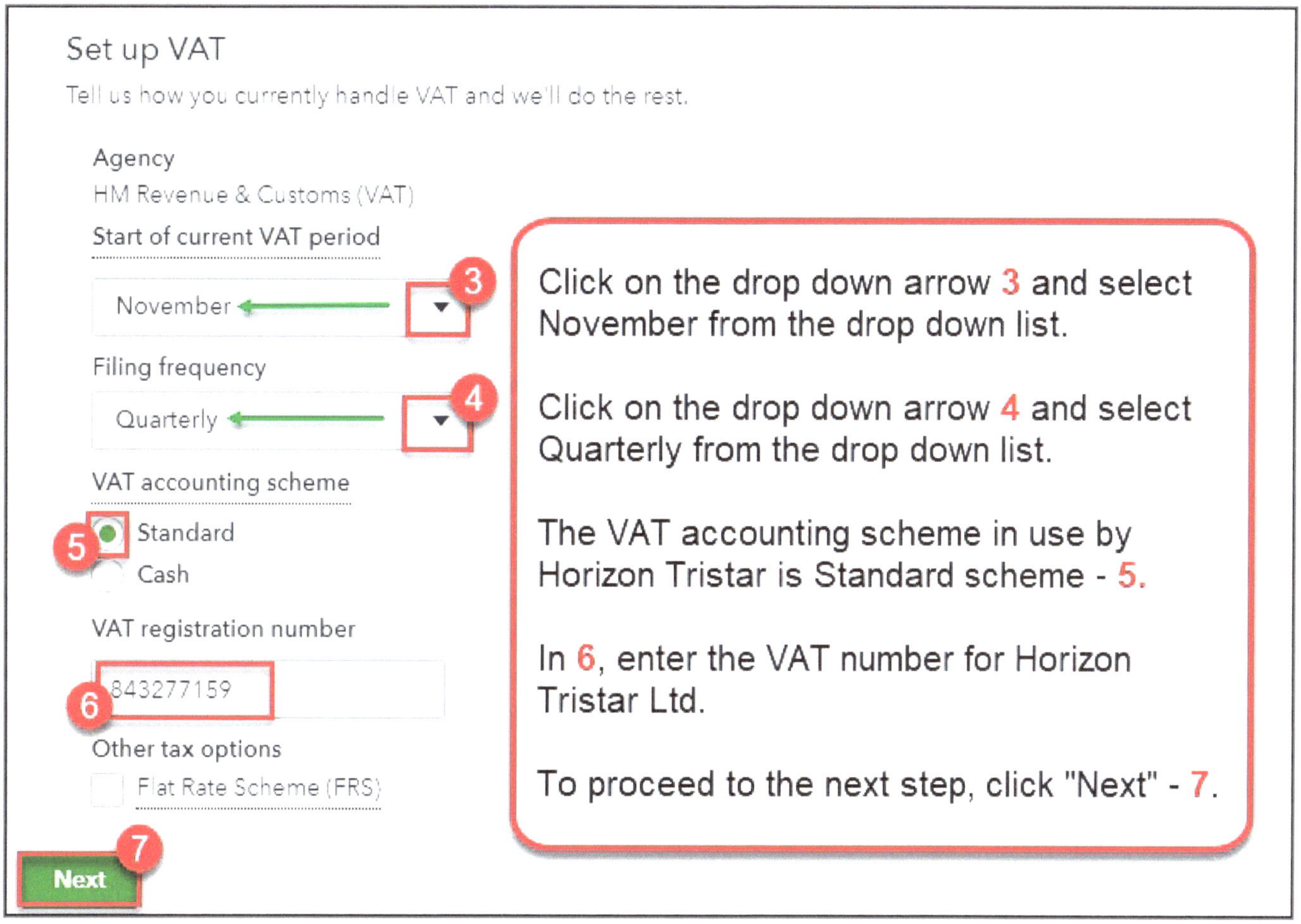

Set up VAT

Tell us how you currently handle VAT and we'll do the rest.

Agency
HM Revenue & Customs (VAT)

Start of current VAT period

November — **3** Click on the drop down arrow **3** and select November from the drop down list.

Filing frequency

Quarterly — **4** Click on the drop down arrow **4** and select Quarterly from the drop down list.

VAT accounting scheme

5 ● Standard
○ Cash

The VAT accounting scheme in use by Horizon Tristar is Standard scheme - **5.**

VAT registration number

6 843277159

In **6**, enter the VAT number for Horizon Tristar Ltd.

Other tax options

☐ Flat Rate Scheme (FRS)

To proceed to the next step, click "Next" - **7**.

7 **Next**

Fig. 20

✓

Now you can add VAT to your transactions, and record your VAT payments in QuickBooks.
Visit the VAT page whenever you want to view your history, run reports, or track payments.

8 **Got it** Click on "Got it" to proceed

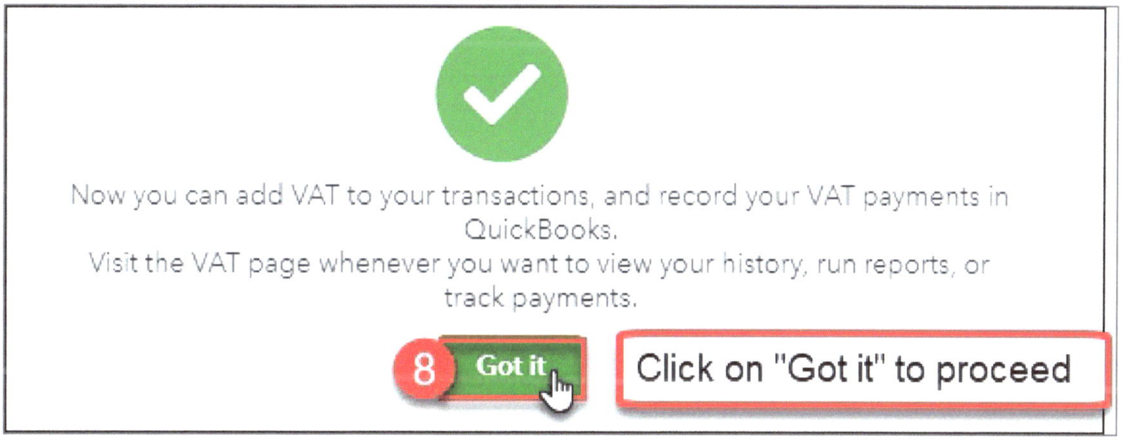

Fig. 21

This space is for notes

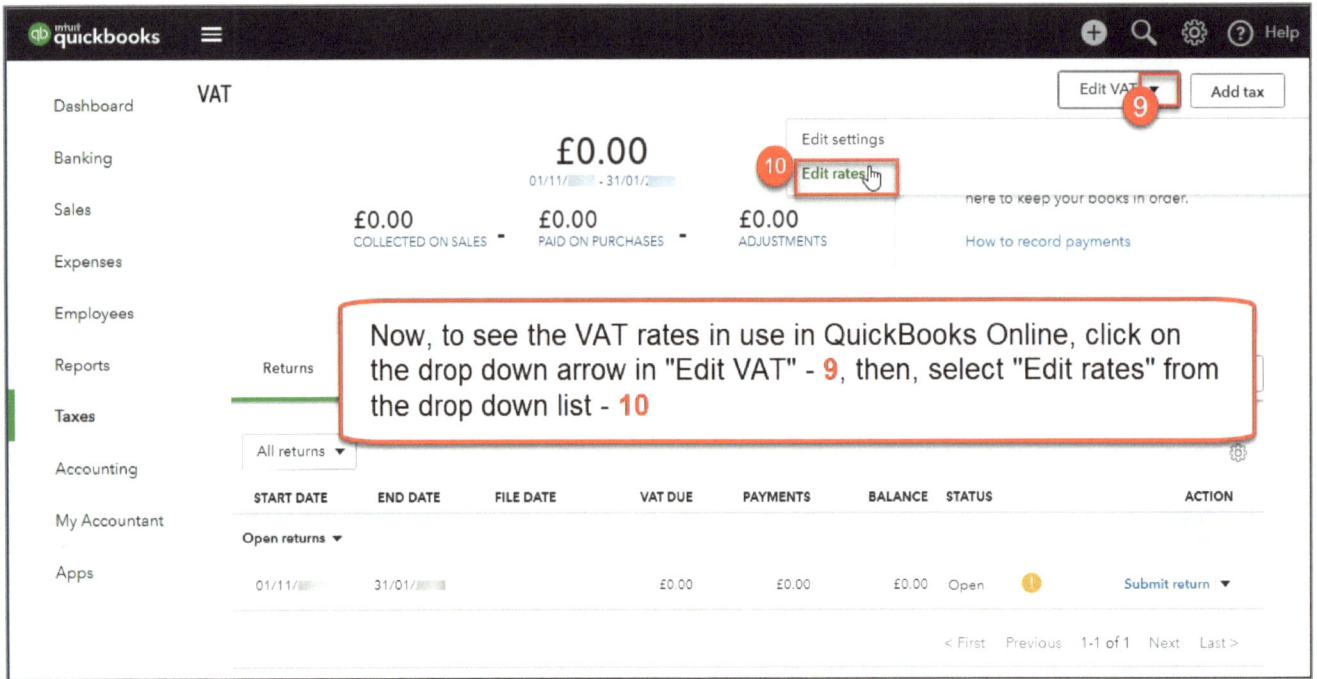

Now, to see the VAT rates in use in QuickBooks Online, click on the drop down arrow in "Edit VAT" - **9**, then, select "Edit rates" from the drop down list - **10**

Fig. 22

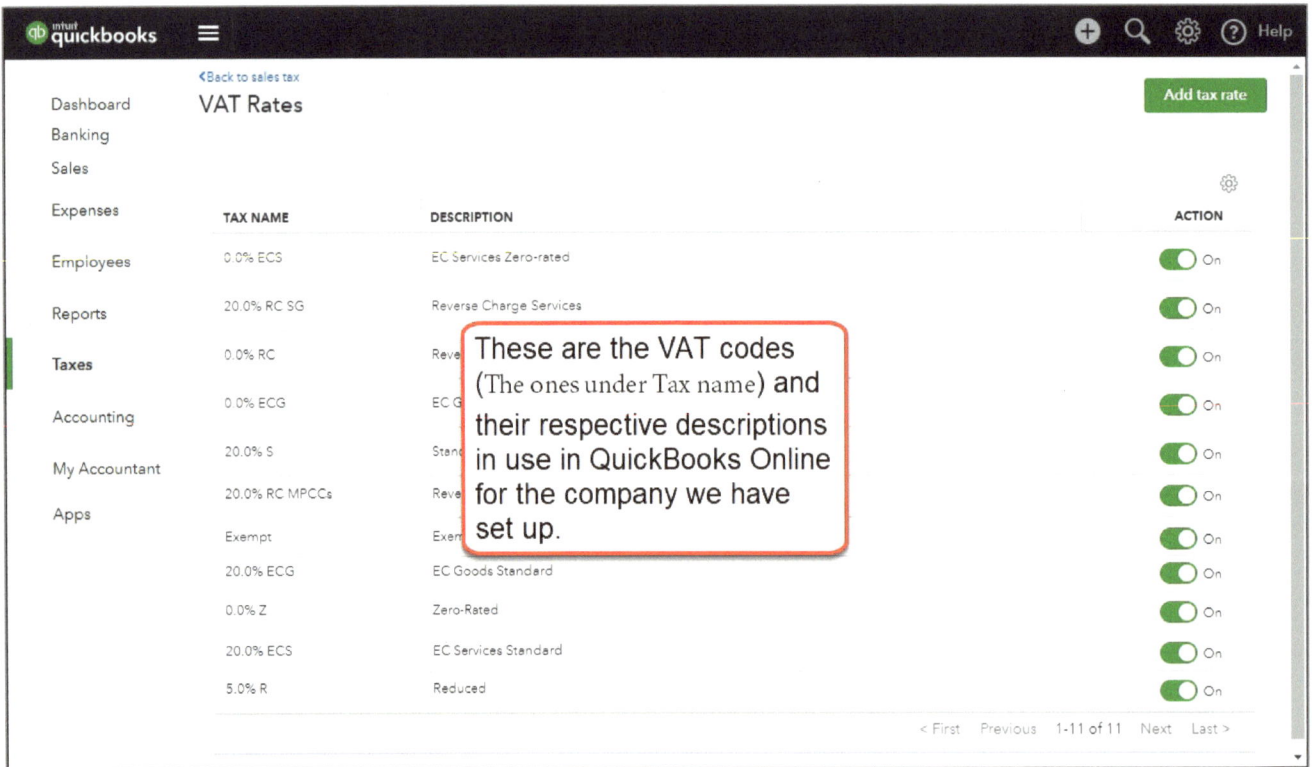

These are the VAT codes (The ones under Tax name) and their respective descriptions in use in QuickBooks Online for the company we have set up.

Fig. 23

The VAT setup is now complete. Let's move on to QuickBooks chart of accounts next.

Task 1a(iii). Understanding QuickBooks Online chart of accounts

Chart of Accounts is the complete list of all the company's accounts and balances. In QuickBooks, it represents and organises the company's assets, liabilities, income, and expense.

QuickBooks Online automatically creates your Chart of Accounts based on the type of company/business you choose when creating your company file.

Let's have a look at the chart of accounts for the company we created – Horizon Tristar Ltd.

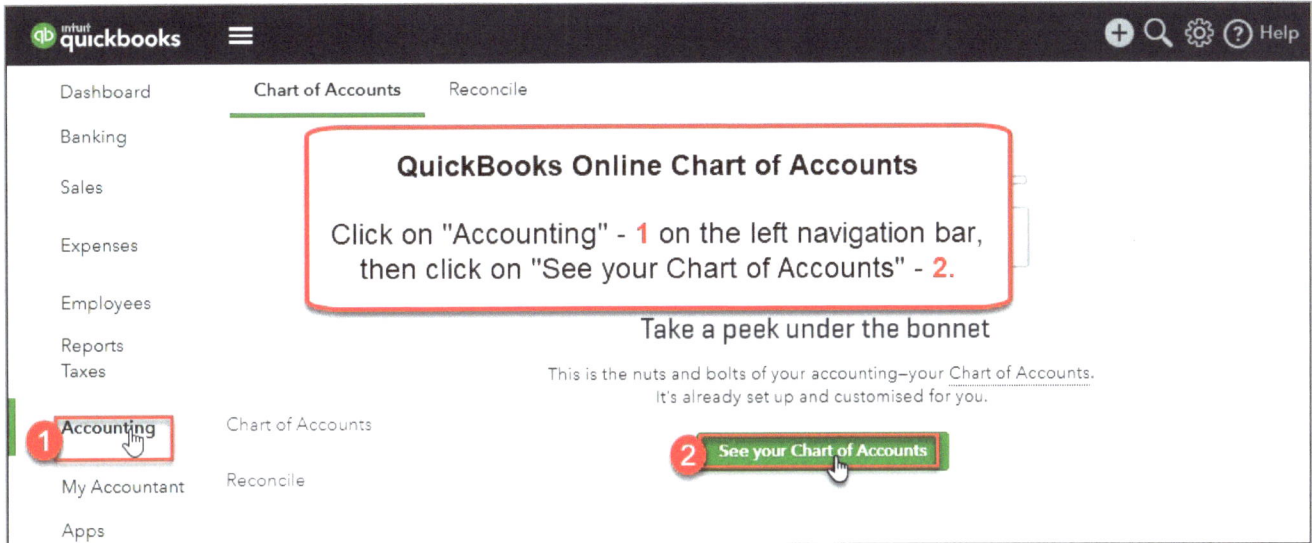

Fig. 24

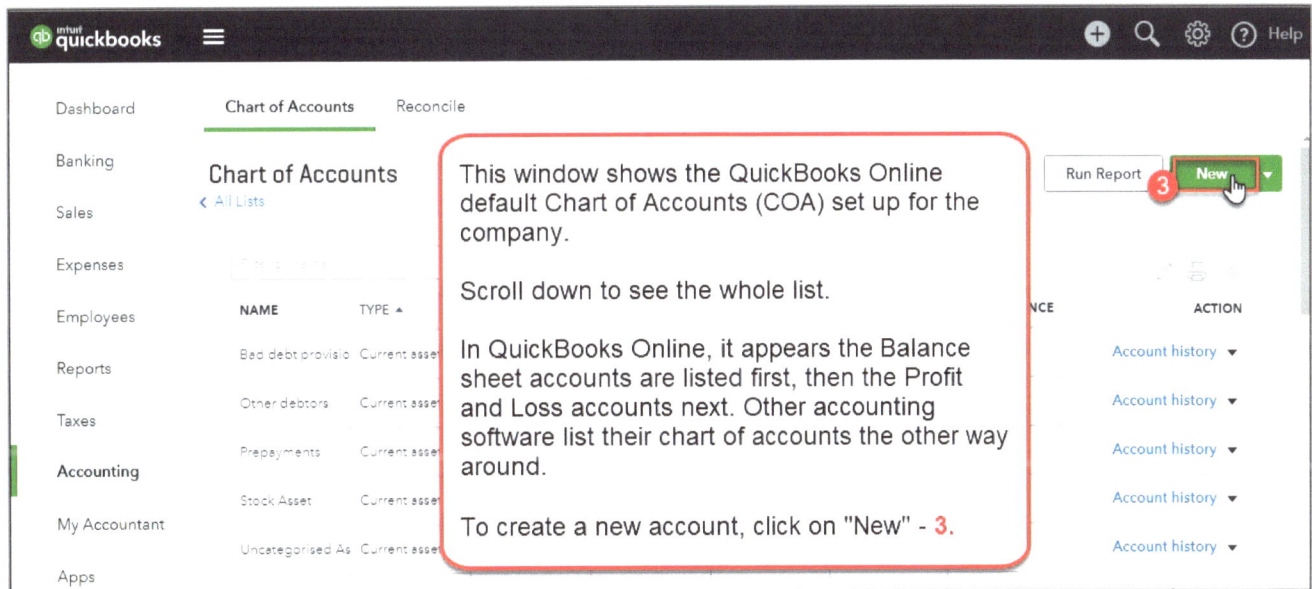

Fig. 25

Here are some new accounts you need to create:

- ✓ The Company Current Bank Account
- ✓ Petty Cash Account
- ✓ The bank Deposit Account
- ✓ Income/Sales account for Office furniture, Office equipment and Consumables.

The Company Current Bank Account

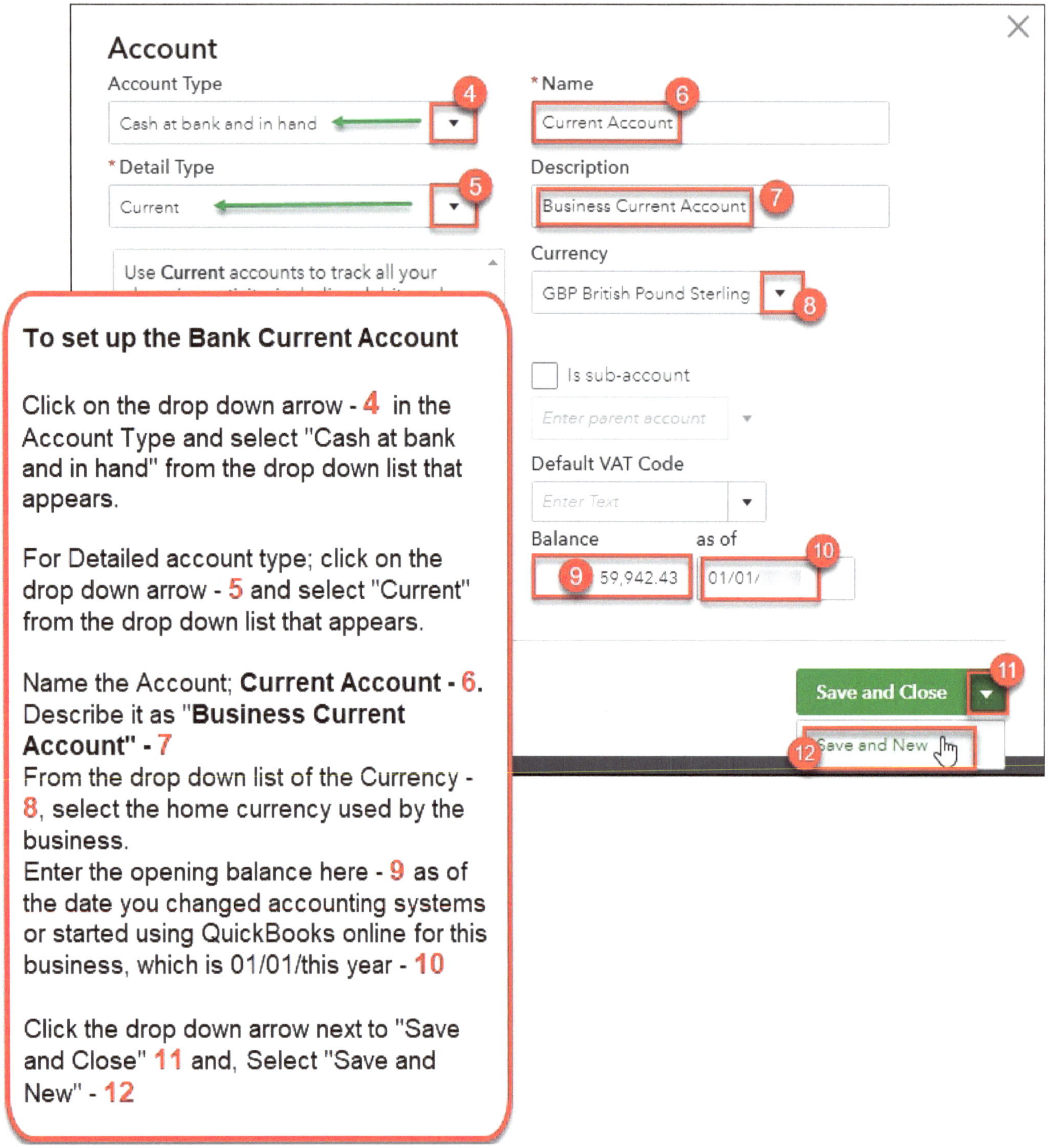

Account

Account Type
Cash at bank and in hand — 4

*Detail Type
Current — 5

Use **Current** accounts to track all your

*Name
Current Account — 6

Description
Business Current Account — 7

Currency
GBP British Pound Sterling — 8

☐ Is sub-account
Enter parent account

Default VAT Code
Enter Text

Balance   as of
9 59,942.43   01/01/ — 10

Save and Close — 11
Save and New — 12

To set up the Bank Current Account

Click on the drop down arrow - 4 in the Account Type and select "Cash at bank and in hand" from the drop down list that appears.

For Detailed account type; click on the drop down arrow - 5 and select "Current" from the drop down list that appears.

Name the Account; **Current Account - 6.** Describe it as "**Business Current Account**" - 7
From the drop down list of the Currency - 8, select the home currency used by the business.
Enter the opening balance here - 9 as of the date you changed accounting systems or started using QuickBooks online for this business, which is 01/01/this year - 10

Click the drop down arrow next to "Save and Close" 11 and, Select "Save and New" - 12

Fig. 26

Next is Petty Cash Account.

Petty Cash Account

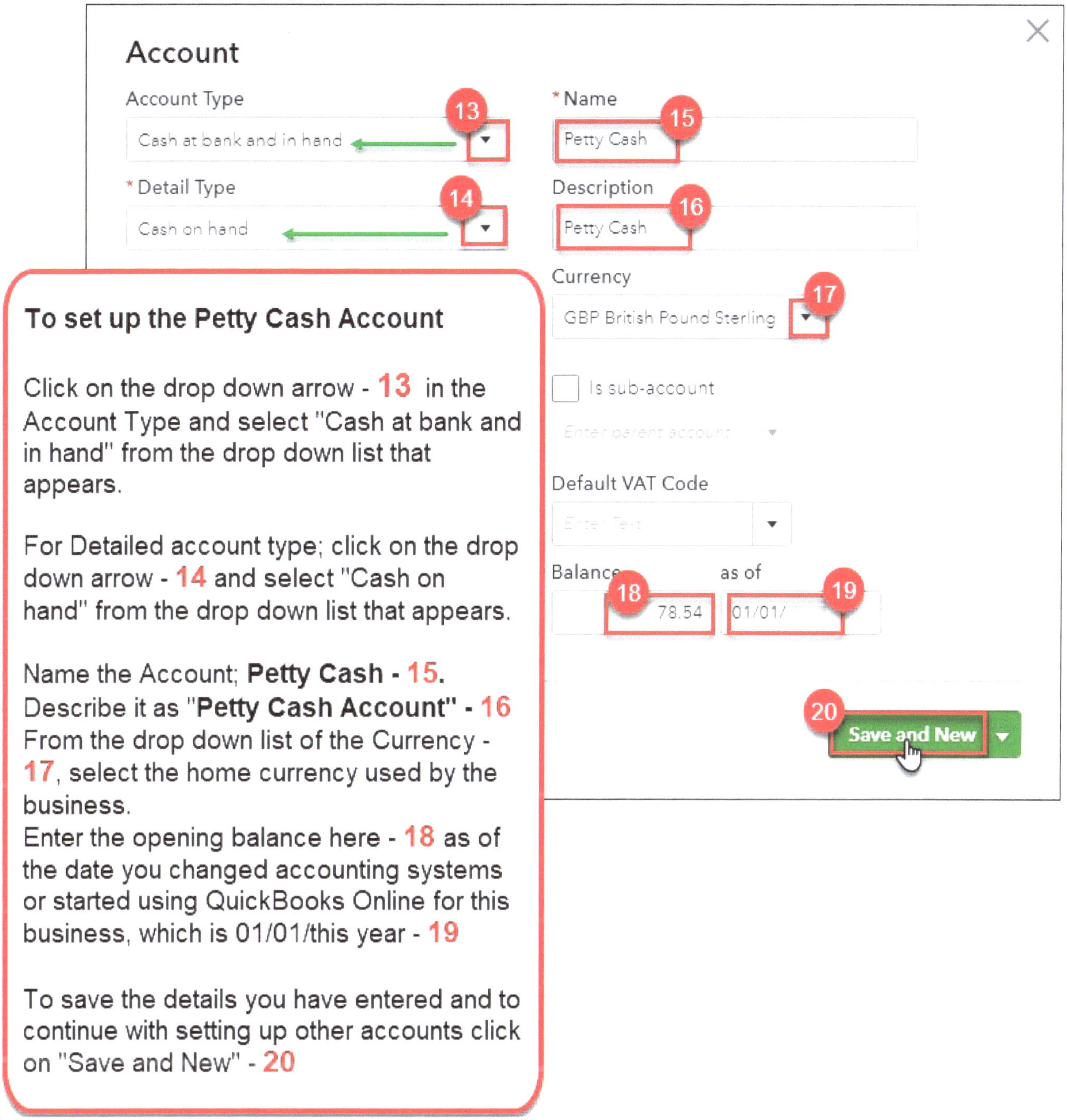

Account

Account Type
⑬
Cash at bank and in hand

*Detail Type
⑭
Cash on hand

*Name
⑮
Petty Cash

Description
⑯
Petty Cash

Currency
⑰
GBP British Pound Sterling

☐ Is sub-account
Enter parent account

Default VAT Code
Enter Text

Balance   as of
⑱ 78.54   ⑲ 01/01/

⑳ Save and New

To set up the Petty Cash Account

Click on the drop down arrow - **13** in the Account Type and select "Cash at bank and in hand" from the drop down list that appears.

For Detailed account type; click on the drop down arrow - **14** and select "Cash on hand" from the drop down list that appears.

Name the Account; **Petty Cash** - **15**.
Describe it as "**Petty Cash Account**" - **16**
From the drop down list of the Currency - **17**, select the home currency used by the business.
Enter the opening balance here - **18** as of the date you changed accounting systems or started using QuickBooks Online for this business, which is 01/01/this year - **19**

To save the details you have entered and to continue with setting up other accounts click on "Save and New" - **20**

Fig. 27

This space is for notes

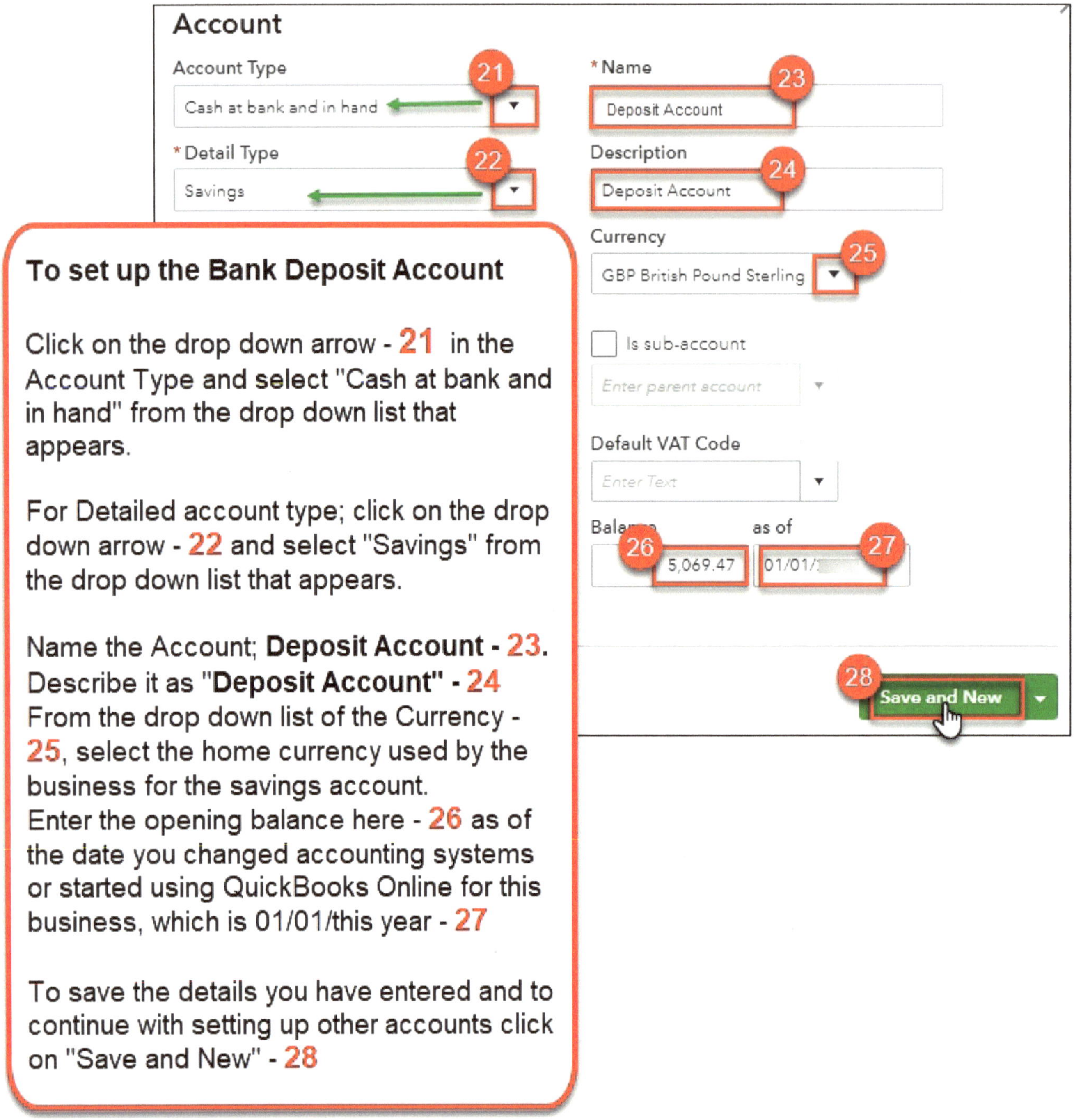

Account

Account Type

Cash at bank and in hand ← (21) ▼

*Detail Type

Savings ← (22) ▼

*Name

Deposit Account (23)

Description

Deposit Account (24)

Currency

GBP British Pound Sterling ▼ (25)

☐ Is sub-account

Enter parent account ▼

Default VAT Code

Enter Text ▼

Balance   **as of**

(26) 5,069.47   01/01/ (27)

(28) **Save and New** ▼

To set up the Bank Deposit Account

Click on the drop down arrow - **21** in the Account Type and select "Cash at bank and in hand" from the drop down list that appears.

For Detailed account type; click on the drop down arrow - **22** and select "Savings" from the drop down list that appears.

Name the Account; **Deposit Account - 23.** Describe it as **"Deposit Account" - 24** From the drop down list of the Currency - **25**, select the home currency used by the business for the savings account.
Enter the opening balance here - **26** as of the date you changed accounting systems or started using QuickBooks Online for this business, which is 01/01/this year - **27**

To save the details you have entered and to continue with setting up other accounts click on "Save and New" - **28**

Fig. 28

Current Account, Petty Cash Account and Bank Deposit Account done. If you needed to create a credit card account and Savings account, you would follow the same steps as above making sure you keep Account type as Cash at bank and in hand and changing all the other entries as required.

Let's move on to creating new accounts for income.

This space is for notes

Income Accounts:

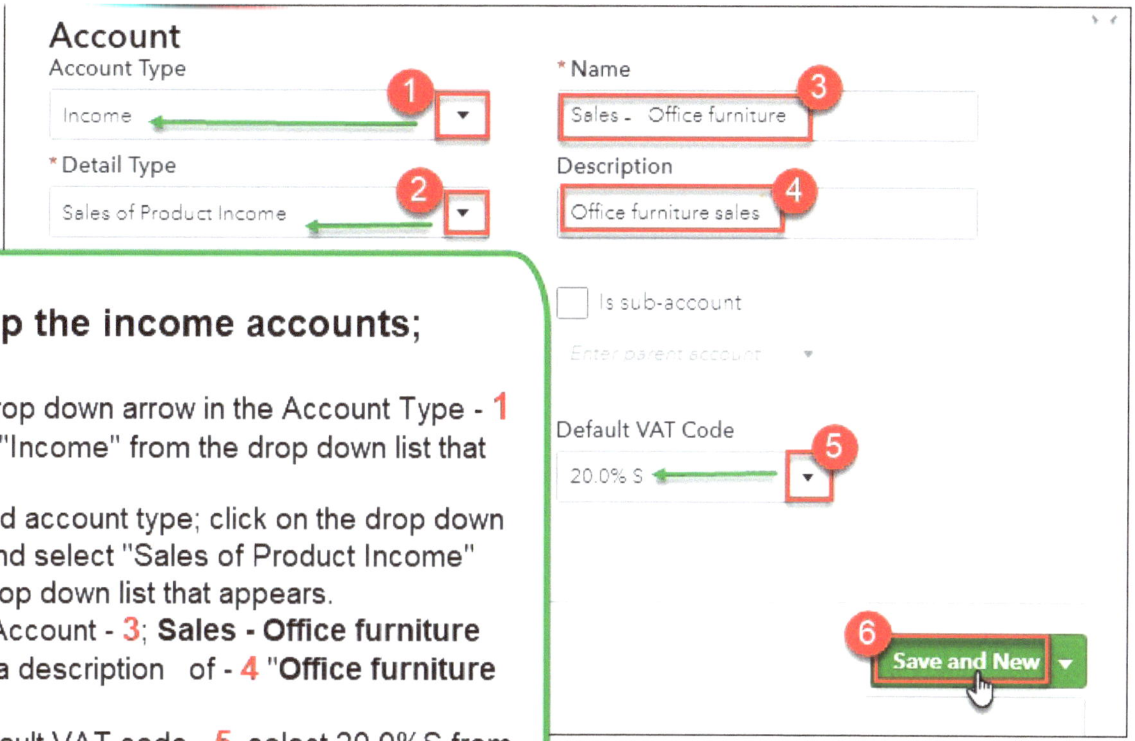

Account

Account Type

Income ← 1 ▼

* Detail Type

Sales of Product Income ← 2 ▼

* Name

Sales - Office furniture 3

Description

Office furniture sales 4

☐ Is sub-account

Enter parent account ▼

Default VAT Code

20.0% S ← 5 ▼

6 **Save and New** ▼

To set up the income accounts;

Click the drop down arrow in the Account Type - 1 and select "Income" from the drop down list that appears.
For Detailed account type; click on the drop down arrow - 2 and select "Sales of Product Income" from the drop down list that appears.
Name the Account - 3; **Sales - Office furniture** and give it a description   of - 4 **"Office furniture sales".**
For the default VAT code - 5, select 20.0%S from the drop down list, then click "Save and New" - 6

From the new window that appears after step 6, keep everything as it is but change 3 & 4. Change them each time to:
1st Change:
Change 3 to: Sales - Office equipment
Change 4 to: Office equipment sales
Then follow steps 5 and 6.

Then again, after step 6, keep everything the same and change 3 & 4 for the second time.
2nd Change:
Change 3 to: Sales - Consumables
Change 4 to: Consumables sales
Then follow steps 5 and 6.

Then again, after step 6, keep everything the same and change 3 & 4 for the third time and also change 2 as well this time as follows:
3rd Change:
Change 2 to: Service/Fee Income, Change 3 to: Expert setup and installation service, Change 4 to: Service sales.

Fig. 29

Task 1b: Setting up Customers & Suppliers

Task 1b(i): Setting up Customers and corresponding opening balances

You can add Customers in QuickBooks online in two ways:

1. Add them directly as shown in the figure below

   or

2. Upload them using a csv template that has the customer details you want to add to QuickBooks Online.

The direct way of adding a Customer to QuickBooks Online is as illustrated in the figure below.

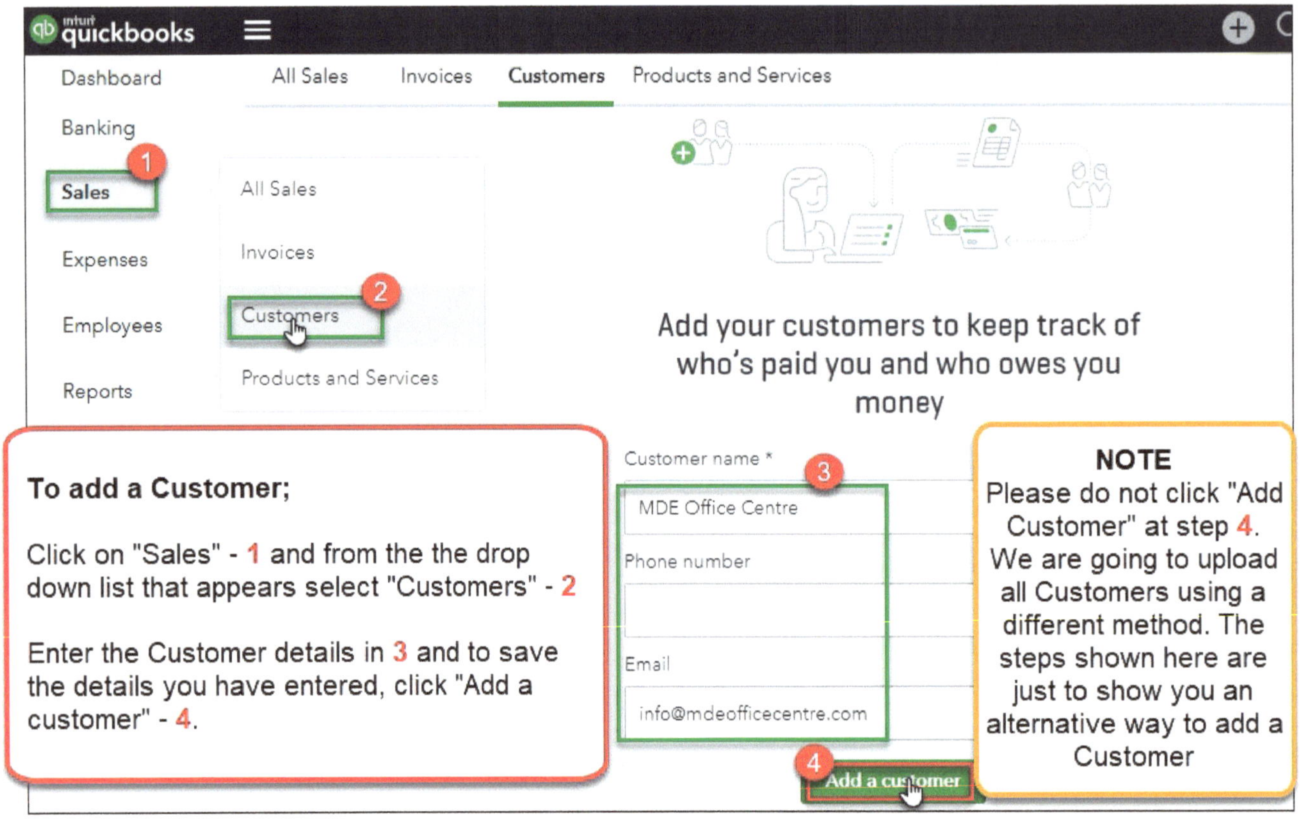

Fig. 30

Let's now look at an alternative way to add a customer to QuickBooks Online – the second option in our tutorial.

The second option is much faster and enables you to add more details about the customer at once. So, we will be using the second method, but I will also show you how to use the first method.

This space is for notes

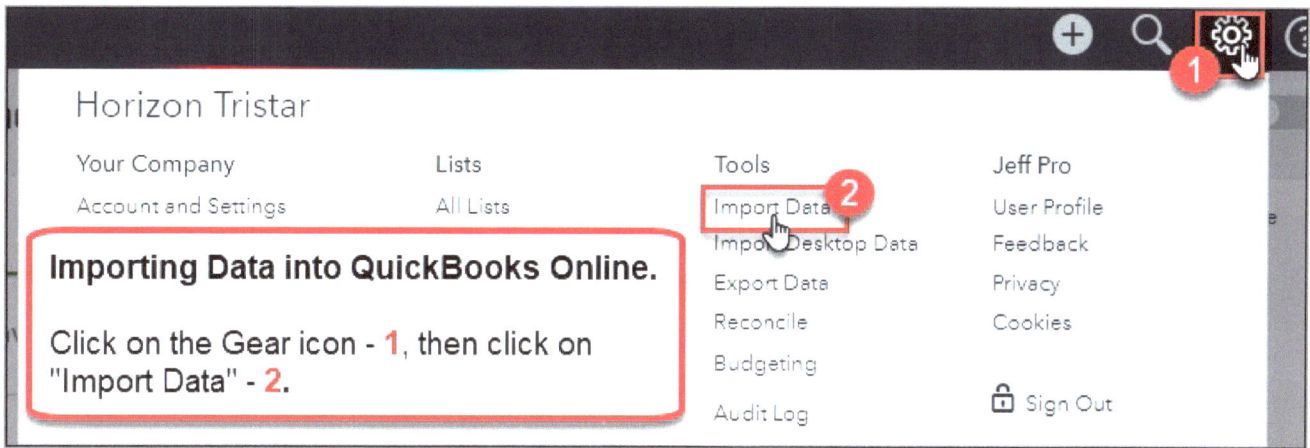

Fig. 31

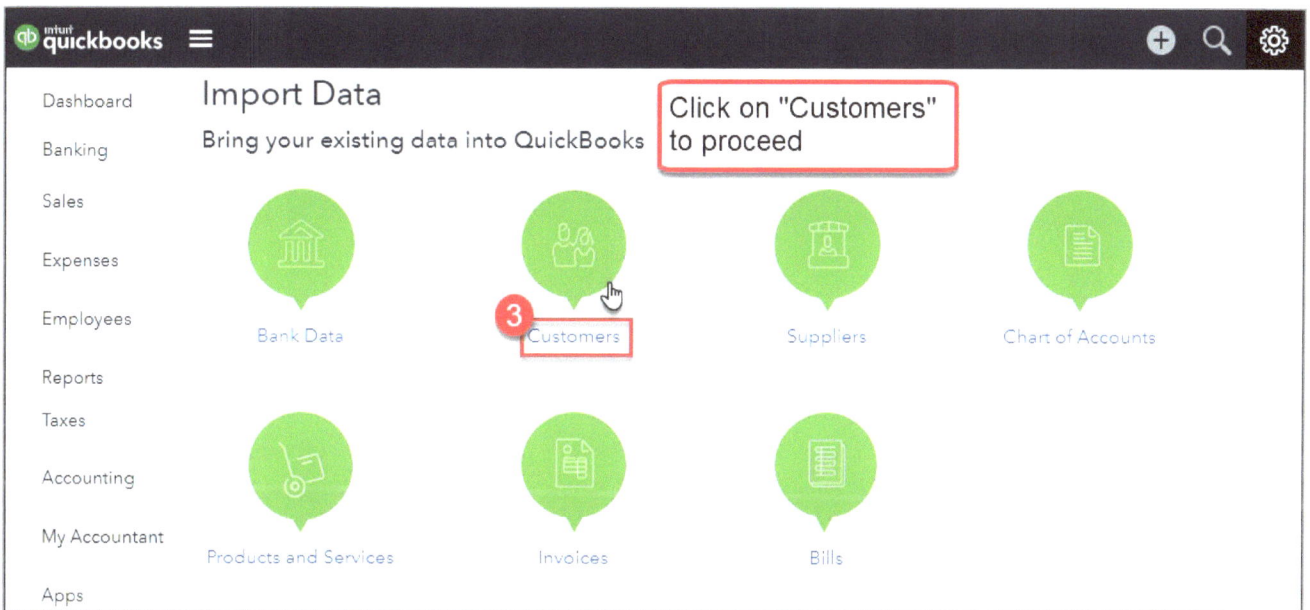

Fig. 32

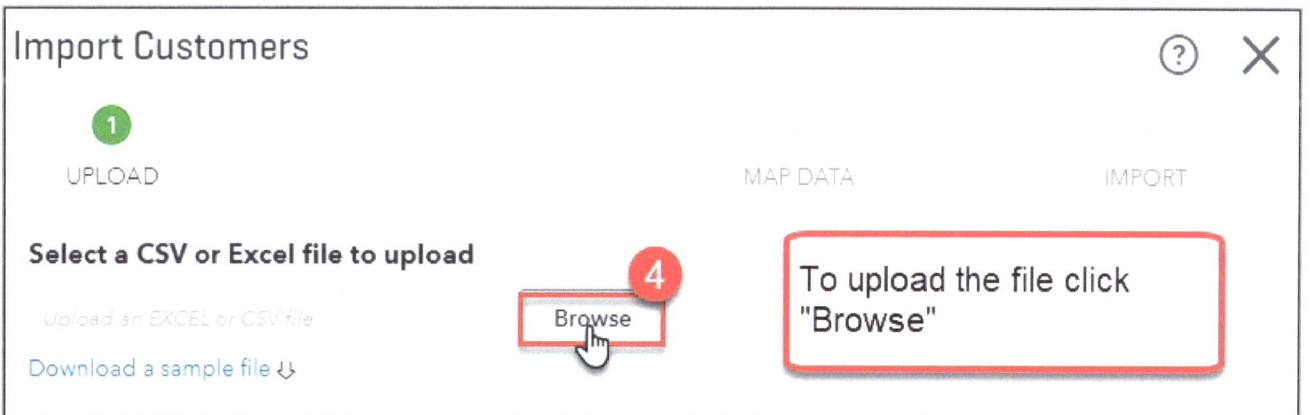

Fig. 33

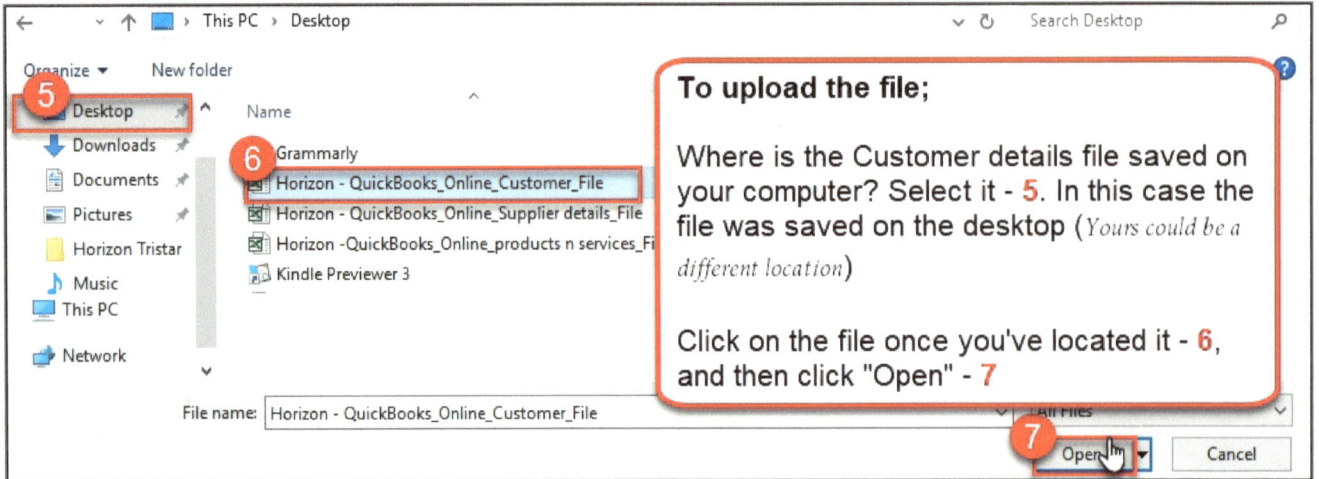

Fig. 34

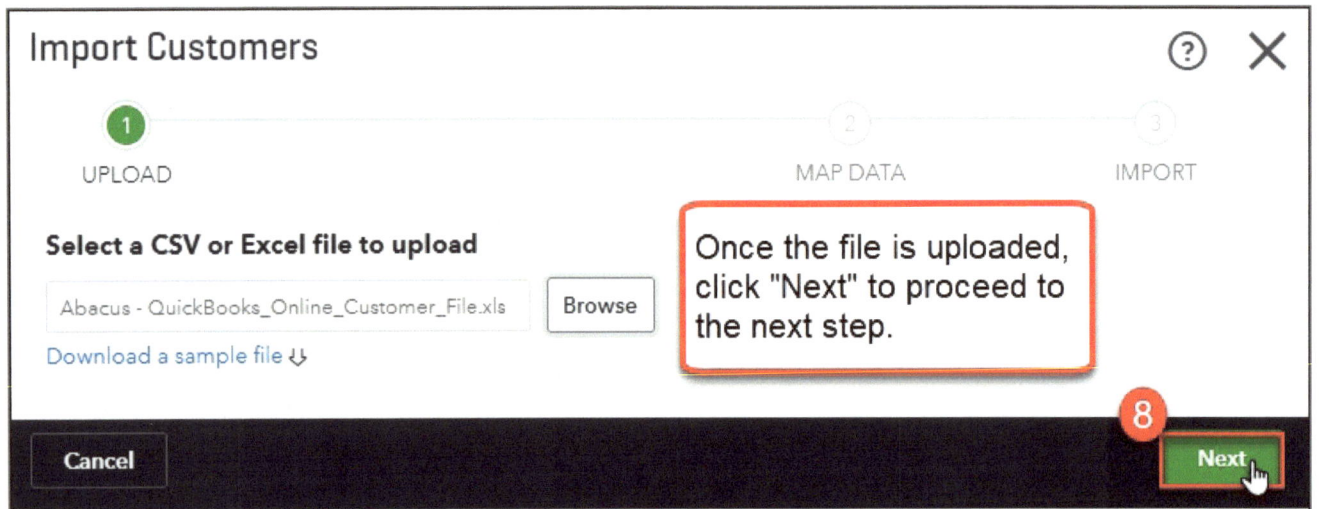

Fig. 35

This space is for notes

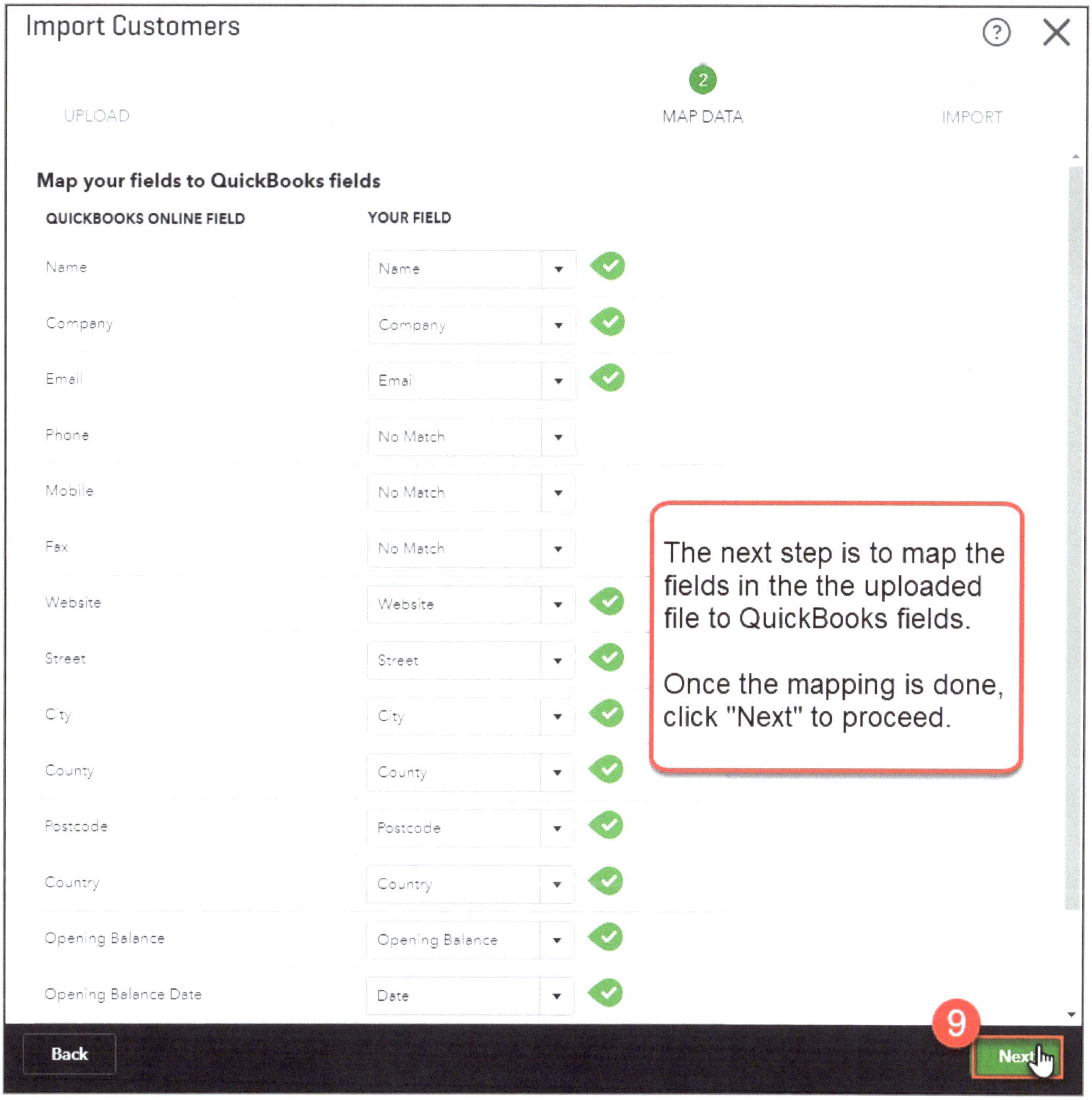

Import Customers

UPLOAD   **2** MAP DATA   IMPORT

Map your fields to QuickBooks fields

QUICKBOOKS ONLINE FIELD	YOUR FIELD	
Name	Name ▼	✓
Company	Company ▼	✓
Email	Email ▼	✓
Phone	No Match ▼	
Mobile	No Match ▼	
Fax	No Match ▼	
Website	Website ▼	✓
Street	Street ▼	✓
City	City ▼	✓
County	County ▼	✓
Postcode	Postcode ▼	✓
Country	Country ▼	✓
Opening Balance	Opening Balance ▼	✓
Opening Balance Date	Date ▼	✓

> The next step is to map the fields in the the uploaded file to QuickBooks fields.
>
> Once the mapping is done, click "Next" to proceed.

Back

9

Next

Fig. 36

This space is for your notes

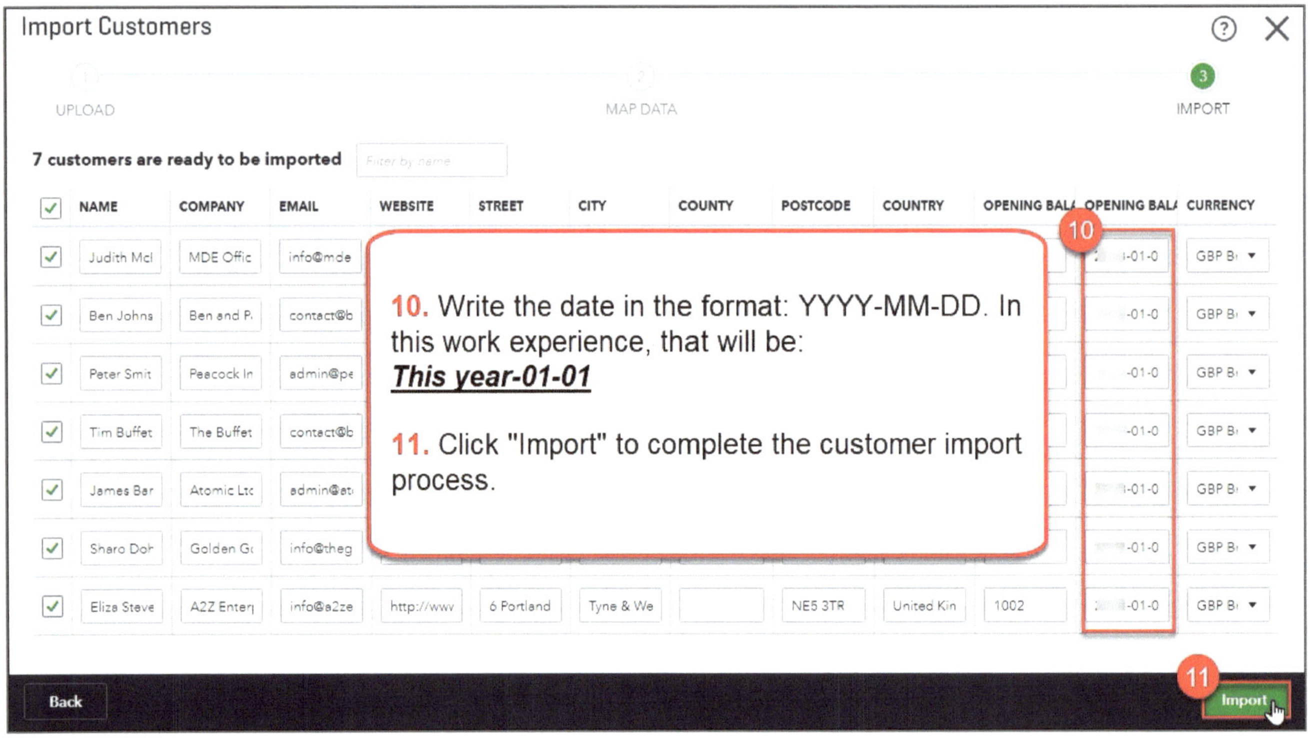

Import Customers

UPLOAD — MAP DATA — ③ IMPORT

7 customers are ready to be imported [Filter by name]

✓	NAME	COMPANY	EMAIL	WEBSITE	STREET	CITY	COUNTY	POSTCODE	COUNTRY	OPENING BAL	OPENING BAL	CURRENCY
✓	Judith McI	MDE Offic	info@mde								-01-0	GBP B ▼
✓	Ben Johns	Ben and P.	contact@b								-01-0	GBP B ▼
✓	Peter Smit	Peacock In	admin@pe								-01-0	GBP B ▼
✓	Tim Buffet	The Buffet	contact@b								-01-0	GBP B ▼
✓	James Bar	Atomic Ltc	admin@at								-01-0	GBP B ▼
✓	Sharo Doh	Golden G	info@theg								-01-0	GBP B ▼
✓	Eliza Steve	A2Z Enter	info@a2ze	http://ww	6 Portland	Tyne & We		NE5 3TR	United Kin	1002	-01-0	GBP B ▼

10

10. Write the date in the format: YYYY-MM-DD. In this work experience, that will be:
This year-01-01

11. Click "Import" to complete the customer import process.

11

Back — Import

Fig. 37

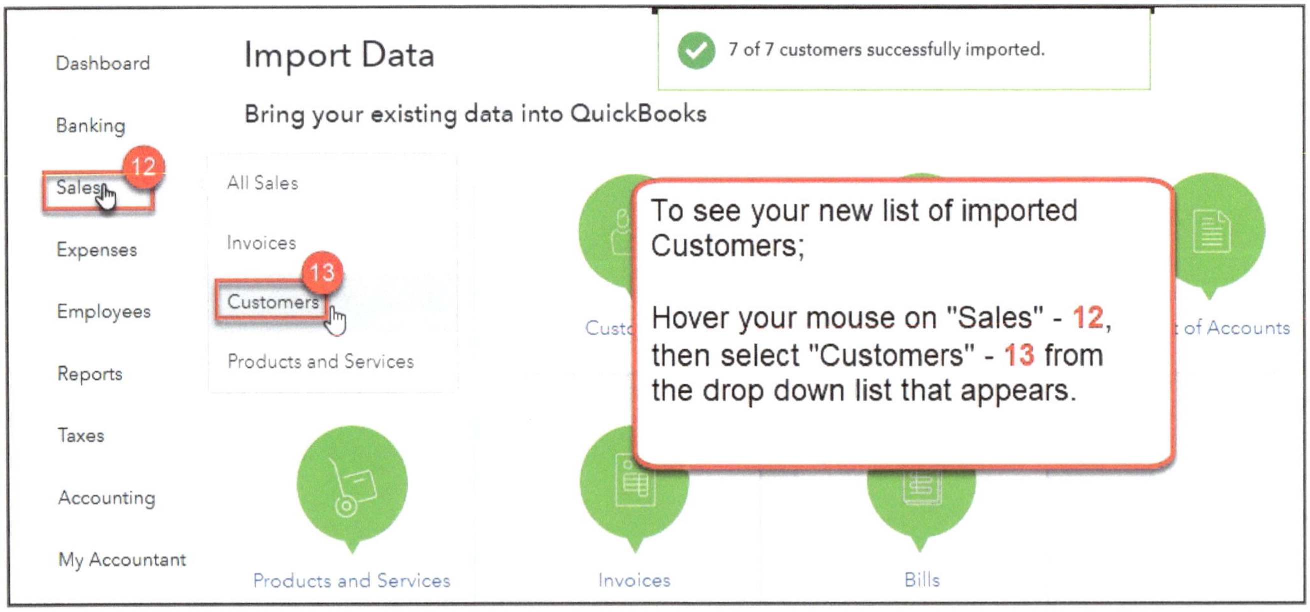

Import Data

Dashboard

Banking

12 Sales

Expenses

Employees

Reports

Taxes

Accounting

My Accountant

✓ 7 of 7 customers successfully imported.

Bring your existing data into QuickBooks

All Sales

Invoices

13 Customers

Products and Services

To see your new list of imported Customers;

Hover your mouse on "Sales" - **12**, then select "Customers" - **13** from the drop down list that appears.

Custo... ...t of Accounts

Products and Services   Invoices   Bills

Fig. 38

This space is for notes

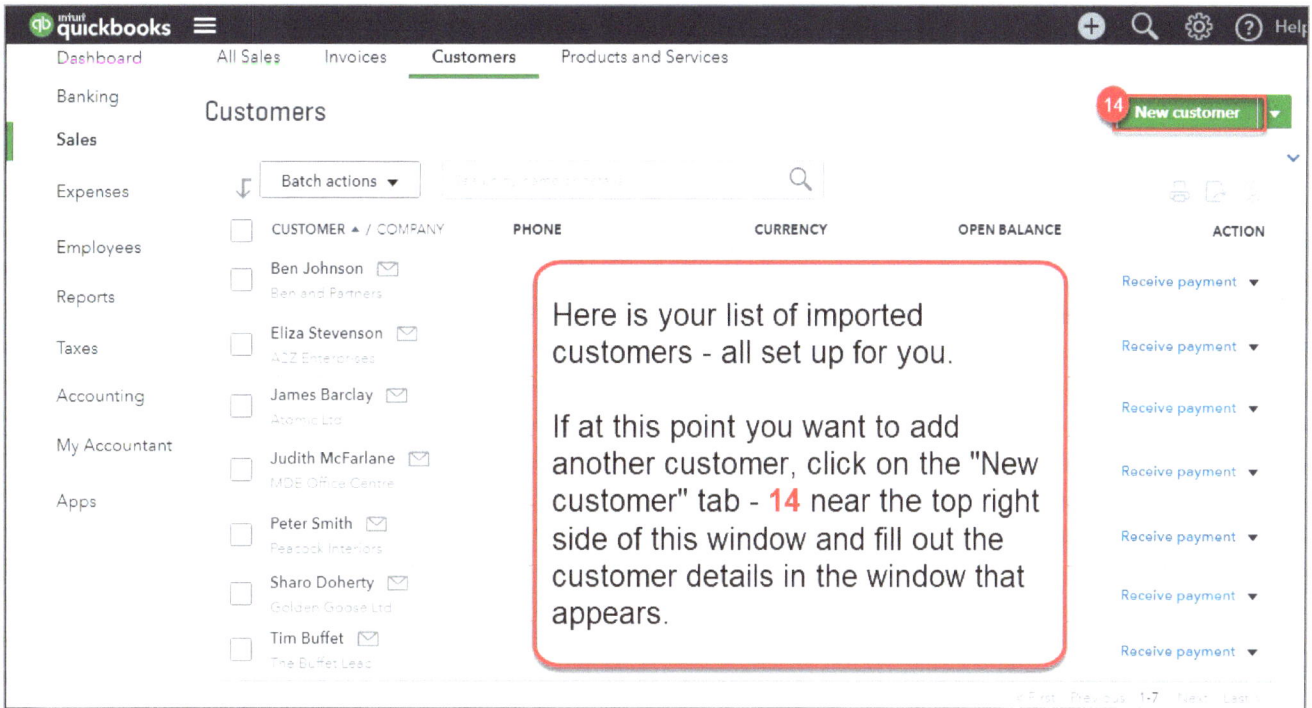

Fig. 39

Please note that when you import Customers to QuickBooks Online the way we have just done, QuickBooks puts the contact persons for each of the Customers you set up as the display names for those respective Customers. It does not pick up the Business names and puts them as display names. So, we will need to edit the Customers details so that the display names reflect the Company/Business name instead of the Customers contact persons name.

Editing Customer details:

The display name for the customers at this point is the Customer contact person. We need to change the display name to the Company name to make it easier later to invoice the customers through the create button.

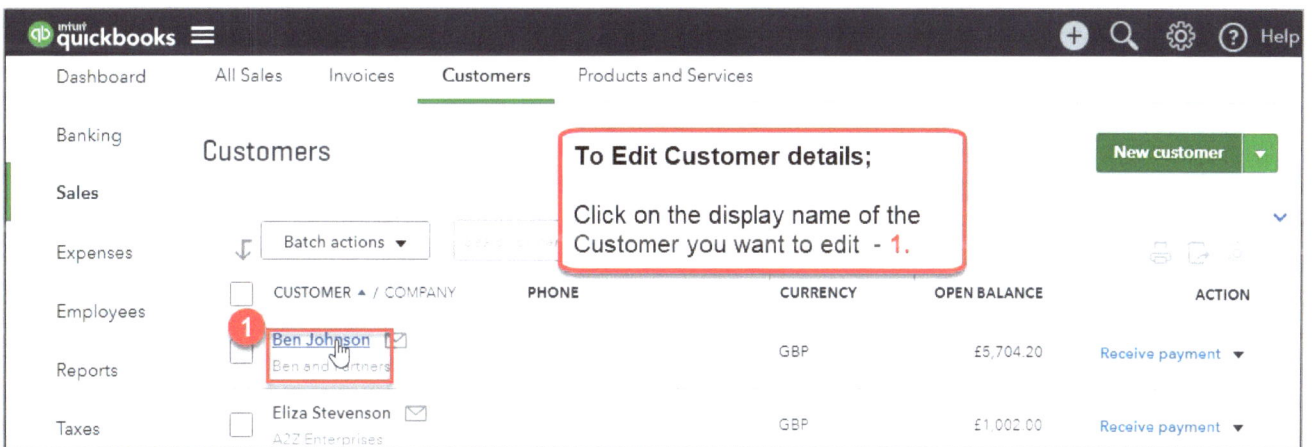

Fig. 40

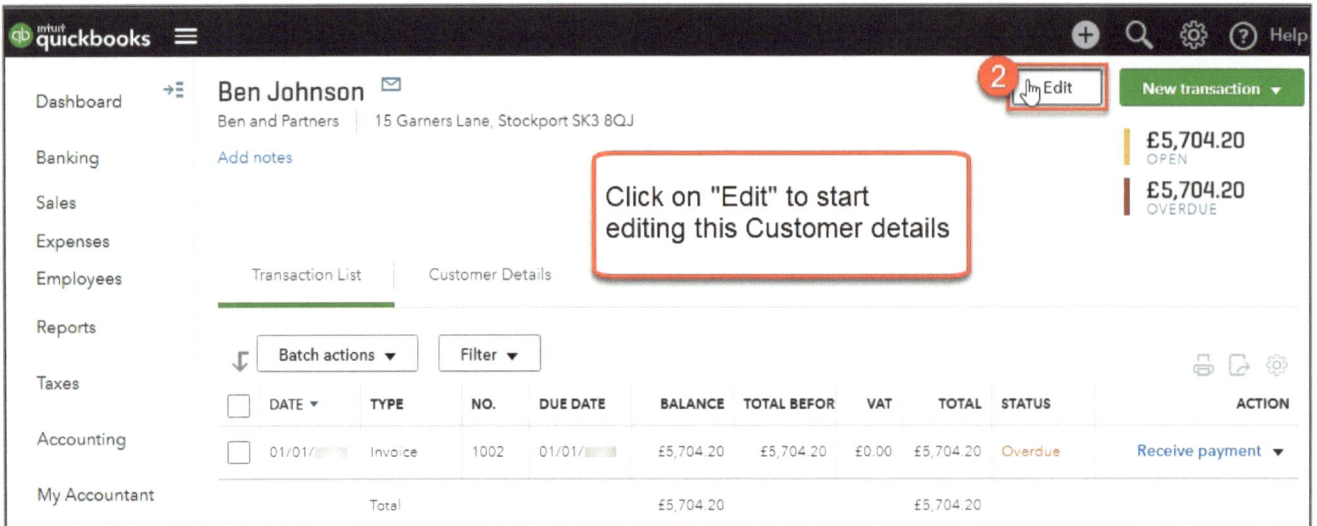

Fig. 41

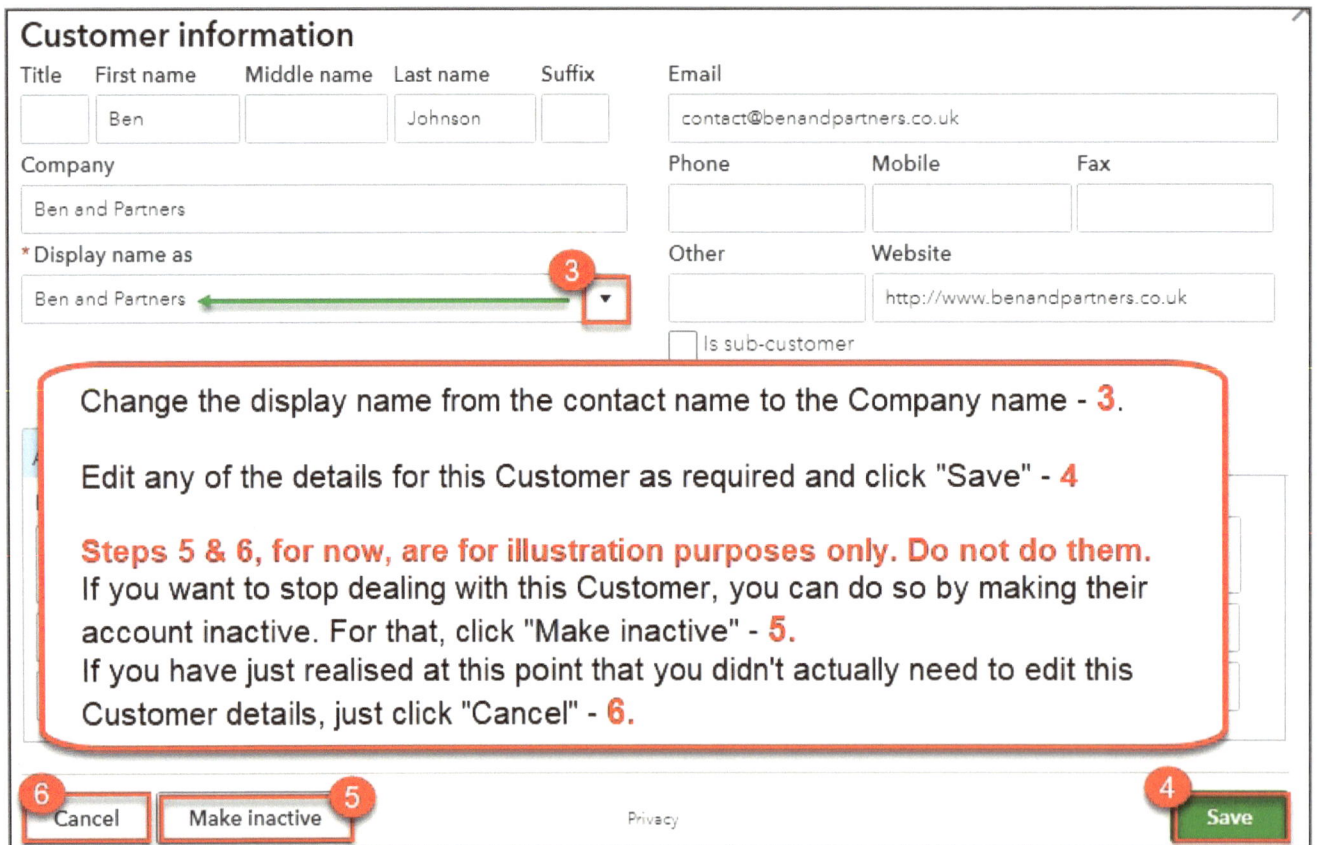

Fig. 42

Please go ahead and edit the display names for the rest of the other Customers. Do not proceed to the next task before editing the display names for all the Customers.

Task 1b(ii): Setting up Suppliers and corresponding opening balances

You can add Suppliers in QuickBooks online in two ways:

i.   Add them directly, or,
ii.   Upload them using a csv template that has the Suppliers details you want to add to QuickBooks Online.

The direct way of adding a Supplier to QuickBooks Online is as illustrated in the figure below.

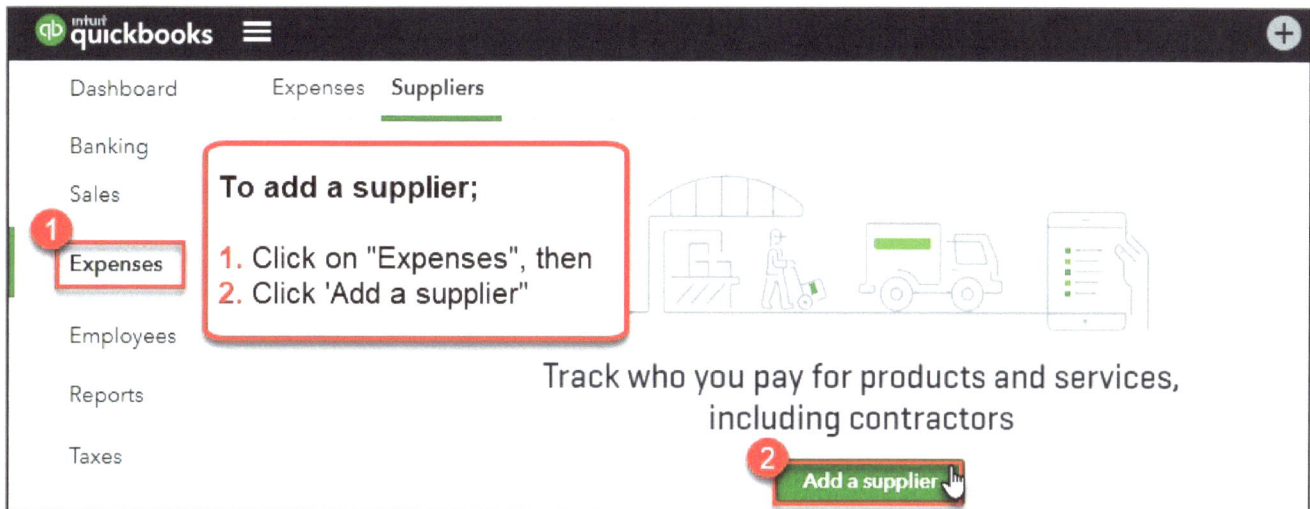

Fig. 43

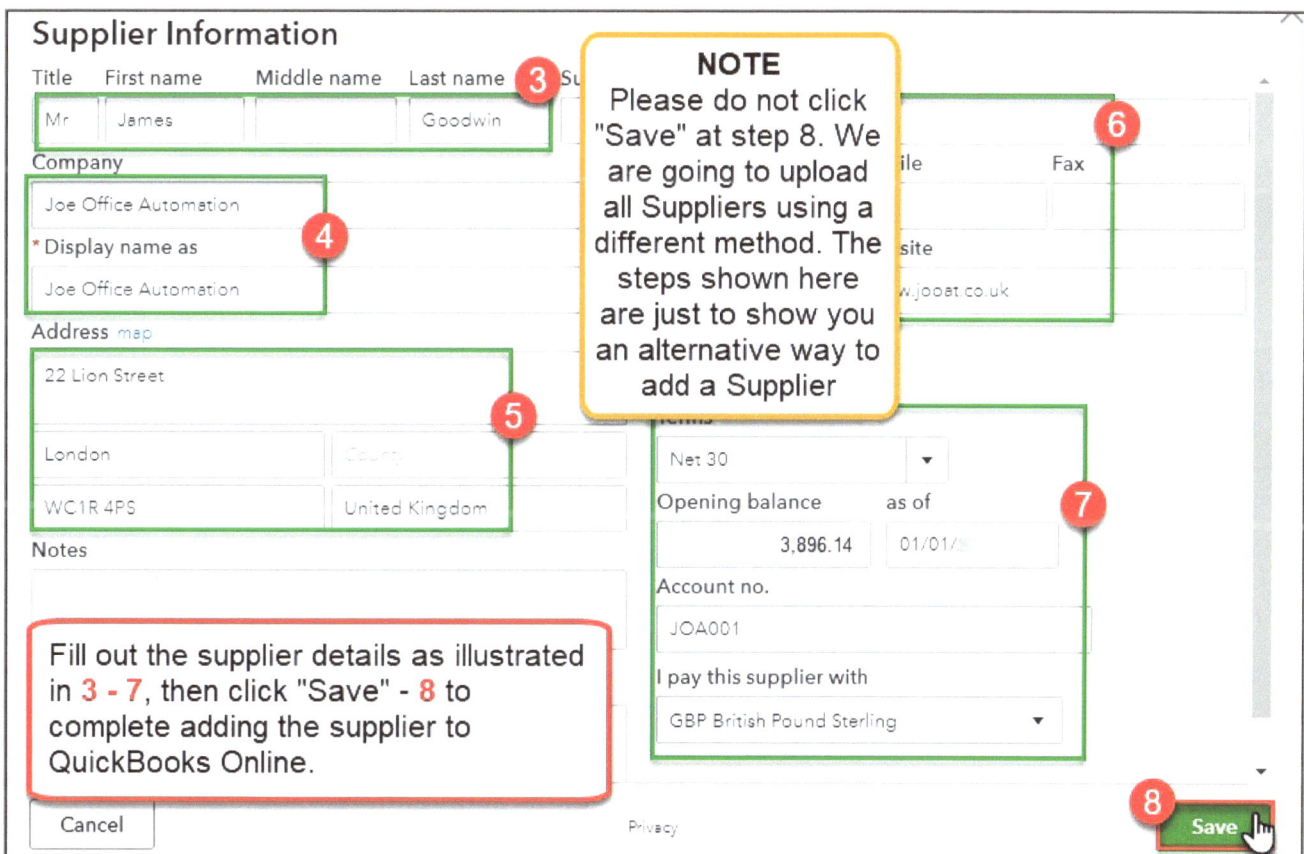

Fig. 44

The second option is much faster and enables you to add more suppliers at once. So, let's do it.

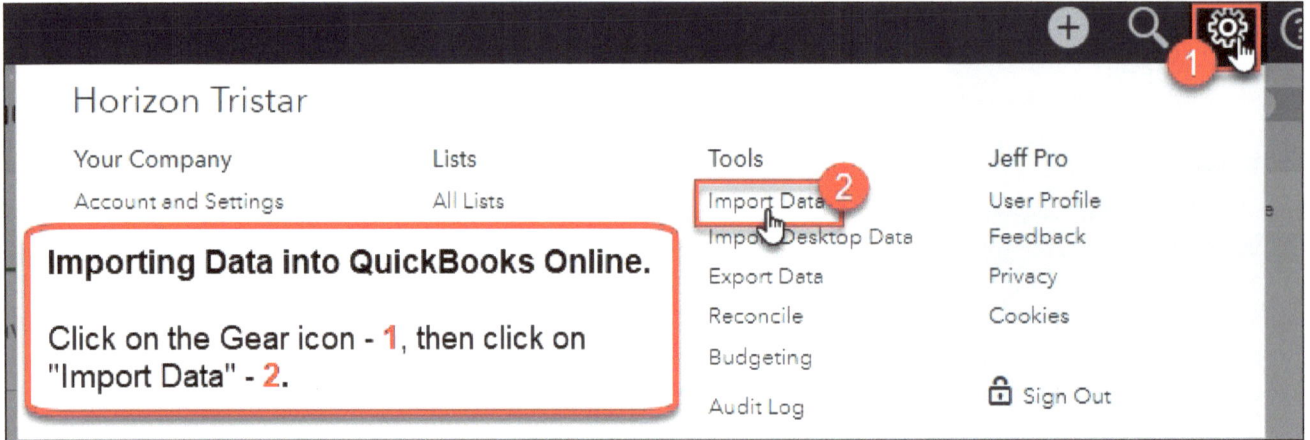

Horizon Tristar

Your Company	Lists	Tools	Jeff Pro
Account and Settings	All Lists	Import Data	User Profile
		Import Desktop Data	Feedback
		Export Data	Privacy
		Reconcile	Cookies
		Budgeting	
		Audit Log	Sign Out

Importing Data into QuickBooks Online.

Click on the Gear icon - 1, then click on "Import Data" - 2.

Fig.45

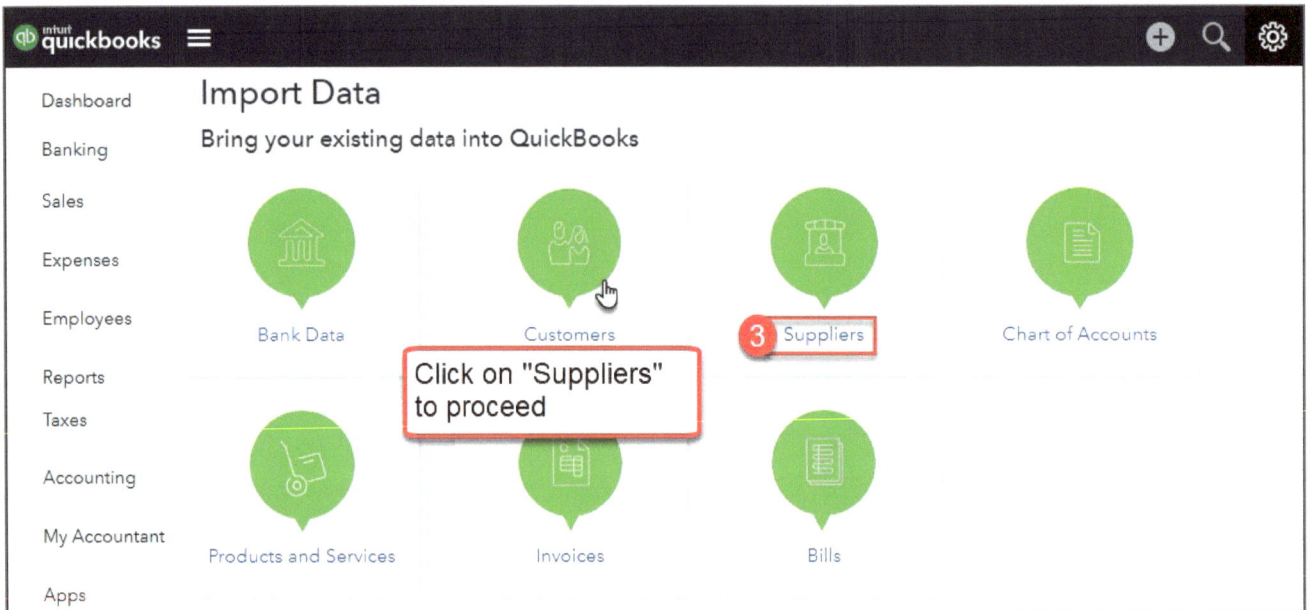

Import Data

Bring your existing data into QuickBooks

Bank Data Customers **3** Suppliers Chart of Accounts

Products and Services Invoices Bills

Click on "Suppliers" to proceed

Fig. 46

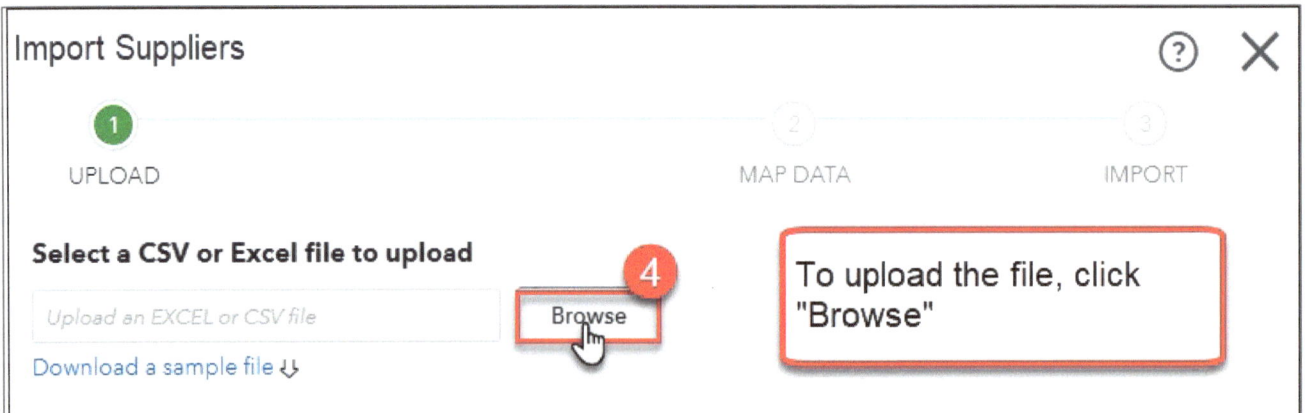

Import Suppliers

1 UPLOAD   **2** MAP DATA   **3** IMPORT

Select a CSV or Excel file to upload

Upload an EXCEL or CSV file   **4** Browse

Download a sample file

To upload the file, click "Browse"

Fig. 47

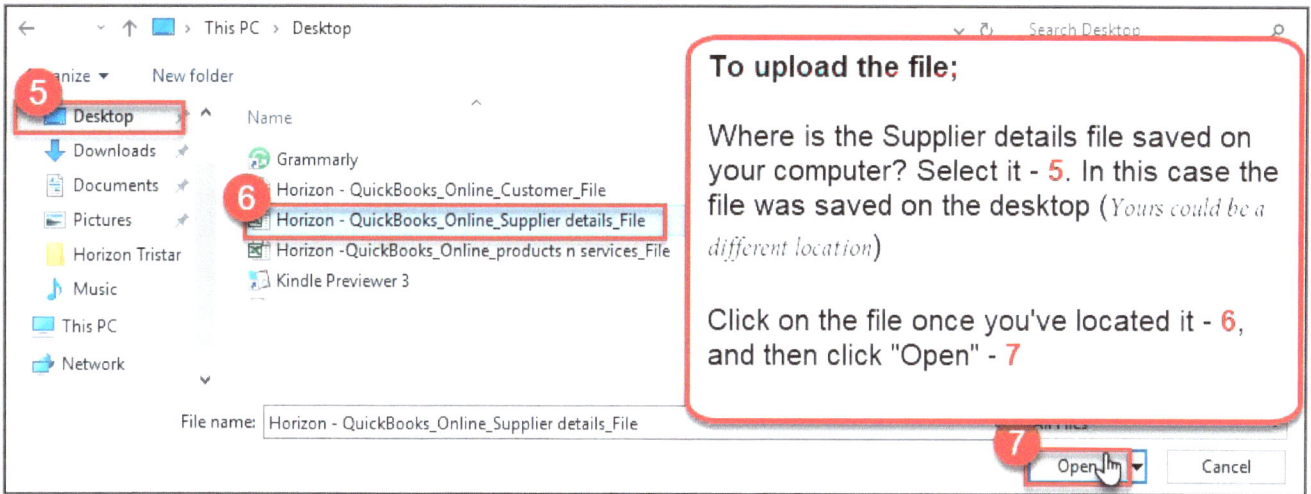

Fig. 48

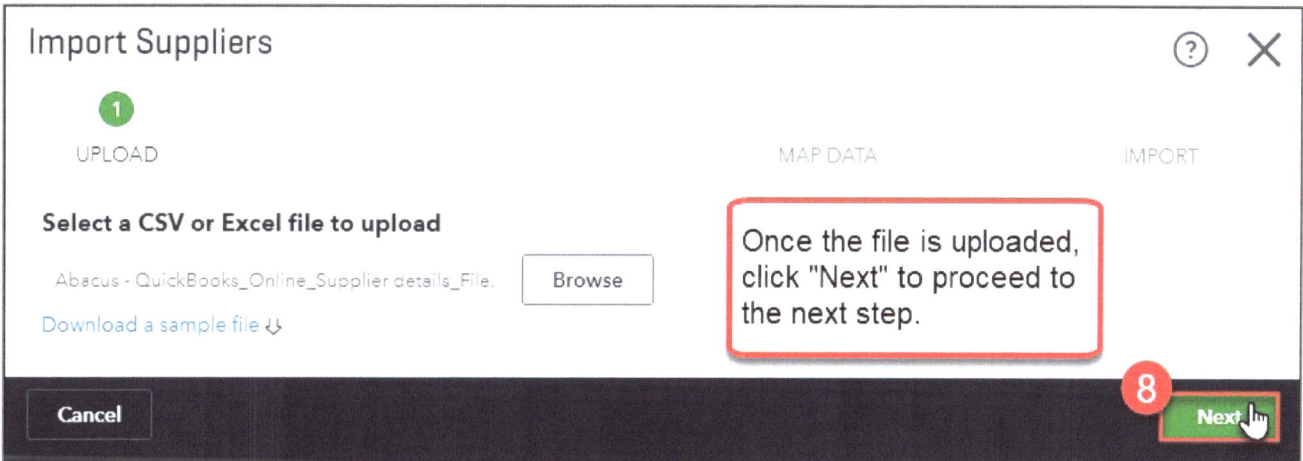

Fig. 49

This space is for your notes

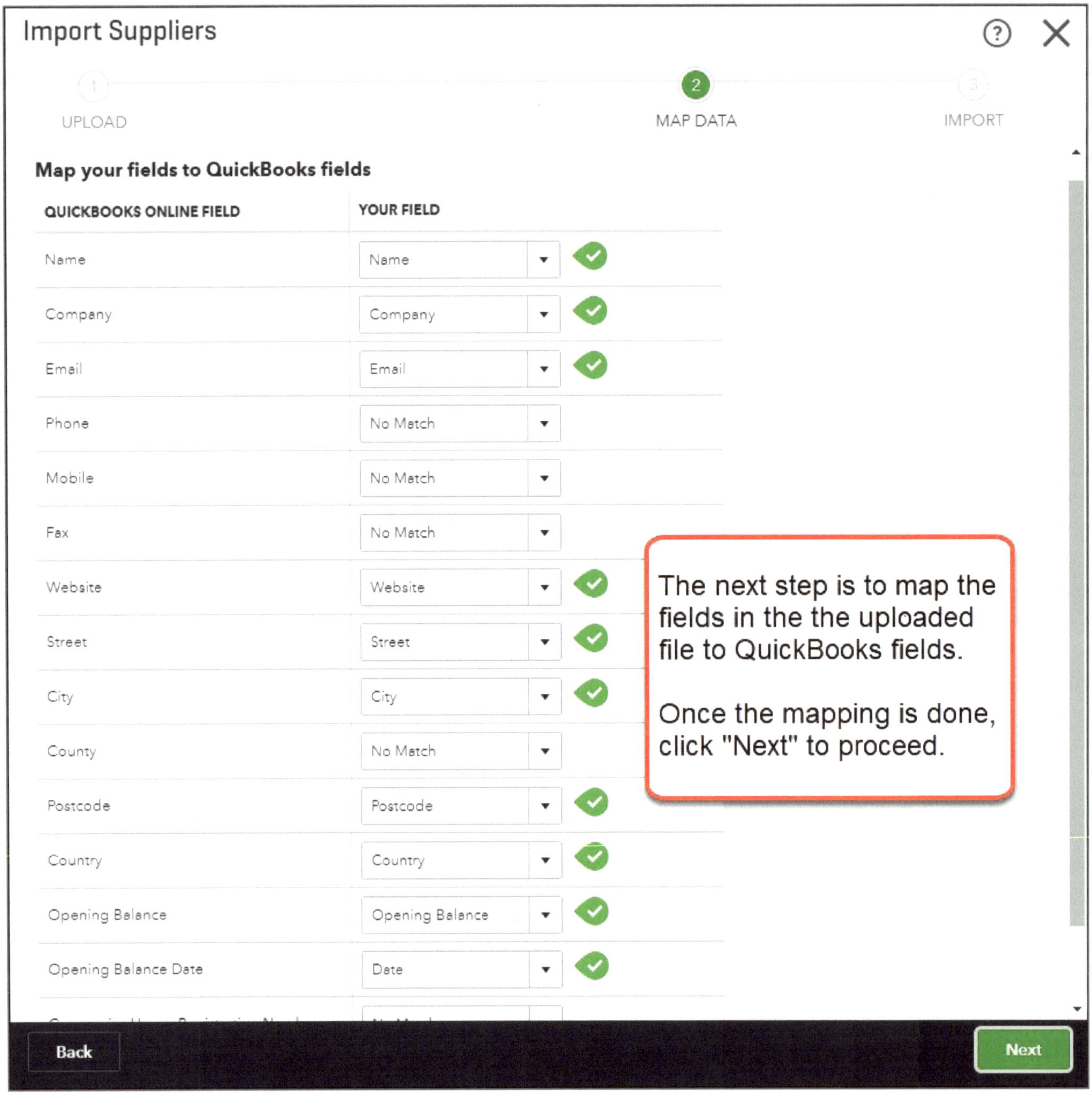

Import Suppliers

| 1 UPLOAD | 2 MAP DATA | 3 IMPORT |

Map your fields to QuickBooks fields

QUICKBOOKS ONLINE FIELD	YOUR FIELD	
Name	Name ▼	✓
Company	Company ▼	✓
Email	Email ▼	✓
Phone	No Match ▼	
Mobile	No Match ▼	
Fax	No Match ▼	
Website	Website ▼	✓
Street	Street ▼	✓
City	City ▼	✓
County	No Match ▼	
Postcode	Postcode ▼	✓
Country	Country ▼	✓
Opening Balance	Opening Balance ▼	✓
Opening Balance Date	Date ▼	✓

The next step is to map the fields in the the uploaded file to QuickBooks fields.

Once the mapping is done, click "Next" to proceed.

Back   **Next**

Fig. 50

This space is for your notes

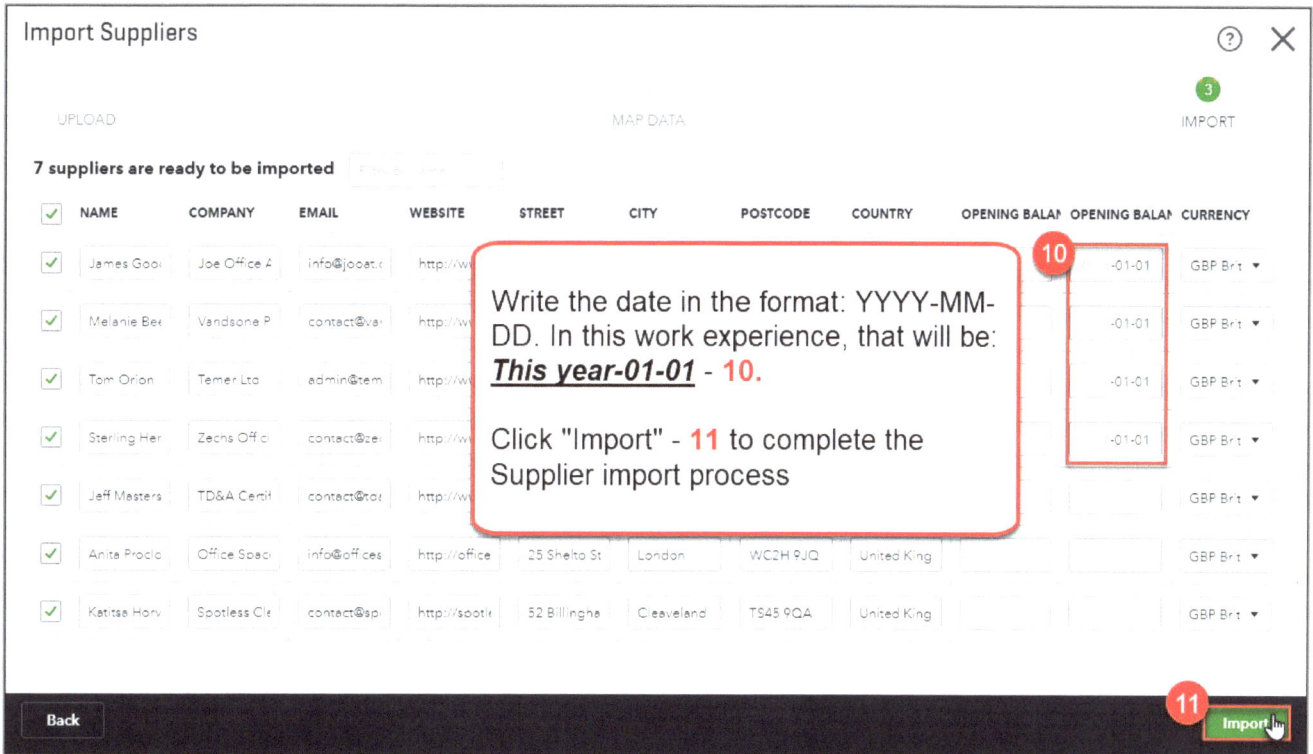

Fig. 51

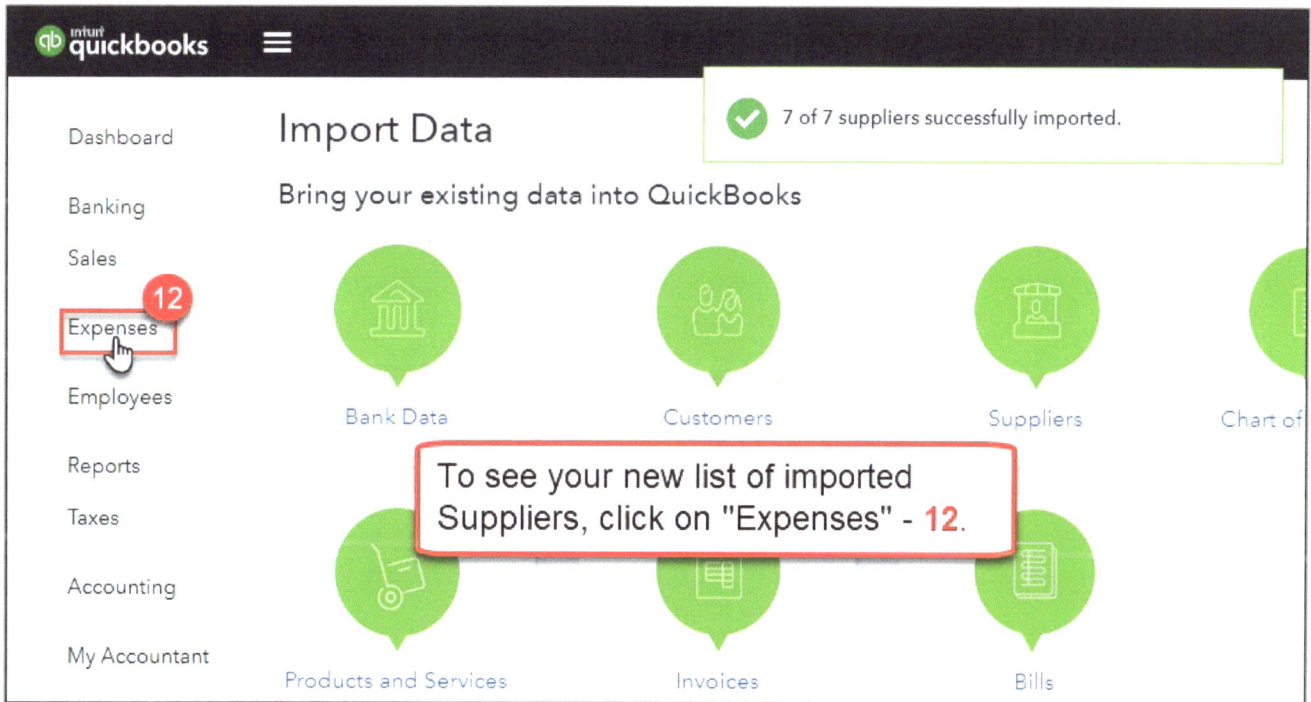

Fig. 52

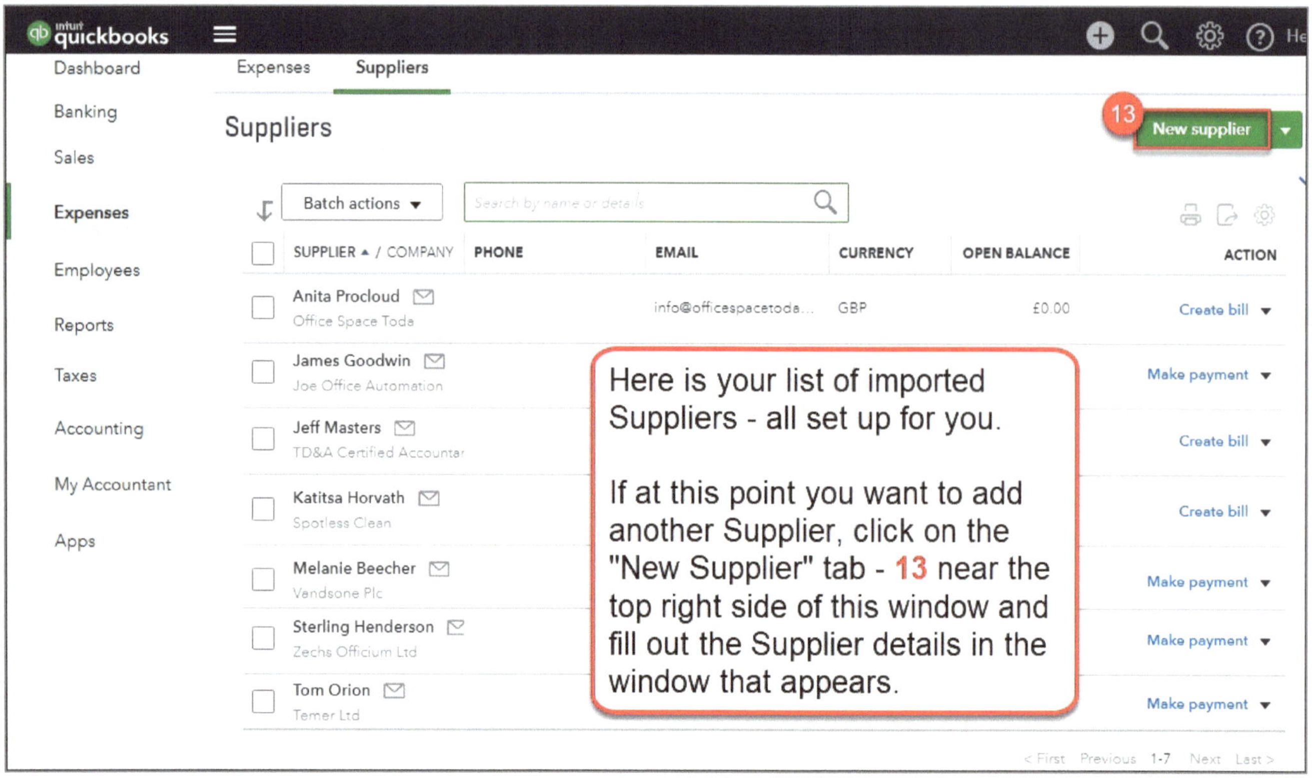

Fig. 53

Please note that when you import Suppliers to QuickBooks Online the way we have just done, QuickBooks puts the contact persons for each of the Suppliers you set up as the display names for those respective Suppliers. It does not pick up the Suppliers business or Company names. So, we will need to edit the supplier details so that the display names reflect the Suppliers Company/Business name instead of the Suppliers contact persons name.

Editing Supplier details:

The display name for the customers at this point is the Supplier contact person. We need to change the display name to the Company name to make it easier later to record invoices/bills from the Suppliers through the create button.

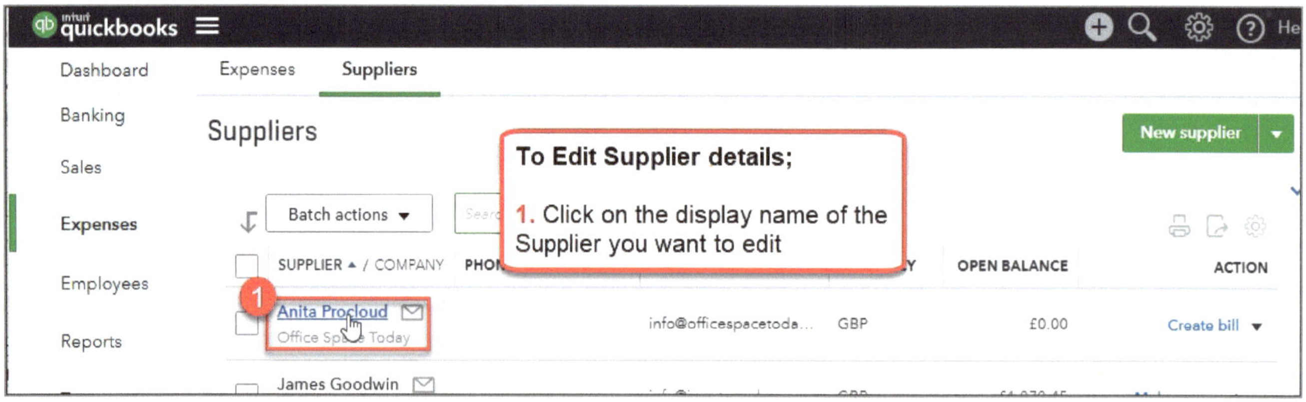

Fig. 54

Fig. 55

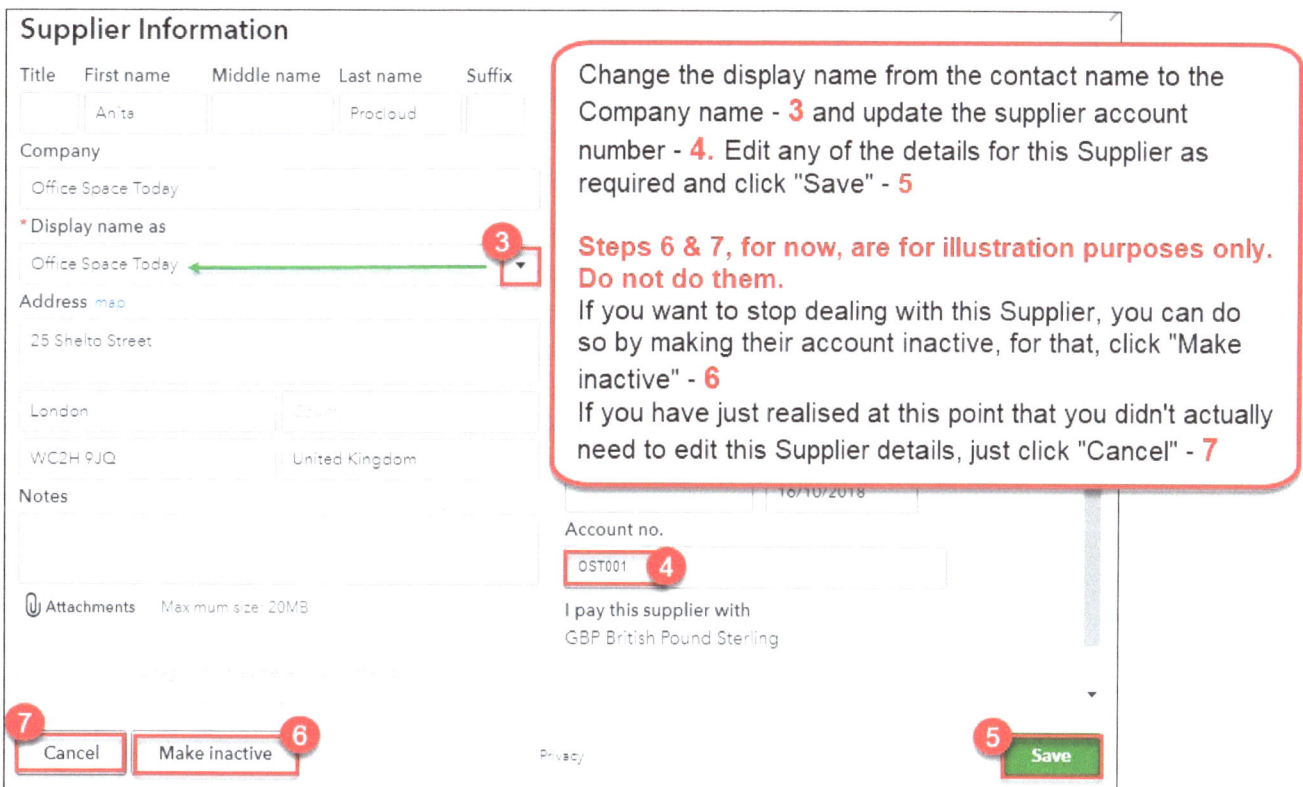

Fig. 56

Please go ahead and edit the display names for the rest of the other Suppliers. Do not proceed to the next task before editing the display names for all the Suppliers.

Task 1c: Setting up products & services

You can get to add a product or service in QuickBooks Online in two ways;

You can do so by clicking the Gear icon, then selecting products and services, then clicking on "Add a product or service" - see below

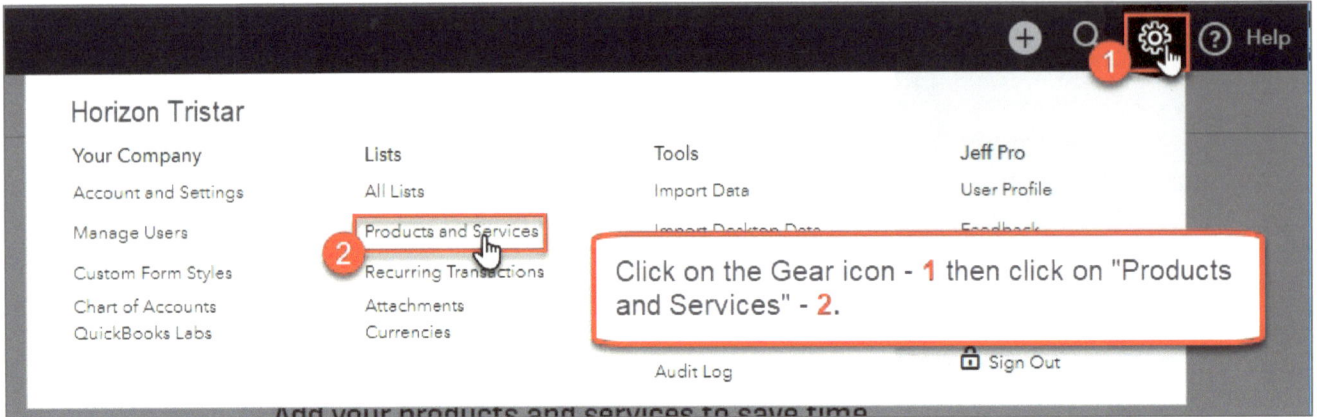

Fig. 57

Or,

You can also get to add a product or service by clicking on Sales, Products and Services, then click on "Add a product or service – see below.

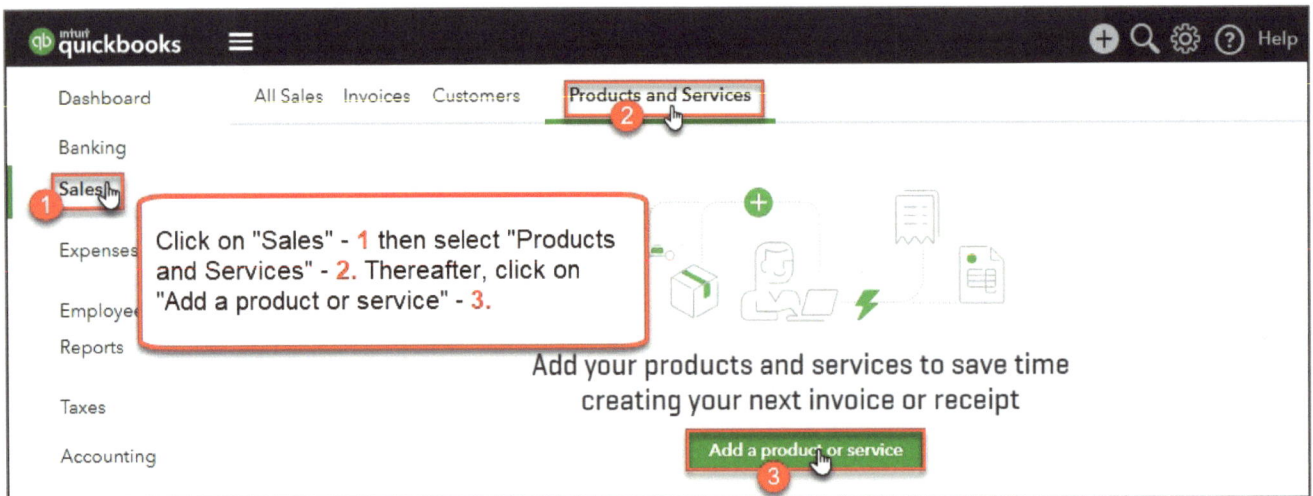

Fig. 58

This space is for notes

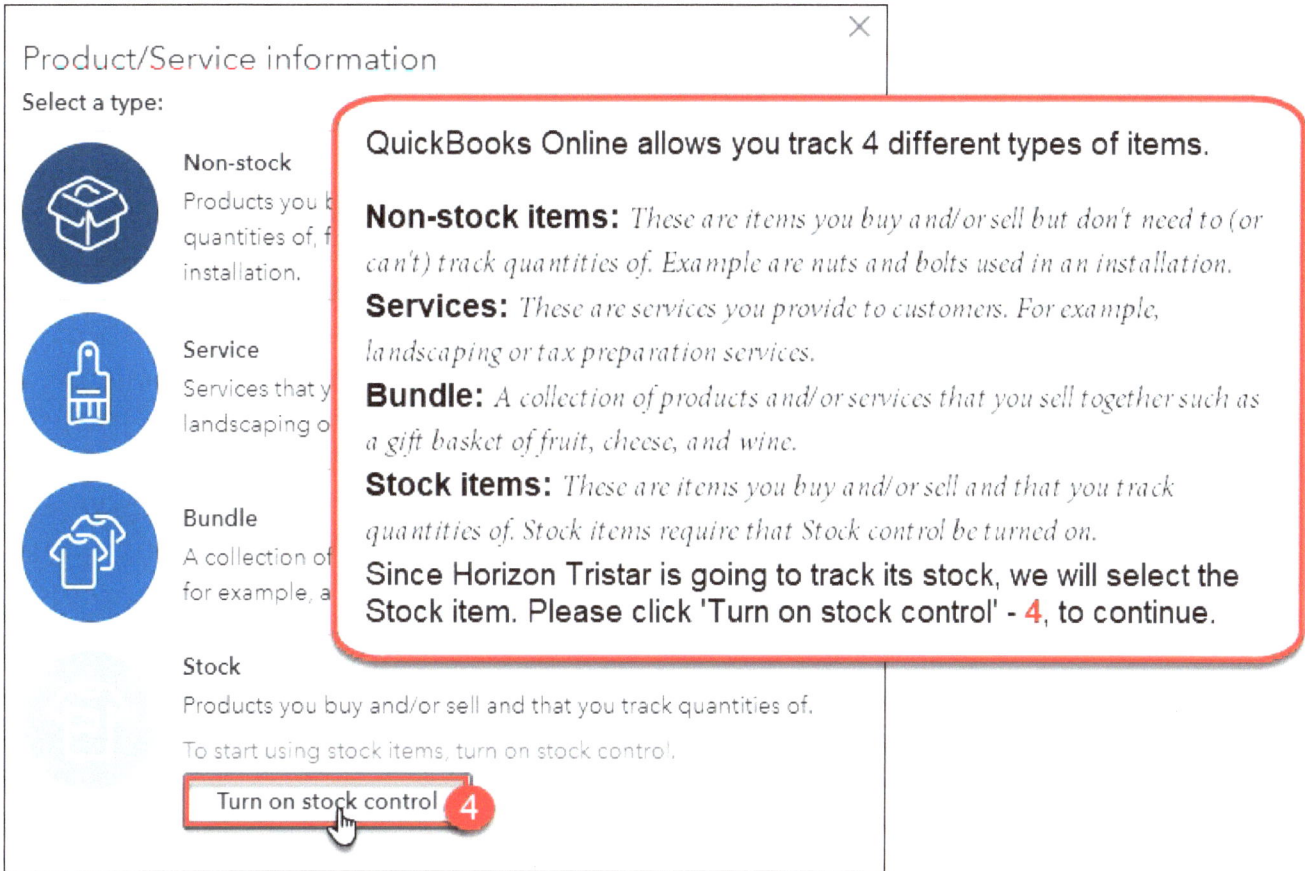

Fig. 59

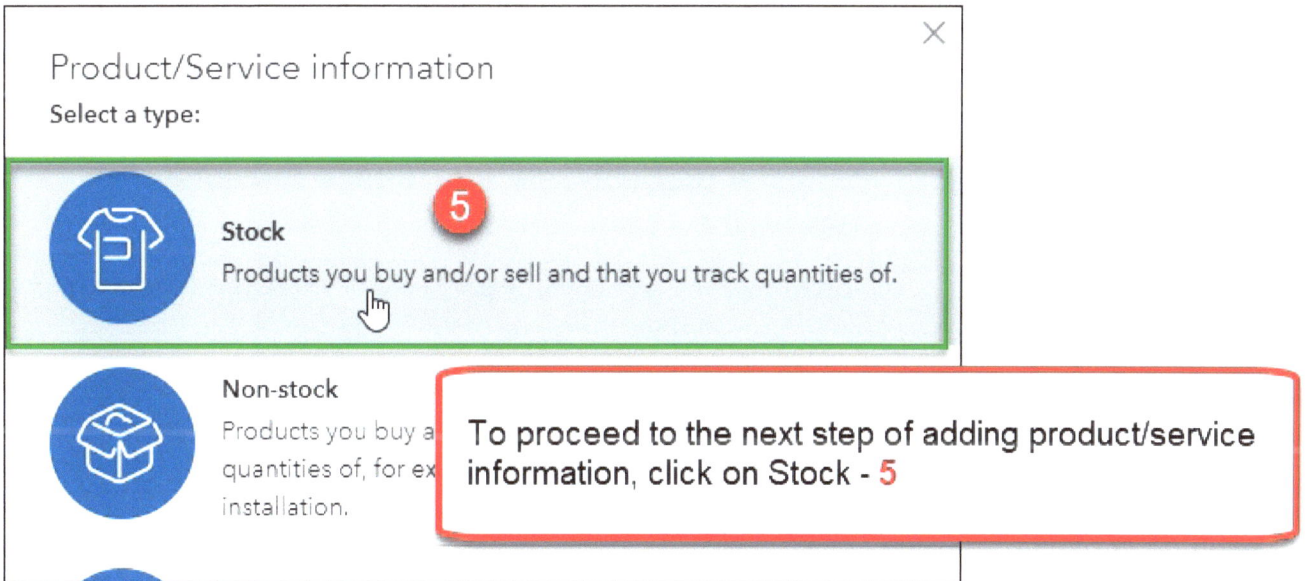

Fig. 60

This space is for notes

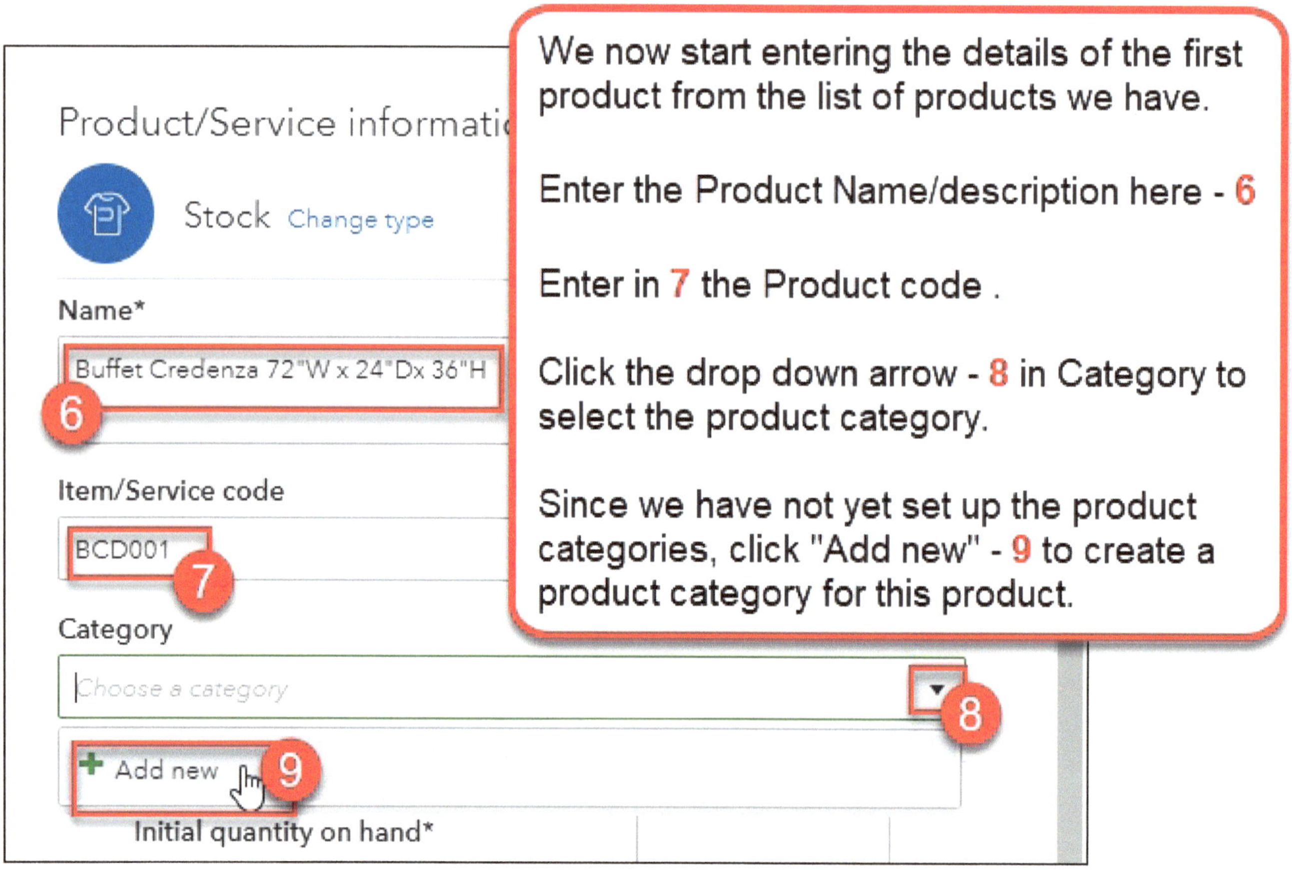

Product/Service information

Stock Change type

Name*

Buffet Credenza 72"W x 24"Dx 36"H

6

Item/Service code

BCD001

7

Category

Choose a category

8

+ Add new **9**

Initial quantity on hand*

We now start entering the details of the first product from the list of products we have.

Enter the Product Name/description here - **6**

Enter in **7** the Product code .

Click the drop down arrow - **8** in Category to select the product category.

Since we have not yet set up the product categories, click "Add new" - **9** to create a product category for this product.

Fig. 61

Category

Choose a category

New category

Name*

10

Office furniture

Cancel **11** Save

Name the product Category: Office furniture - step **10**, then click "Save" - **11**

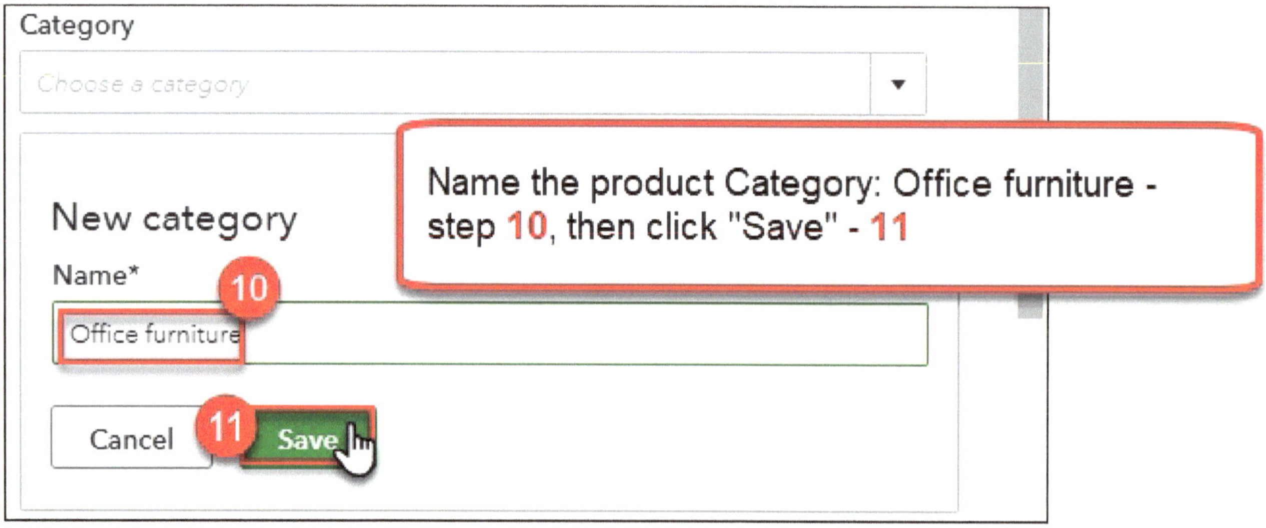

Fig. 62

This space is for notes

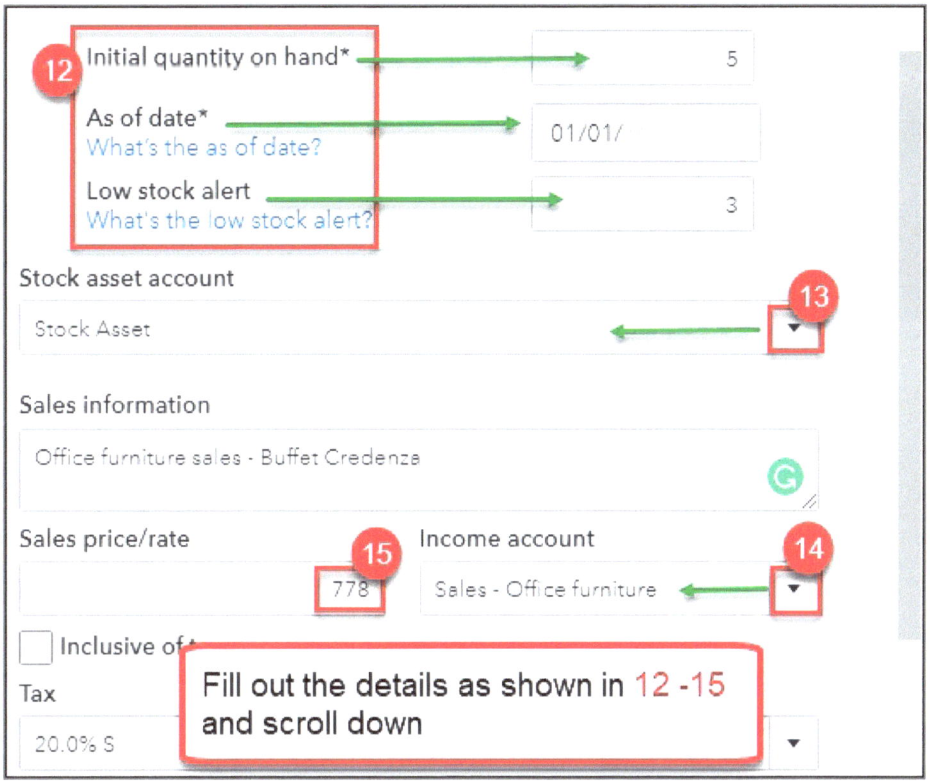
12
Initial quantity on hand*
5
As of date*
What's the as of date?
01/01/
Low stock alert
What's the low stock alert?
3
Stock asset account
Stock Asset
13
Sales information
Office furniture sales - Buffet Credenza
Sales price/rate
15
778
Income account
Sales - Office furniture
14
Inclusive of
Tax
20.0% S
Fill out the details as shown in 12 -15 and scroll down

Fig. 63

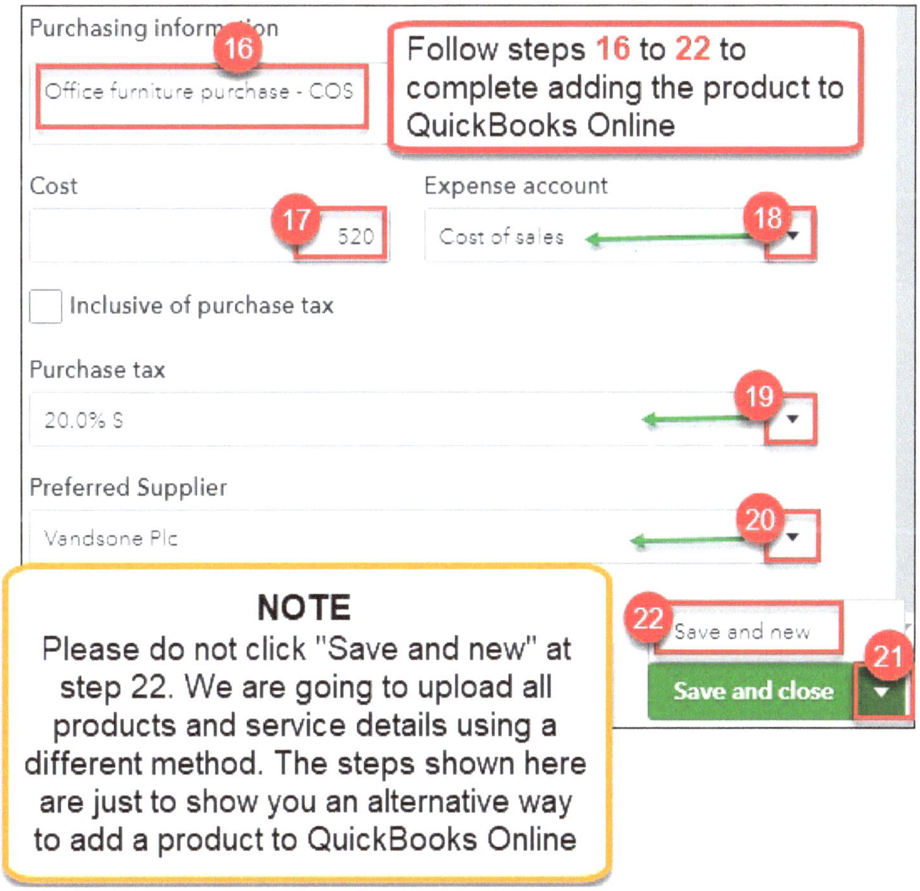
Purchasing information
16
Office furniture purchase - COS
Follow steps 16 to 22 to complete adding the product to QuickBooks Online
Cost
17
520
Expense account
Cost of sales
18
Inclusive of purchase tax
Purchase tax
20.0% S
19
Preferred Supplier
Vandsone Plc
20
NOTE
Please do not click "Save and new" at step 22. We are going to upload all products and service details using a different method. The steps shown here are just to show you an alternative way to add a product to QuickBooks Online
22
Save and new
21
Save and close

Fig. 64

The alternative way to add products and services to QuickBooks Online is by uploading a CSV or excel file that has all the products and services already added. Let me show you how to do it.

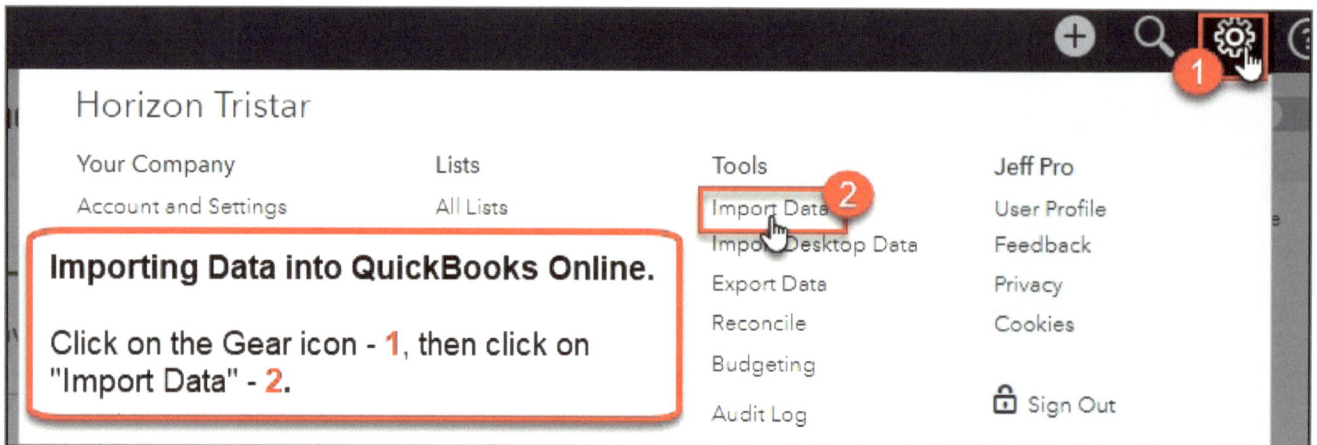

Fig. 65

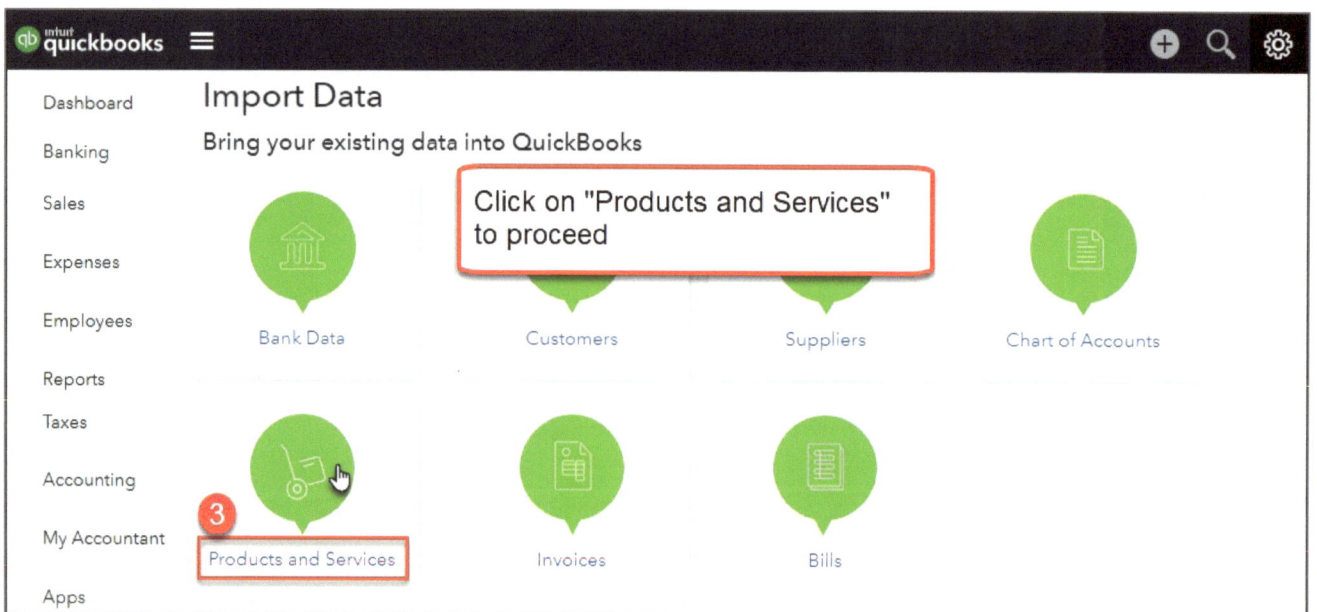

Fig. 66

This space is for notes

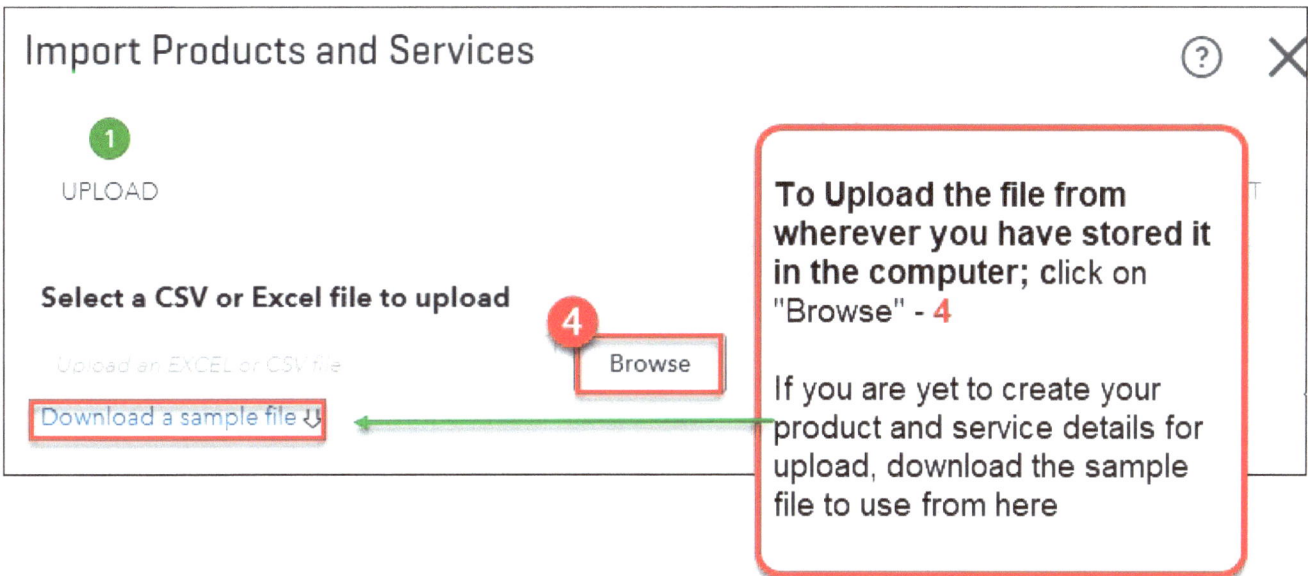

Fig. 67

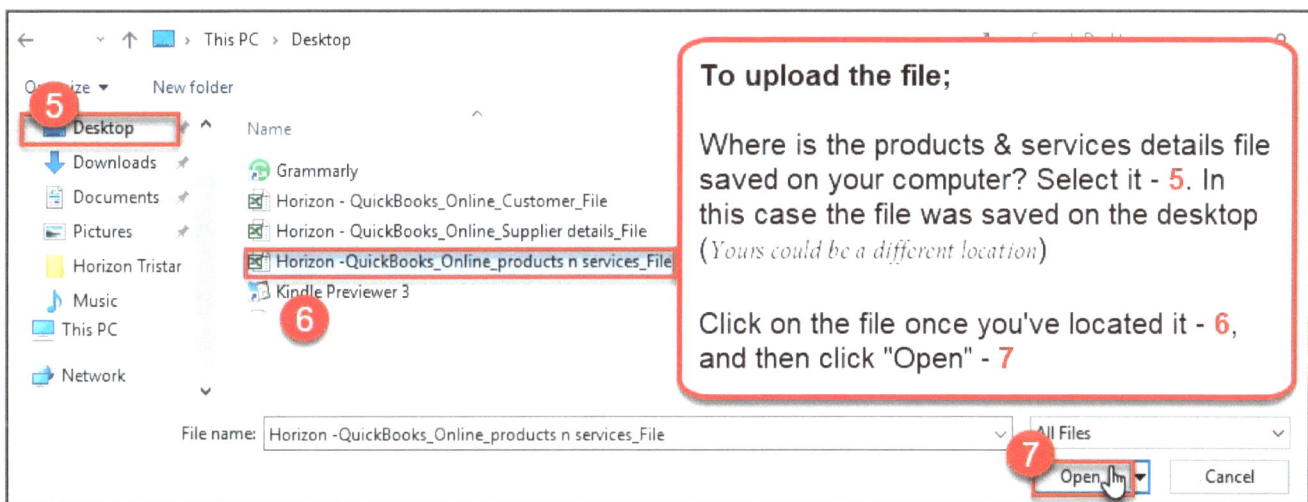

Fig. 68

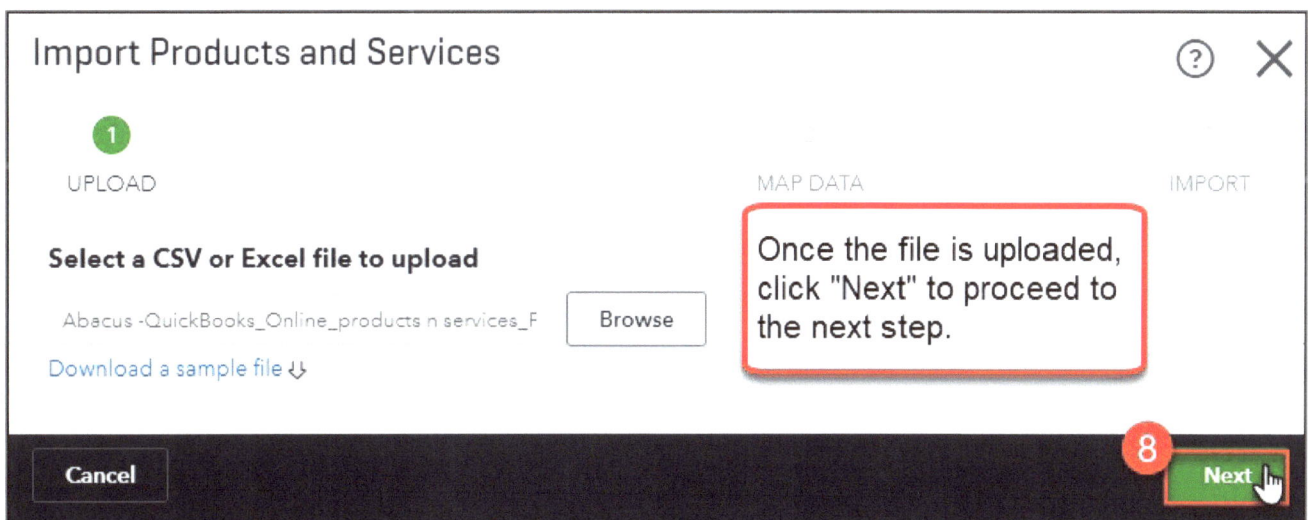

Fig. 69

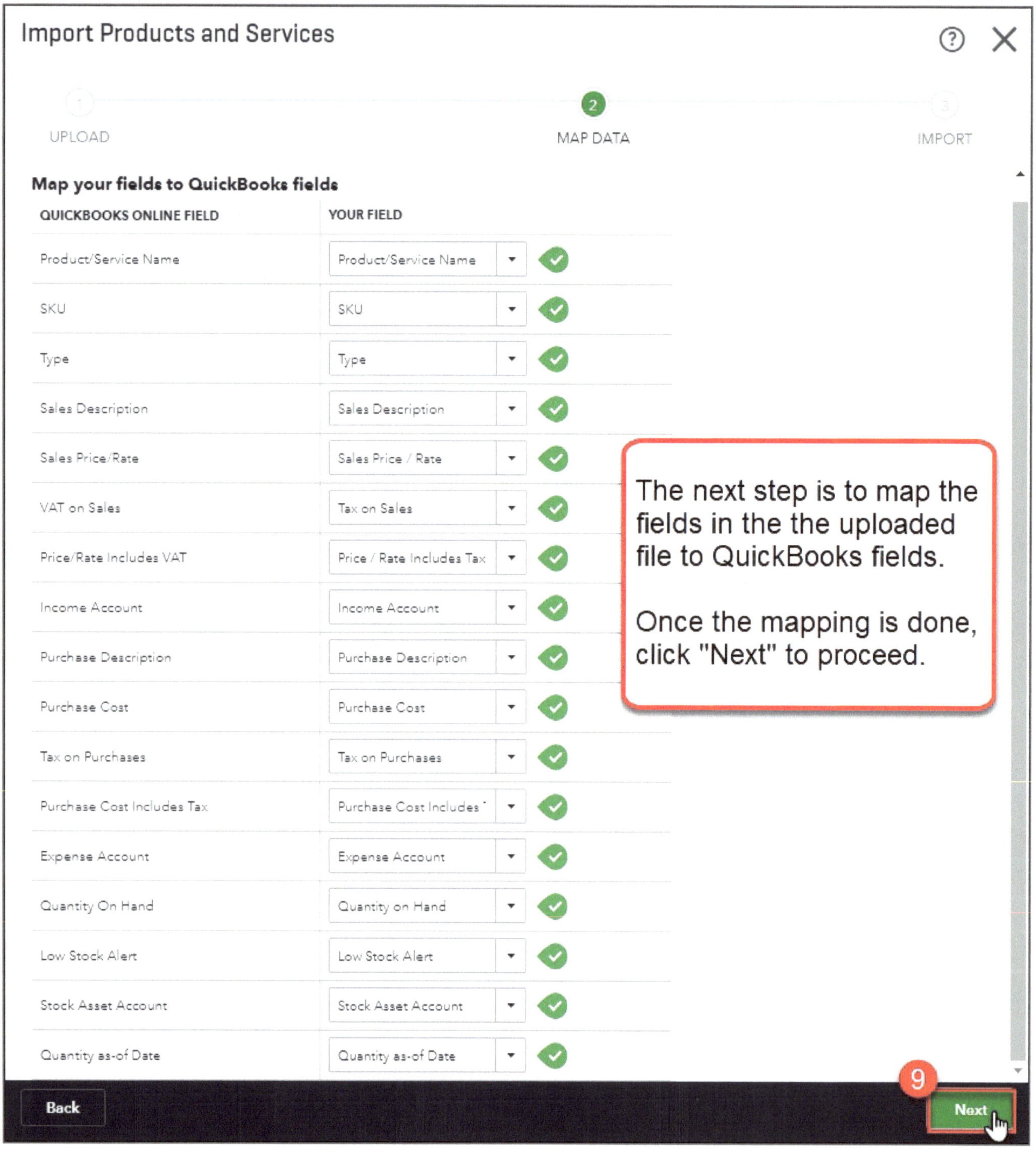

Import Products and Services

UPLOAD · MAP DATA (2) · IMPORT

Map your fields to QuickBooks fields

QUICKBOOKS ONLINE FIELD	YOUR FIELD	
Product/Service Name	Product/Service Name	✓
SKU	SKU	✓
Type	Type	✓
Sales Description	Sales Description	✓
Sales Price/Rate	Sales Price / Rate	✓
VAT on Sales	Tax on Sales	✓
Price/Rate Includes VAT	Price / Rate Includes Tax	✓
Income Account	Income Account	✓
Purchase Description	Purchase Description	✓
Purchase Cost	Purchase Cost	✓
Tax on Purchases	Tax on Purchases	✓
Purchase Cost Includes Tax	Purchase Cost Includes	✓
Expense Account	Expense Account	✓
Quantity On Hand	Quantity on Hand	✓
Low Stock Alert	Low Stock Alert	✓
Stock Asset Account	Stock Asset Account	✓
Quantity as-of Date	Quantity as-of Date	✓

The next step is to map the fields in the the uploaded file to QuickBooks fields.

Once the mapping is done, click "Next" to proceed.

Back

9 Next

Fig. 70

This space is for notes

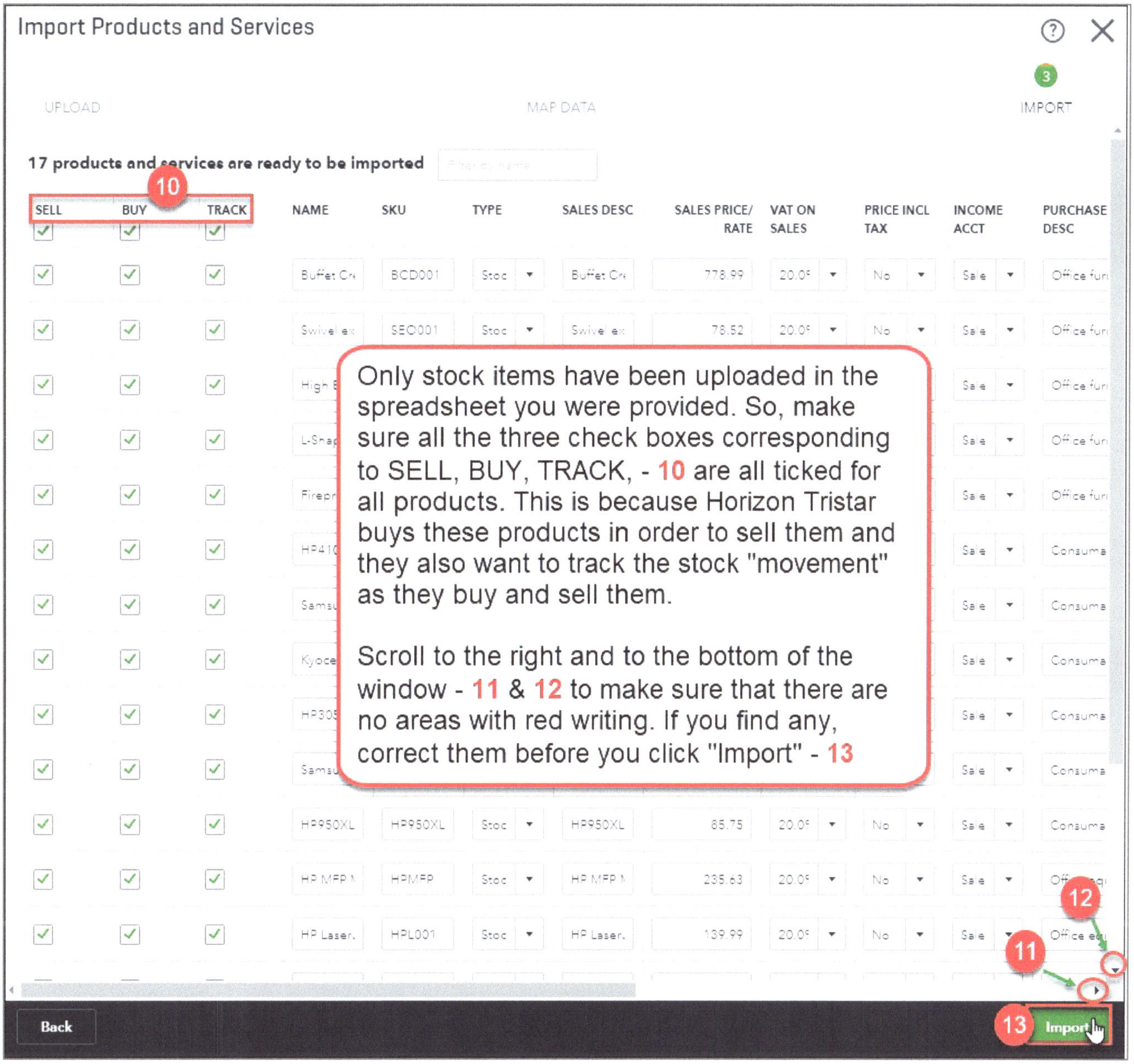

Fig. 71

This space is for notes

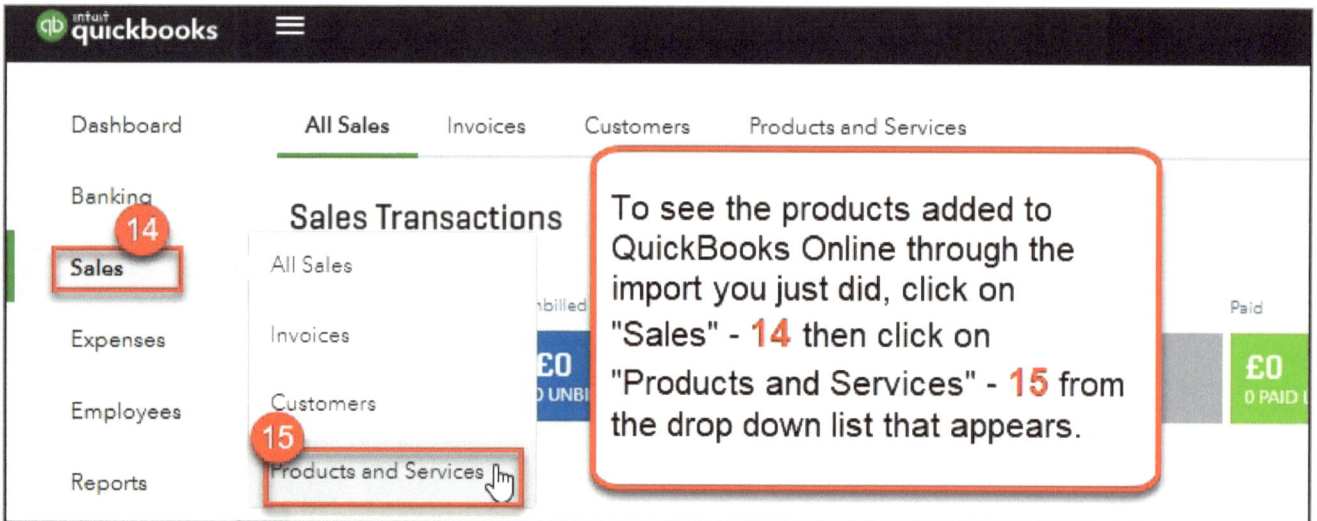

Fig. 72

The callout in Fig. 72 reads:

> To see the products added to QuickBooks Online through the import you just did, click on "Sales" - **14** then click on "Products and Services" - **15** from the drop down list that appears.

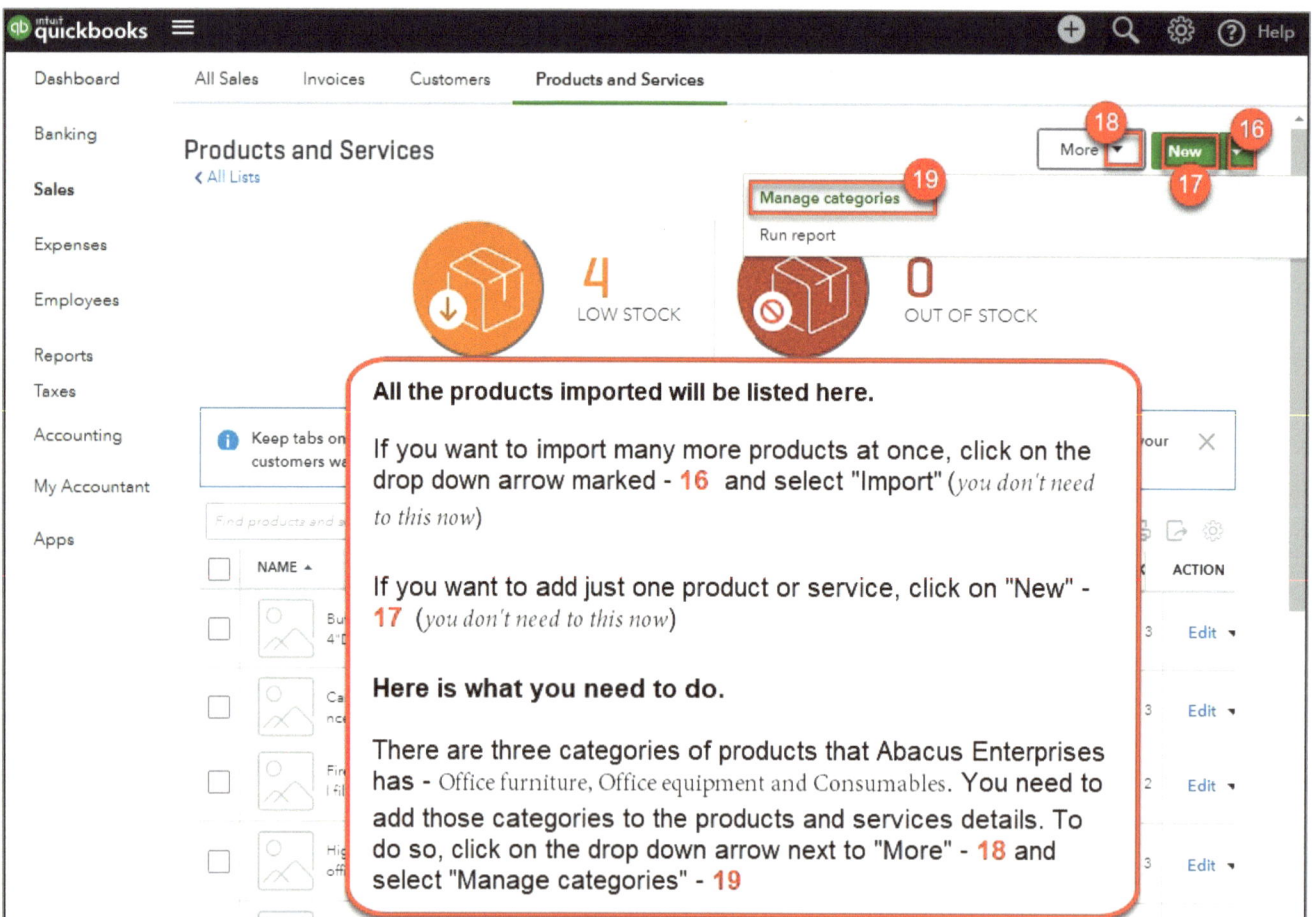

The callout in Fig. 73 reads:

> **All the products imported will be listed here.**
>
> If you want to import many more products at once, click on the drop down arrow marked - **16** and select "Import" (*you don't need to this now*)
>
> If you want to add just one product or service, click on "New" - **17** (*you don't need to this now*)
>
> **Here is what you need to do.**
>
> There are three categories of products that Abacus Enterprises **has -** Office furniture, Office equipment and Consumables. **You need to** add those categories to the products and services details. To do so, click on the drop down arrow next to "More" - **18** and select "Manage categories" - **19**

Fig. 73

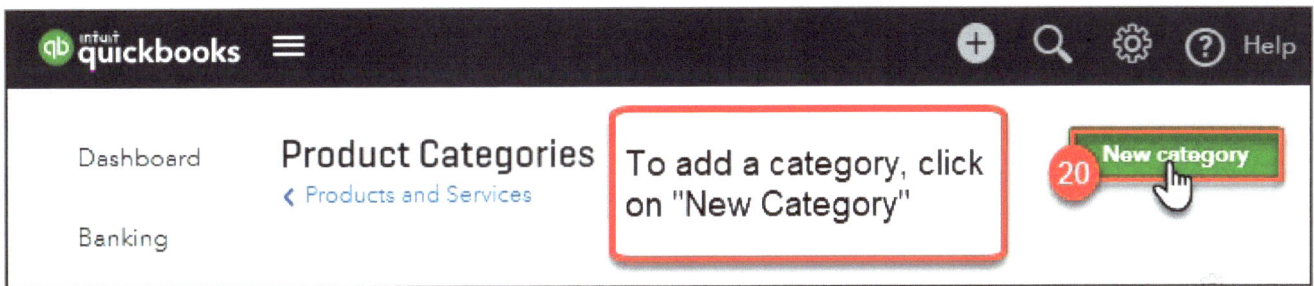

Fig. 74

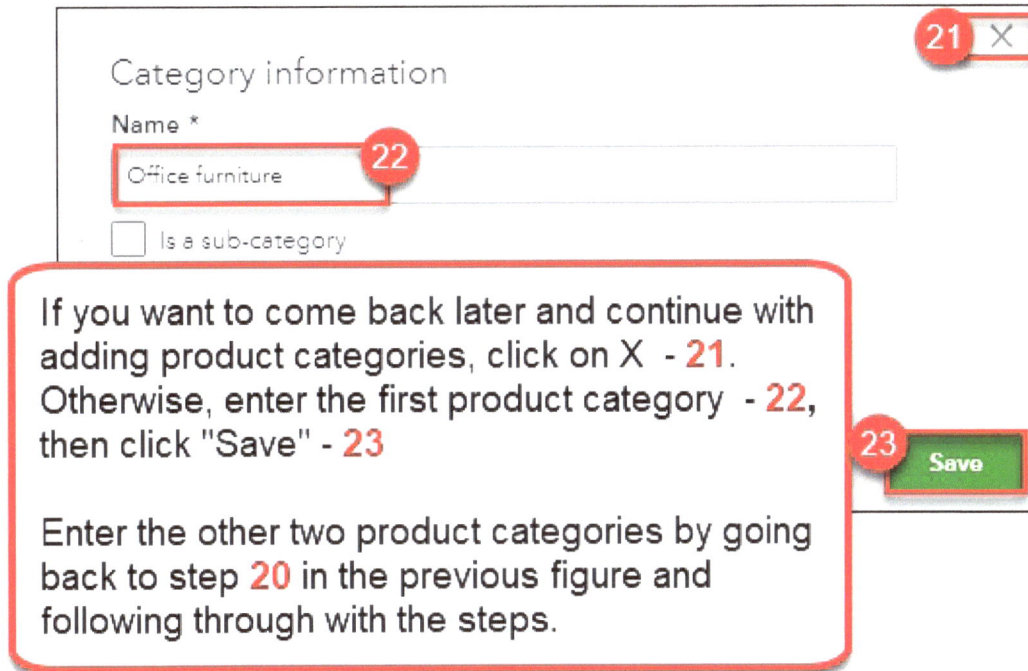

Fig. 75

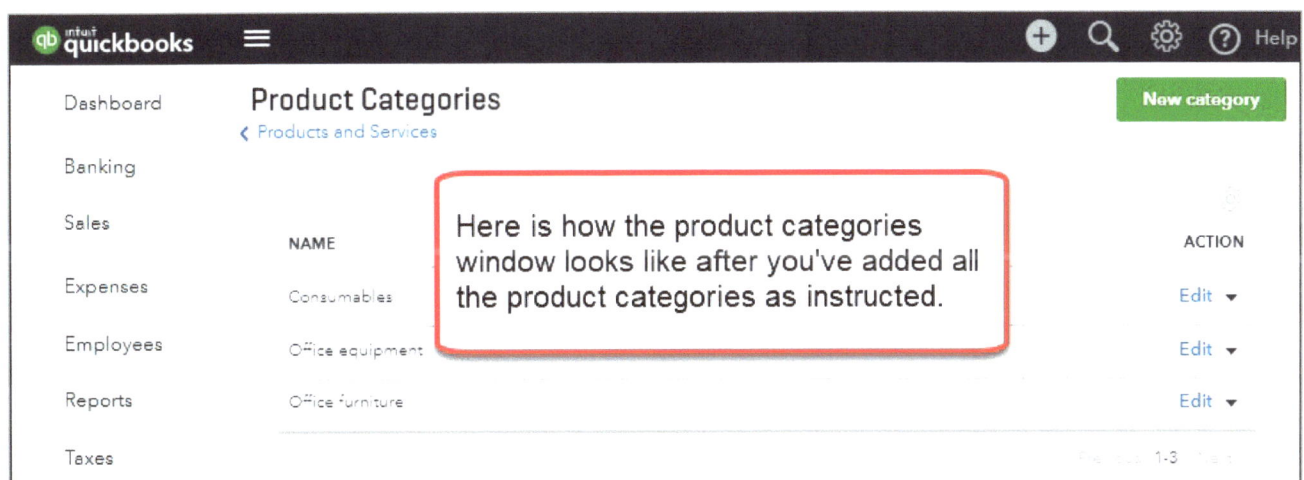

Fig. 76

Task 1d: Setting up the fixed assets register

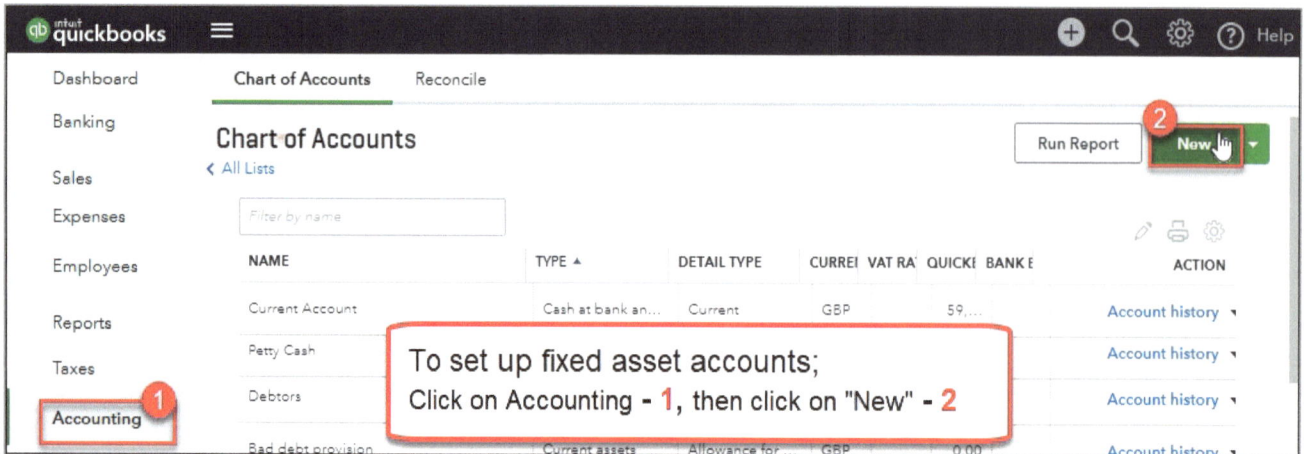

Fig. 77

Using the list of the Fixed assets you have been given, here is how to set up the fixed asset accounts for them. I will do the first one with you; then you can carry on with the rest.

> *Fixed assets are any assets that cannot be easily converted to cash. They are typically tangible, physical things that have an economic life of longer than a year. These include buildings, vehicles, furniture and office equipment. Fixed assets normally don't include intangible things like royalties and brand names.*
>
> *Fixed assets are also known as non-current and long-term assets. They may also be referred to as property, plant and equipment. They are assets intended to be used within the business, not sold or converted to cash.*

This space is for notes

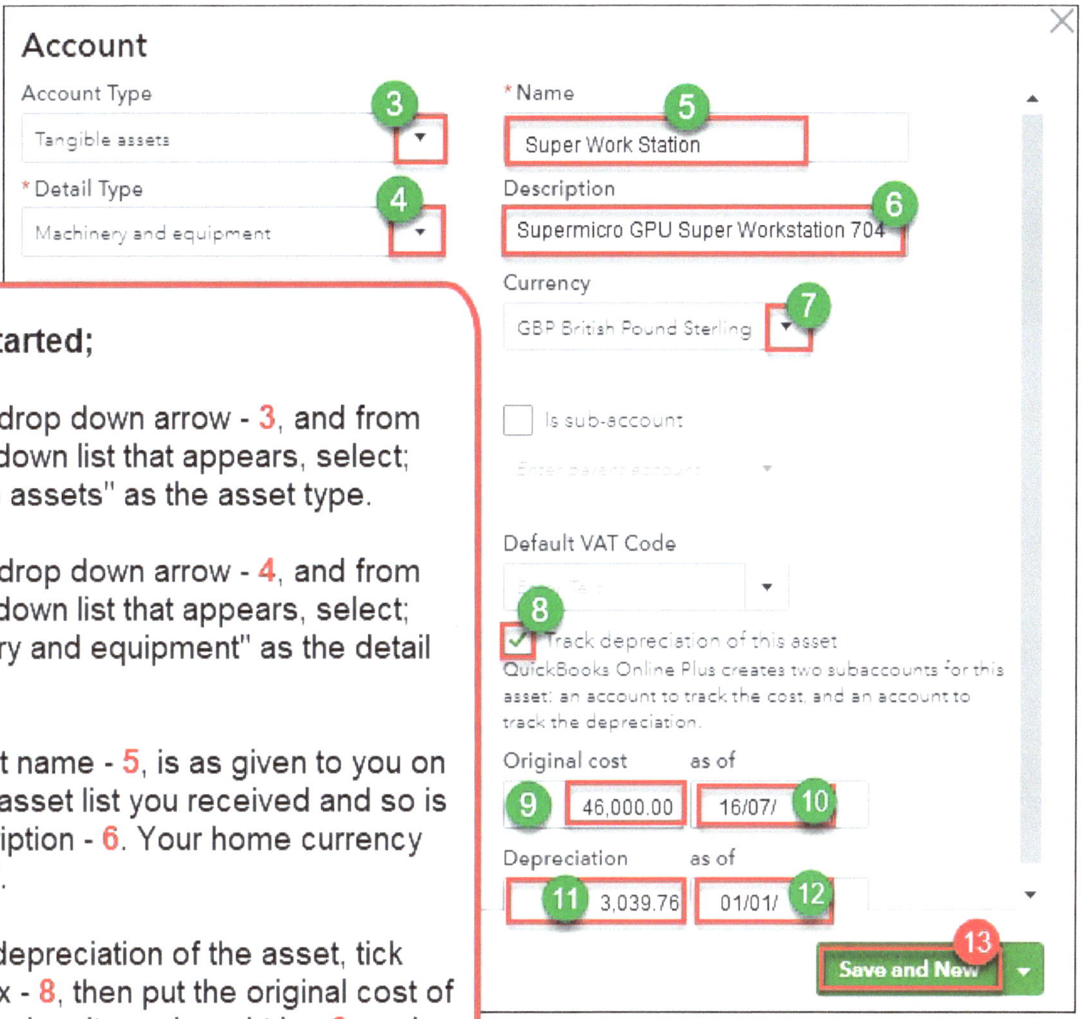

Account

Account Type

Tangible assets ▼ ③

*Detail Type

Machinery and equipment ▼ ④

*Name ⑤

Super Work Station

Description ⑥

Supermicro GPU Super Workstation 704

Currency ⑦

GBP British Pound Sterling ▼

☐ Is sub-account

Enter parent account ▼

Default VAT Code

☑ ⑧ Track depreciation of this asset
QuickBooks Online Plus creates two subaccounts for this asset; an account to track the cost, and an account to track the depreciation.

Original cost   as of

⑨ 46,000.00   16/07/ ⑩

Depreciation   as of

⑪ 3,039.76   01/01/ ⑫

Save and New ⑬ ▼

To get started;

Click the drop down arrow - **3**, and from the drop down list that appears, select; "Tangible assets" as the asset type.

Click the drop down arrow - **4**, and from the drop down list that appears, select; "Machinery and equipment" as the detail type.

The asset name - **5**, is as given to you on the fixed asset list you received and so is the description - **6**. Your home currency will be - **7**.

To track depreciation of the asset, tick check box - **8**, then put the original cost of the asset when it was bought in - **9**, and the date it was bought in - **10**.
If the asset has already been depreciated, put the depreciation amount in - **11** and the corresponding date of that depreciation to date value in - **12**.

Check your entries, ensure that they are correct and click "Save and New" - **13**.

Fig. 78

This space is for notes

Task 1e: Setting up opening balances from the Trial balance

Overview of this task

The opening balance is the balance that is brought forward from the end of one accounting period to the beginning of a new accounting period or from one accounting system to a new accounting system.

The funds in a company's/business accounts at the start of a new financial period are called the opening balances. The opening balance is the first entry in a company's accounts, either when they are first starting up or at the start of a new financial year or when changing accounting systems.

In the case of a new company, the opening balances usually are just two: one is the cash on hand, and the other is the capital contributed by the company's founders or loan from investors.

Opening balances are entered into the accounting system using the double entry accounting principles.
The best way to gather your opening balances is to prepare an opening trial balance. This is done by listing all your nominal accounts and the value (balance) on each account.

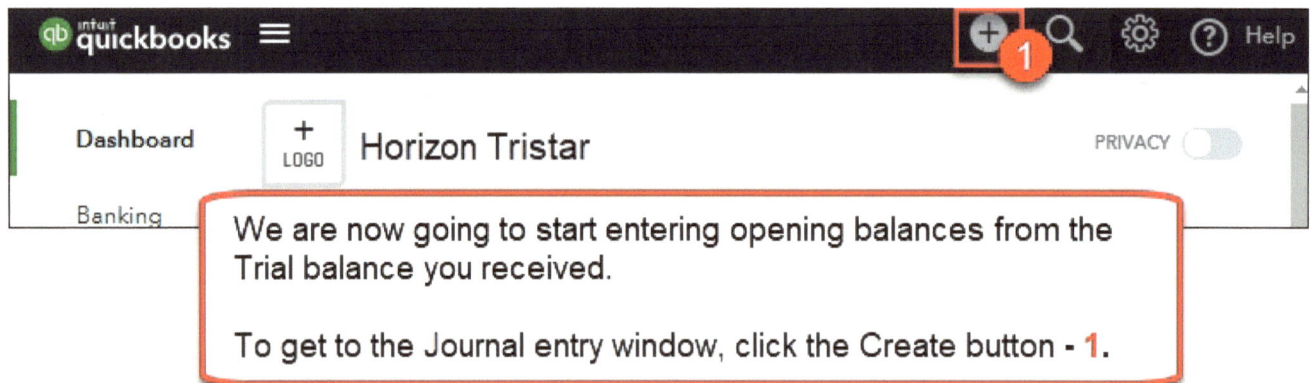

We are now going to start entering opening balances from the Trial balance you received.

To get to the Journal entry window, click the Create button - 1.

Fig. 79

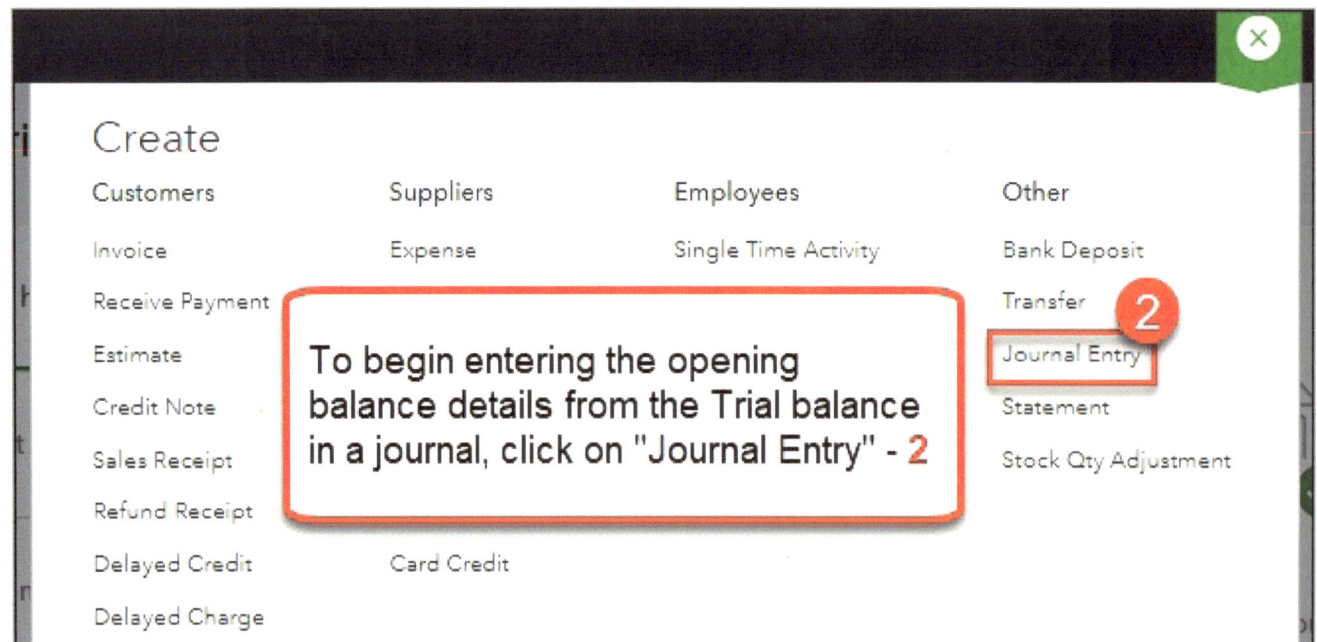

To begin entering the opening balance details from the Trial balance in a journal, click on "Journal Entry" - 2

Fig. 80

In the set-up steps earlier on did record opening balances for the items in the trial balance up until Creditors Control Account, we will continue from Sales tax Control Account (Credit balance of 22,182.53 in the Trial balance) and then enter the rest of the balances as shown in the Trial balance.

Journal Entry no.1 - Opening balances

Currency: GBP British Pound Sterling

Journal date: 01/01/ **1**

Journal no.: 1 - Opening balances **2**

#	ACCOUNT	DEBITS (GBP)	CREDITS (GBP)	DESCRIPTION
1	VAT Control		22.182.53	Sales tax control acc
2	Retained profit balance forward	22.182.53		Sales tax control acc
3	VAT Control	12.903.64		Purchase tax contro
4	Retained profit balance forward		12.903.64	Purchase tax contro
5	VAT Control	14.800.35		VAT Liability
6	Retained profit balance forward		14.800.35	VAT Liability
7	Wages and salaries control		5.396.79	P.A.Y.E
8	Retained profit balance forward	5.396.79		P.A.Y.E
9	Wages and salaries control		2.006.98	National Insurance
10	Retained profit balance forward	2.006.98		National Insurance
11	Wages and salaries control		120.00	Pension fund
12	Retained profit balance forward	120.00		Pension fund
13	Loans		6.895.00	Loans
14	Retained profit balance forward	6.895.00		Loans
15	Hire Purchase		6.160.00	Loans
16	Retained profit balance forward	6.160.00		Loans
17	Ordinary share capital		35.250.00	Ordinary Share Capital
18	Retained profit balance forward	35.250.00		Ordinary Share Capital
19	Retained Earnings		61.082.00	Reserves
20	Retained profit balance forward	61.082.00		Reserves
21	Sales - Office furniture		80.706.82	Sales - Office furniture
22	Retained profit balance forward	80.706.82		Sales - Office furniture
23	Sales - Office equipment		71.021.10	Sales - Office equipment
24	Retained profit balance forward	71.021.10		Sales - Office equipment
25	Sales - Consumables		31.772.11	Sales - Consumables
26	Retained profit balance forward	31.772.11		Sales - Consumables
27	Uncategorised Income	50.00		Discounts allowed
28	Retained profit balance forward		50.00	Discounts allowed
29	Uncategorised Income		50.03	Miscellaneous Income
30	Retained profit balance forward	50.03		Miscellaneous Income
31	Uncategorised Income		870.00	Distribution and Carriage
32	Retained profit balance forward	870.00		Distribution and Carriage
33	Purchases	76.088.01		Purchases
34	Retained profit balance forward		76.088.01	Purchases
35	Shipping Freight and Delivery	251.26		Carriage
36	Retained profit balance forward		251.26	Carriage
37	Advertising	50.00		Sales Promotion
38	Retained profit balance forward		50.00	Sales Promotion

Write the correct journal date in **1** (*in this case the date is 01/01/thisyear*).
The Journal reference should be entered in - **2**.

When you enter the balances from the Trial balance to QuickBooks Online for Horizon Tristar Ltd, the offsetting account for every other account balance you use is the - Retained profit balance forward account - Equity.

For example;
when you record the Sales tax opening balance in the VAT Control account on the credit side, the corresponding debit entry to complete the double entry will be in the "Retained profit balance forward account-Equity" account

⠿	39	Advertising	465.00		Advertising			🏛
⠿	40	Retained profit balance forward		465.00	Advertising			🏛
⠿	41	Advertising	115.00		Gifts and Samples			🏛
⠿	42	Retained profit balance forward		115.00	Gifts and Samples			🏛
⠿	43	Advertising	1,050.00		P.R. (Literature & Brochures)			🏛
⠿	44	Retained profit balance forward		1,050.00	P.R. (Literature & Brochures)			🏛
⠿	45	Gross Wages	32,472.11		Gross wages			🏛
⠿	46	Retained profit balance forward		32,472.11	Gross wages			🏛
⠿	47	Employer's NI contributions	3,327.24		Employers NI			🏛
⠿	48	Retained profit balance forward		3,327.24	Employers NI			🏛
⠿	49	SSP	107.60		Statutory Sick Pay reclaimed			🏛
⠿	50	Retained profit balance forward		107.60	Statutory Sick Pay reclaimed			🏛
⠿	51	SMP	255.00		Statutory Maternity Pay			🏛
⠿	52	Retained profit balance forward		255.00	Statutory Maternity Pay			🏛
⠿	53	Rent	12,720.00		Rent			🏛
⠿	54	Retained profit balance forward		12,720.00	Rent			🏛
⠿	55	Light and heat	1,052.00		Electricity			🏛
⠿	56	Retained profit balance forward		1,052.00	Electricity			🏛
⠿	57	Motor running expenses	620.95		Fuel and Oil			🏛
⠿	58	Retained profit balance forward		620.95	Fuel and Oil			🏛
⠿	59	Motor running expenses	492.15		Repairs & Servicing			🏛
⠿	60	Retained profit balance forward		492.15	Repairs & Servicing			🏛
⠿	61	Motor running expenses	67.50		Miscellaneous Motor Expen			🏛
⠿	62	Retained profit balance forward		67.50	Miscellaneous Motor Expen			🏛
⠿	63	Motor running expenses	90.27		Scale Charges			🏛
⠿	64	Retained profit balance forward		90.27	Scale Charges			🏛
⠿	65	Travelling expenses	201.00		Travelling Expenses			🏛
⠿	66	Retained profit balance forward		201.00	Travelling Expenses			🏛
⠿	67	Travelling expenses	150.00		Car hire			🏛
⠿	68	Retained profit balance forward		150.00	Car hire			🏛
⠿	69	Travelling expenses	720.00		Hotels			🏛
⠿	70	Retained profit balance forward		720.00	Hotels			🏛
⠿	71	Entertaining	149.50		U.K. Etertainment			🏛
⠿	72	Retained profit balance forward		149.50	U.K. Etertainment			🏛
⠿	73	Printing, postage and stationer	54.10		Printing			🏛
⠿	74	Retained profit balance forward		54.10	Printing			🏛
⠿	75	Printing, postage and stationer	102.50		Postage and Carriage			🏛
⠿	76	Retained profit balance forward		102.50	Postage and Carriage			🏛
⠿	77	Telephone	178.72		Telephone			🏛
⠿	78	Retained profit balance forward		178.72	Telephone			🏛

Fig. 81

This space is for notes

58

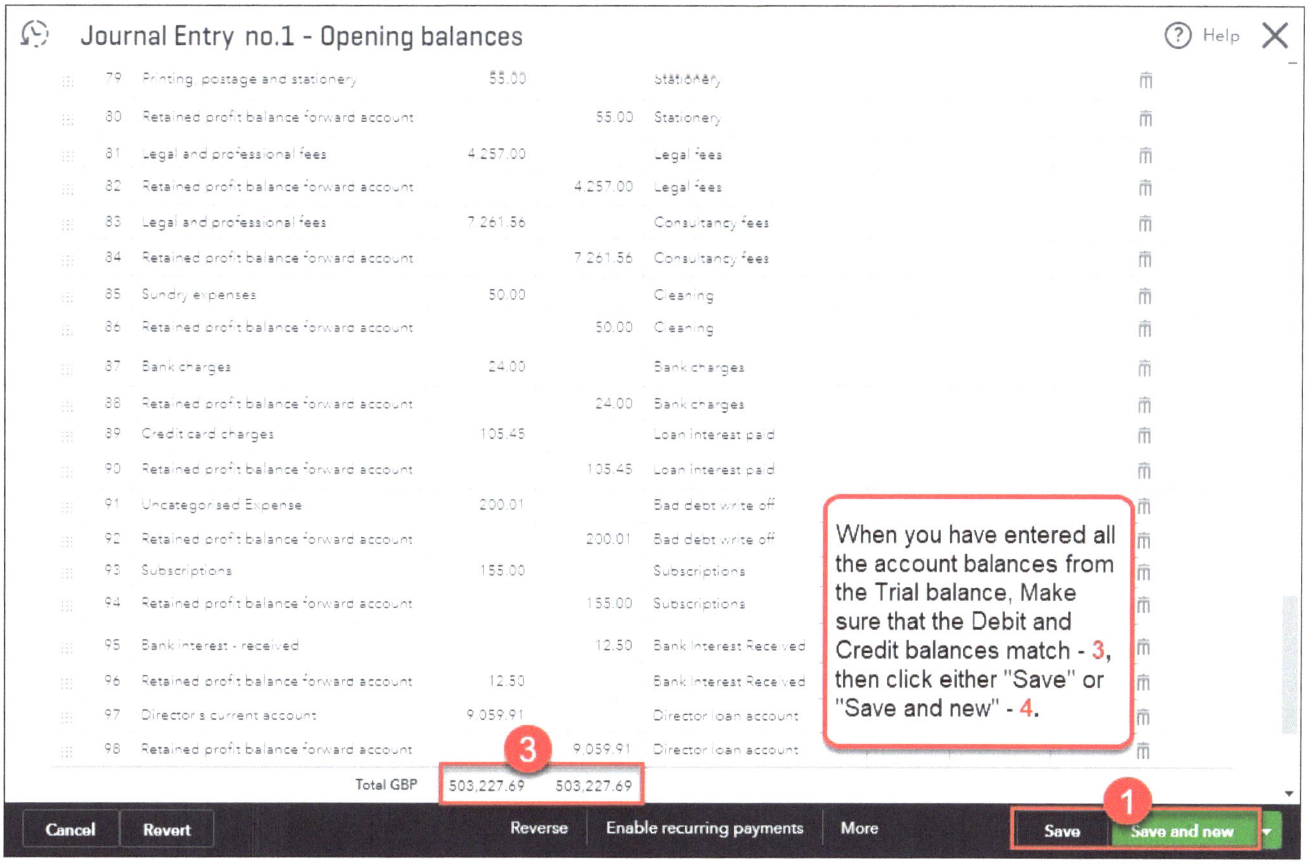
Journal Entry no.1 - Opening balances
Help
79 Printing, postage and stationery 55.00 Stationery
80 Retained profit balance forward account 55.00 Stationery
81 Legal and professional fees 4,257.00 Legal fees
82 Retained profit balance forward account 4,257.00 Legal fees
83 Legal and professional fees 7,261.56 Consultancy fees
84 Retained profit balance forward account 7,261.56 Consultancy fees
85 Sundry expenses 50.00 Cleaning
86 Retained profit balance forward account 50.00 Cleaning
87 Bank charges 24.00 Bank charges
88 Retained profit balance forward account 24.00 Bank charges
89 Credit card charges 105.45 Loan interest paid
90 Retained profit balance forward account 105.45 Loan interest paid
91 Uncategorised Expense 200.01 Bad debt write off
92 Retained profit balance forward account 200.01 Bad debt write off
93 Subscriptions 155.00 Subscriptions
94 Retained profit balance forward account 155.00 Subscriptions
95 Bank interest - received 12.50 Bank Interest Received
96 Retained profit balance forward account 12.50 Bank Interest Received
97 Director's current account 9,059.91 Director loan account
98 Retained profit balance forward account 9,059.91 Director loan account
Total GBP 503,227.69 503,227.69
When you have entered all the account balances from the Trial balance, Make sure that the Debit and Credit balances match - 3, then click either "Save" or "Save and new" - 4.
3
1
Cancel
Revert
Reverse
Enable recurring payments
More
Save
Save and new

Fig. 82

Notes

What is Opening balance?

Opening balance is the balance that is brought forward from the end of one accounting period to the beginning of a new accounting period or from one accounting system to a new accounting system.

TASK 2: HOW TO DO BUDGETING IN QUICKBOOKS ONLINE

In the context of business management, the purpose of budgeting includes the following three aspects:
- A forecast of income and expenditure (and thereby profitability)
- A tool for decision making
- A means to monitor business performance

A carefully constructed budget allows a business to continually track where they are financially. This allows for strategic, long-term planning for everything from current operating costs to potential expansion. Knowing where the budget stands opens up the ability to hire new staffers, invest in new product lines and set earning goals in line with the organisations' corporate financial objectives.

Let's get going with producing Horizon Tristar's budget.

To create, access, edit, or delete budgets in QuickBooks Online, you must have Administrator Access Rights (All Access Rights).

Your budget will start with the first month of the fiscal year you have set up in QuickBooks Online (For Horizon Tristar Ltd it is November of last year). Therefore, you should check that the Fiscal Year setting is accurate before continuing with the Budget set up process.

Here is what you need to do to check Fiscal Year settings:

1. Select the **Gear icon** at the top, then choose **Account and Settings** (or **Company Settings**).
2. Select **Advanced**.
3. Check if the first month of fiscal year is **November**. If not, select the pencil icon in the Accounting section and set it to November last year.
4. Select **Save**.

With that done, let's proceed.

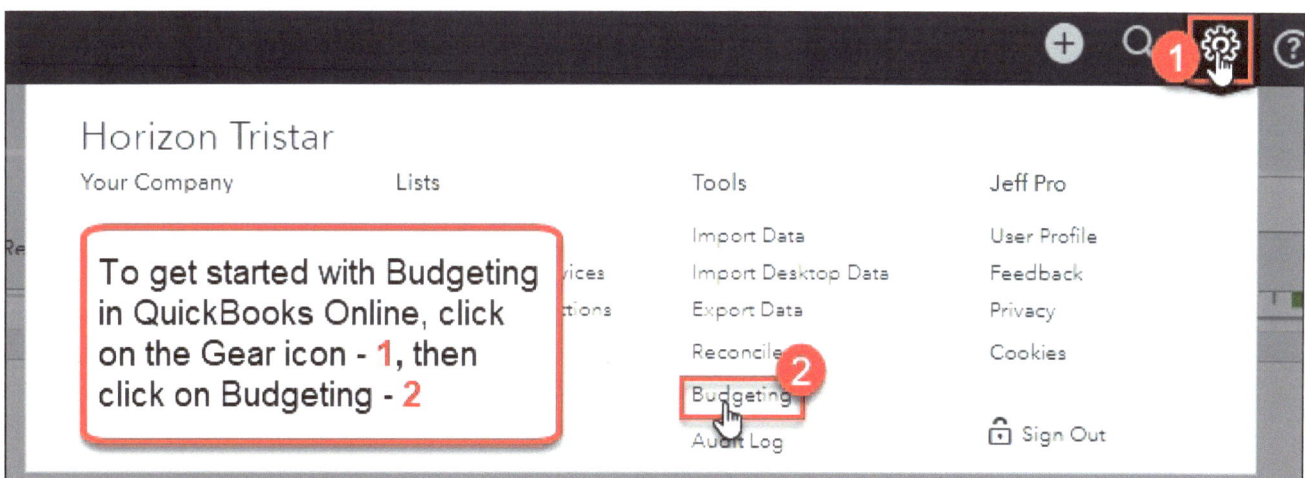

Fig. 83

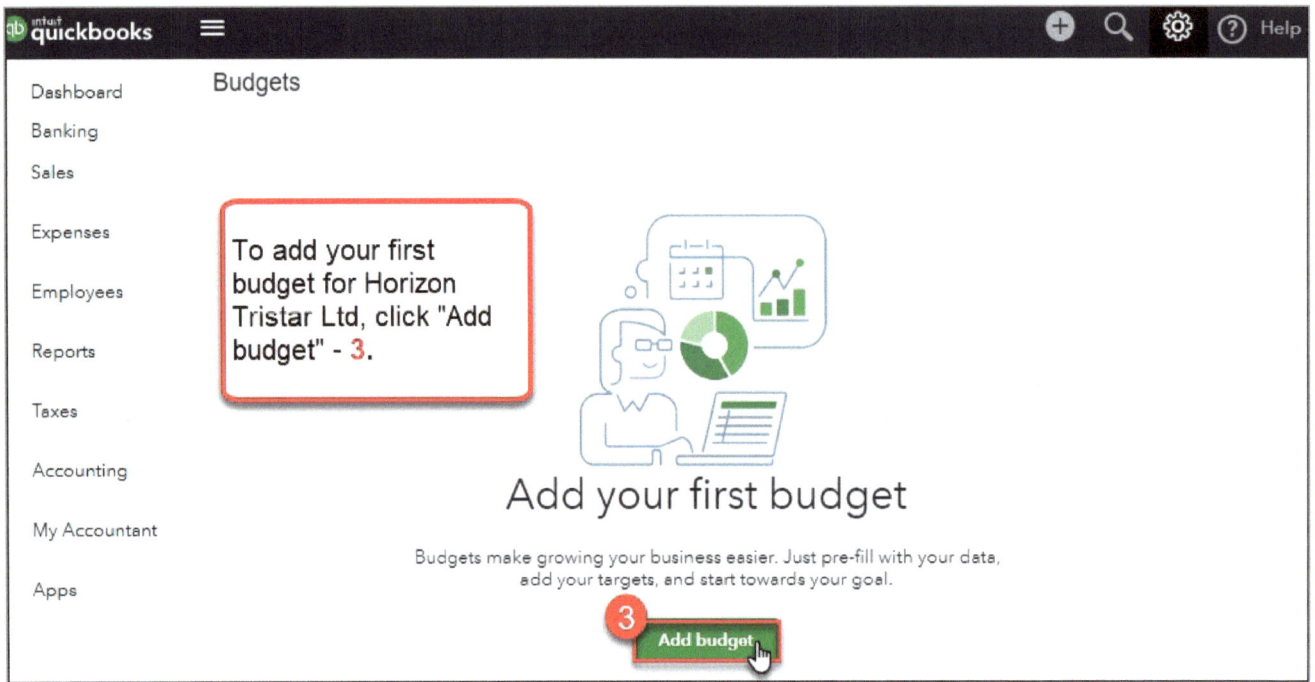

To add your first budget for Horizon Tristar Ltd, click "Add budget" - **3**.

Fig. 84

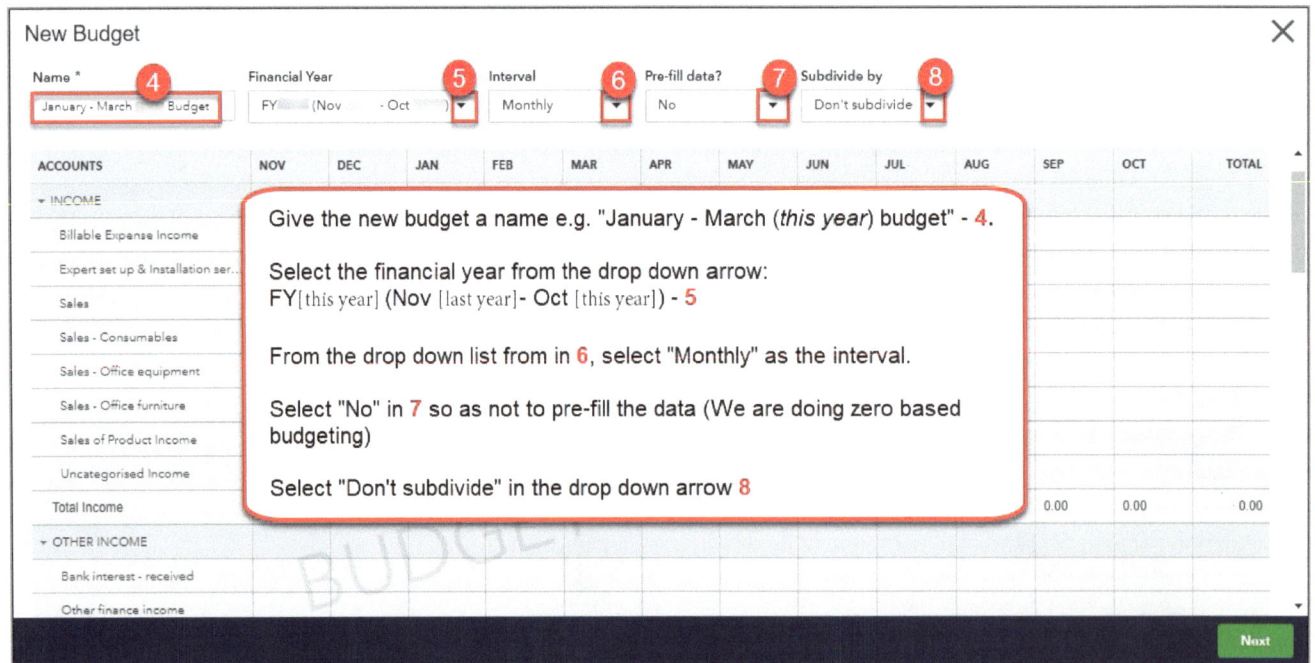

Give the new budget a name e.g. "January - March (*this year*) budget" - **4**.

Select the financial year from the drop down arrow:
FY[this year] (Nov [last year]- Oct [this year]) - **5**

From the drop down list from in **6**, select "Monthly" as the interval.

Select "No" in **7** so as not to pre-fill the data (We are doing zero based budgeting)

Select "Don't subdivide" in the drop down arrow **8**

Fig. 85

This space is for notes

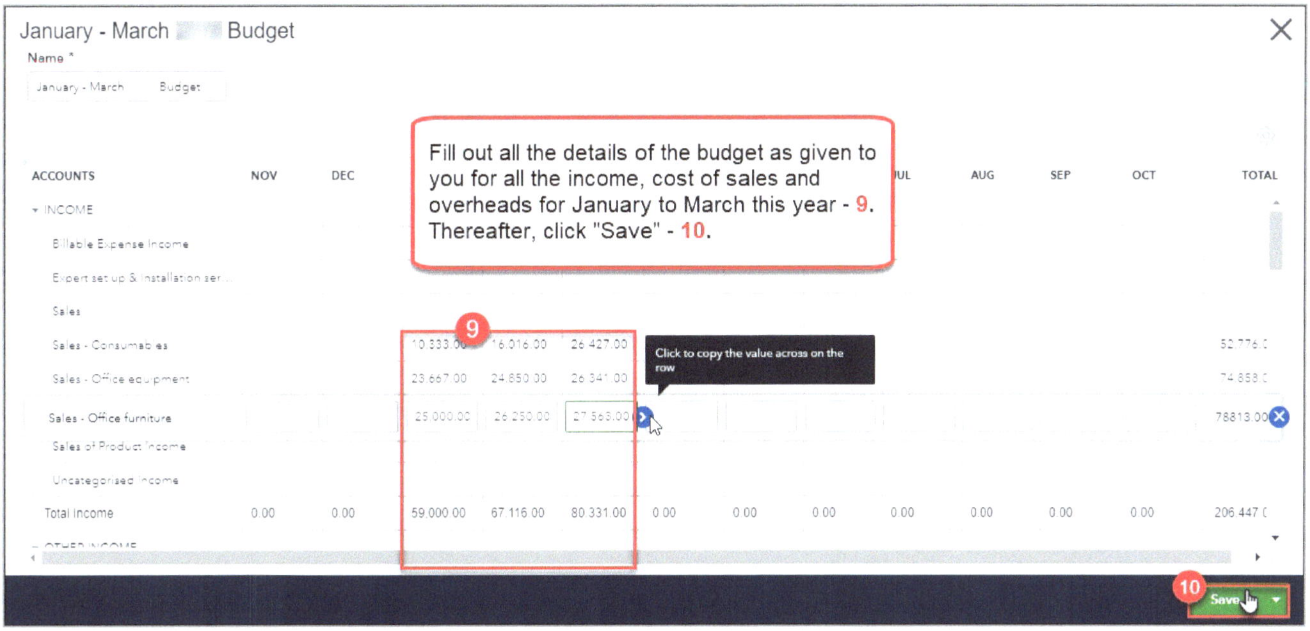

Fig. 86

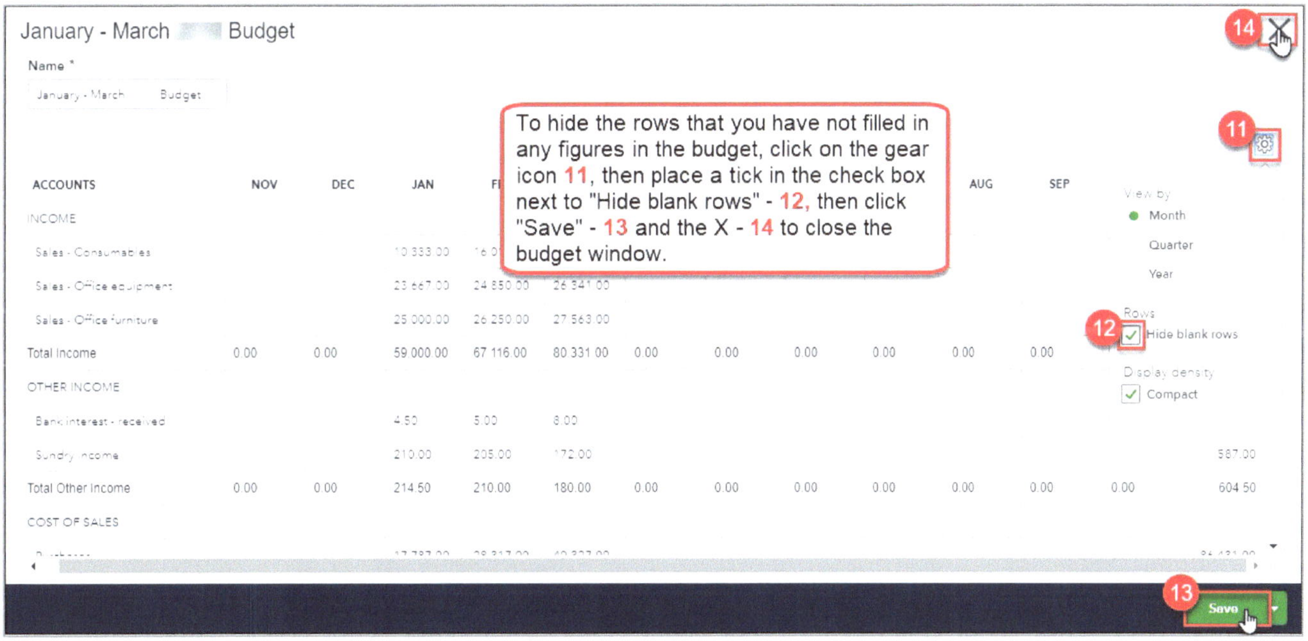

Fig. 87

Notes

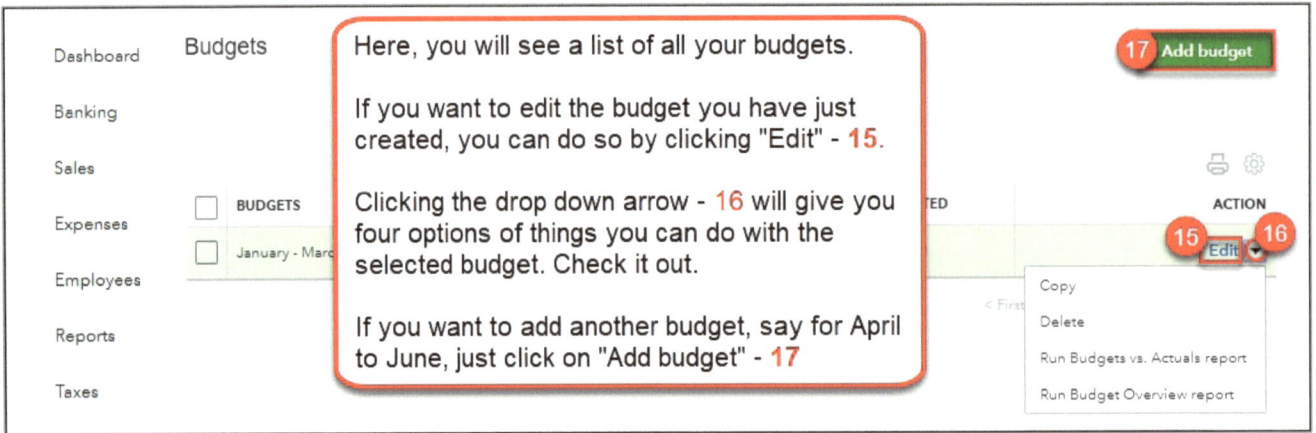

Fig. 88

That's it, you have managed to set up Horizon Tristar's budget for January to March this year. You will have the opportunity in March to compare the budget figures you have just entered to the actual figures that will reflect the actual performance of the business and with that, do some variance analysis.

We will now move on to the next task – Doing Accounts payable tasks.

Notes

TASK 3: DOING THE ACCOUNTS PAYABLE TASKS

How to analyse a financial document before recording it.

Let's do this task by analysing one of the invoices received by Horizon Tristar Ltd.

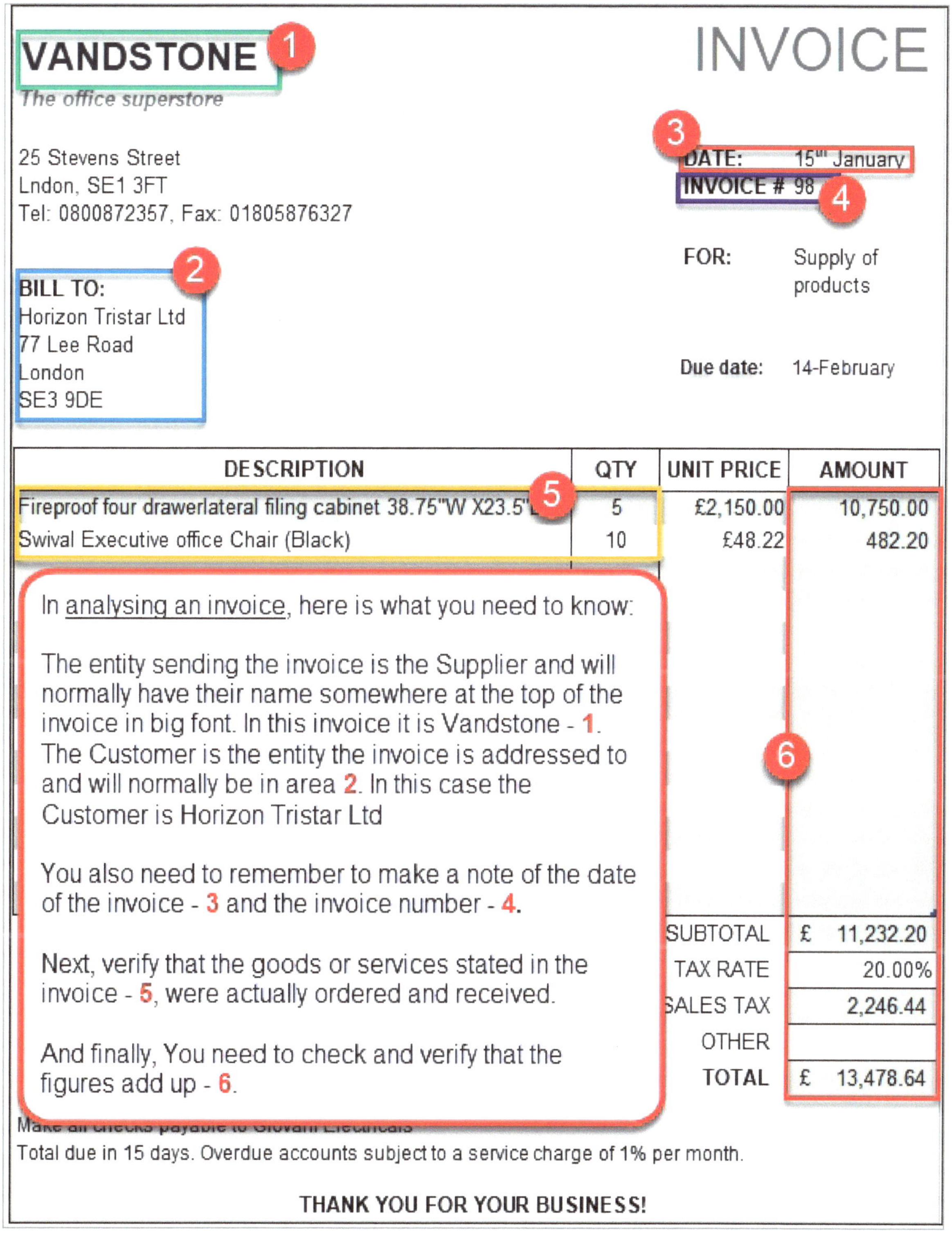

VANDSTONE — **1**
The office superstore

25 Stevens Street
Lndon, SE1 3FT
Tel: 0800872357, Fax: 01805876327

BILL TO: — **2**
Horizon Tristar Ltd
77 Lee Road
London
SE3 9DE

INVOICE

3 DATE: 15ᵗʰ January
INVOICE # 98 **4**

FOR: Supply of products

Due date: 14-February

DESCRIPTION	QTY	UNIT PRICE	AMOUNT
Fireproof four drawerlateral filing cabinet 38.75"W X23.5" **5**	5	£2,150.00	10,750.00
Swival Executive office Chair (Black)	10	£48.22	482.20

In analysing an invoice, here is what you need to know:

The entity sending the invoice is the Supplier and will normally have their name somewhere at the top of the invoice in big font. In this invoice it is Vandstone - **1**.
The Customer is the entity the invoice is addressed to and will normally be in area **2**. In this case the Customer is Horizon Tristar Ltd

You also need to remember to make a note of the date of the invoice - **3** and the invoice number - **4**.

Next, verify that the goods or services stated in the invoice - **5**, were actually ordered and received.

And finally, You need to check and verify that the figures add up - **6**.

SUBTOTAL	£	11,232.20
TAX RATE		20.00%
SALES TAX		2,246.44
OTHER		
TOTAL	£	13,478.64

6

Make all checks payable to Giovani Electricals
Total due in 15 days. Overdue accounts subject to a service charge of 1% per month.

THANK YOU FOR YOUR BUSINESS!

Fig. 89

Here are further details on the analysis of an invoice for your consideration.

Features of a valid invoice	
Address details	Invoices must be addressed to the business or department within the organisation. The name of an individual may also appear as long as this is an authorised signatory
Status of document	The document must be an invoice rather than a delivery note, order acknowledgement or statement. Some invoices from smaller entities may not contain all of the details for VAT purposes. If the word 'invoice' appears on the document, then it should be treated as an invoice.
Accurate	The Gross value in the invoice should be arithmetically correct [Subtotal plus Tax (if any)].
VAT invoice	Invoices that charge VAT must contain all of the following details in addition to those given above: • *The entity's VAT number;* • *The entity's trading name and address;* • *Description of goods or services;* • *Invoice number;* • *Invoice date;* • *Time of supply - 'tax point' if different from the invoice date;* • *Analysis of VAT charged, including value and rate used*

Task 3a: A brief overview of the Accounts payable process:

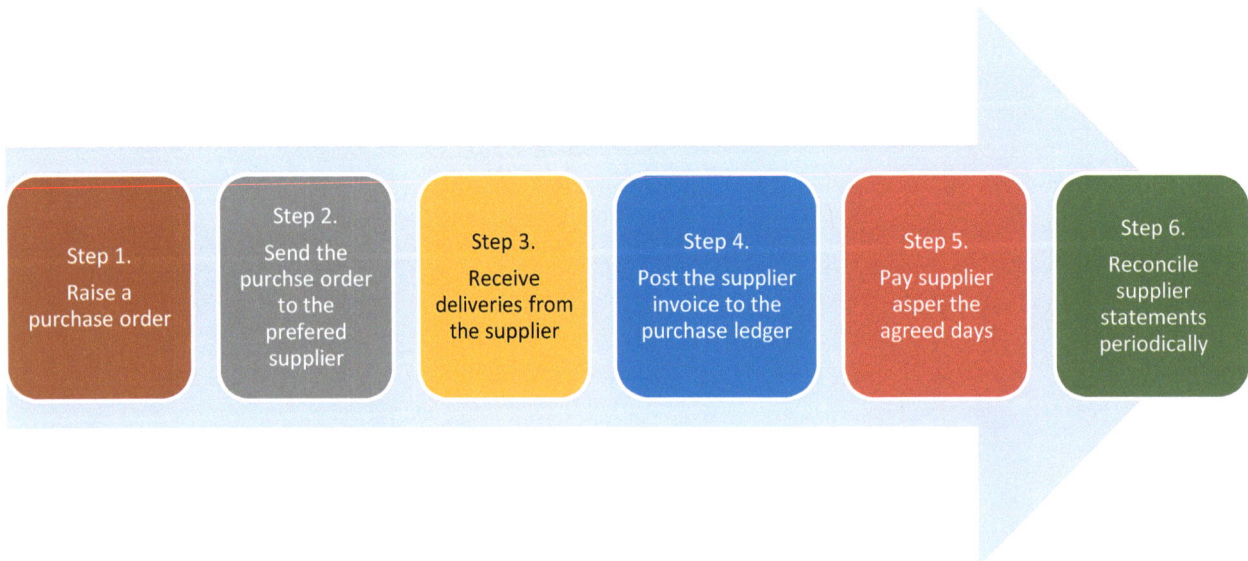

Fig. 90

> **A Note**
>
> When a company orders and receives goods (or services) in advance of paying for them, we say that the company is purchasing the goods *on account* or *on credit*. The supplier (or vendor) of the goods on credit is also referred to as a creditor. If the company receiving the goods does not sign a promissory note, the vendor's bill or invoice will be recorded by the company in its liability account Accounts Payable (or Trade Payables).
>
> Accounts Payable will normally have a credit balance. Hence, when a Supplier/vendor invoice is recorded, Accounts Payable will be credited and another account must be debited (as required by double-entry accounting). When an account payable is paid, Accounts Payable will be debited and Cash will be credited. Therefore, the credit balance in Accounts Payable should be equal to the amount of vendor invoices that have been recorded but have not yet been paid.
>
> Under the *accrual method of accounting*, the company receiving goods or services on credit must report the liability no later than the date they were received. The same date is used to record the debit entry to an expense or asset account as appropriate. Hence, accountants say that under the accrual method of accounting expenses are reported when they are *incurred* (not when they are paid).

Let's spend some time exploring the steps mentioned in the figure above, shall we?

To begin with, it is essential to know that a business can buy goods & services both in cash and on credit. When it buys on credit, it creates – a payable (which means something purchased on credit and payment will be due at a later date). When it buys in cash, that's different; it has made a cash payment.

Let's look at those steps in the figure above.

Step 1: Raising a purchase order

First, let's define a purchase order, shall we?

Of course, here is what it is:

A purchase order is a legally binding document between a supplier and a buyer. It details the items the buyer agrees to purchase at a certain price point. It also outlines the delivery/shipping date and terms of payment for the buyer.

Purchase orders are often used when a buyer wants to purchase supplies or inventory on account; this means that the supplier delivers or ships the purchased items before payment, with the purchase order serving as its risk protection.

How should you go about raising a purchase order?

First, a purchase requisition for the details of what needs to be purchased should be raised by the person or department that needs the goods or services. The request should then be sent to the appropriate budget holder(s) for approval.

When the Budget Holder approves the requisition, it should then be sent to the purchasing department, and a Purchase Order will be raised. The order will typically have:
- Purchase Order (PO) number
- Delivery/Shipping date
- Billing address
- Delivery/Shipping address
- Requested terms

- A list of products/services with quantities and price

Step 2: Placing the order with the preferred supplier.

The Purchase Order can then be faxed or emailed to the supplier if necessary.

Suppliers should not be asked/requested to supply goods until the purchase order has been generated. The purchase order number should be given to the supplier who should in turn quote this number on their invoice.

Step 3: Receiving delivery of goods/services from a supplier

When the supplier delivers the goods, you should then raise a Goods Received Note (GRN). A GRN is a record of goods received at the point of receipt. You should raise the GRN after inspecting delivery for proof of order receipt. It's used by stores, procurement and finance to raise any issues, update your stock records and it should be matched against the original purchase order and supplier invoice, to allow payment to be made.

GRNs play an essential part in the accounts payable process by confirming that items have been received as expected, in accordance with the original purchase order, and that the items can, therefore, be invoiced by the supplier and subsequently paid for by the buyer.

Step 4: Post the invoice from supplier to the purchase ledger

The "Tax Invoice" received from the supplier should now be posted to the accounting software.

An invoice is a document that a business issues to its customers, asking the customers to pay for the goods or services that the business has supplied to them. Invoices can be issued either before or after the goods or services are supplied.

If the business issuing the invoices is registered for VAT, the invoices must comply with specific requirements as laid down by HMRC.

Many accounting software these days are used to raise purchase orders, and they seamlessly allow you to update the records with the supplier invoices received and thus easily record the supplier invoices.

Step 5: Pay the supplier as per the agreed days

Just as you expect others to pay you on time, it's just as important that you pay your bills on time.

A supplier invoice should ideally not be paid without a matching purchase order (except for utility bills like gas, electricity, telephone – which generally might be paid by direct debit/standing order). This ensures both that the organisation does not pay for unauthorised purchases and that authorised purchases will be paid in a timely fashion.

Suppose that today is the end of the month, and you have to pay for 200 invoices from 50 suppliers. You can process each payment individually by going into the supplier accounts - select the invoices, generate the payment list, write out the cheques, get the manager to authorise, send the cheques to the suppliers together with remittance advise notes.

This process will probably take you hours to complete manually.

There could be a better way.

If your purchase ledger system has a Batch Payments to Suppliers facility, all this is going to take you is the best part of 10 minutes. Just display a list of the 200 invoices on the screen, scan through them to note down the ones you don't want to pay, press the Select All button to highlight the lot, double-click on the two or more invoices you want to deselect, then press the button.

Here is how you go about it in detail; typically, the process will involve several stages, with the opportunity to review and correct at each stage. Below is a step by step example of how you might want to handle a batch payment run:

1. *Print a report of invoices due for payment and send this report to the manager requesting authorisation to pay.*
2. *Manager returns report indicating invoices approved or refused.*
3. *Display the list of all invoices due for payment on the Accounts software on-screen, press select to highlight all invoices and then deselect any invoices that have not been authorised for payment.*
4. *Print off resultant remittance advice note(s) in the draft to check for errors. Any necessary corrections should be done. Use the software to recalculate payments and reprint remittances.*
5. *Check and reprint until satisfied and then finalise the payment. Many Accounts packages allocate reference numbers to each payment. [Note - Payment transactions are now committed and cannot be changed]*
6. *The software prints final remittance advice and outputs BACS file, output onto an external disk.*
7. *Load file from external disk into your banks BACS system and complete the process.*

Batch Payments to Suppliers is one of the biggest time-savers in any accounts package, and it is handy if you process many payments at one time. However, if you only issue a dozen or so payments, you might as well keep doing them manually.

Send suppliers remittance advice slips

A remittance advice note is a note sent from a customer to his supplier, informing the supplier that he/she has paid the invoice. The advice may contain elements such as a text note, the invoice number and the invoice amount, among others.

Remittance advice notes are not required, but they are seen as a courtesy since they make it easier for the supplier to match invoices with payments.

Remittance advice note could be compared to a receipt from a cash register, in that they serve as a record of received payment.

At its simplest, a remittance advice note can be a letter or a note that outlines the invoice number and the payment amount sent or enclosed (such as when attached to a cheque).

Send your suppliers' remittance advice notes. It's a courteous business practice.

Step 6: Supplier statement reconciliation

Most organisations have to reconcile supplier accounts as part of their audit processes, which is an arduous task.

In principle, the process for reconciling supplier accounts is very straightforward. The supplier's credit control department sends a statement of account, which contains the unpaid invoices on their sales ledger, to the buyer's accounts payable department. The accounts payable team at the buyer's organisation compare the statement to their accounts payable in the creditors' ledger should be immediately debited. However, the money might not arrive at the supplier's account for a few days (especially if you are paying by cheque). In the meantime, the supplier will be showing that amount still owing, and the supplier thus will send you a statement showing unpaid invoices.

When you receive a supplier's statement, you should try to reconcile it to the supplier's account in your creditors' ledger. The term 'reconcile' means that you try to explain the difference between the two figures.

Any differences that you cannot explain are probably caused by errors – either yours or the suppliers.

To reconcile a supplier's statement to the balance on an account, you must go through the entries on each, marking off the ones which match. Any entries which don't match, whether on the statement or the account, need to be investigated and explained.

The first stage in the reconciliation is to 'tick off' all the items in common between the account and the statement. These items cannot be contributing to the difference. Whatever is left unticked should be "investigated."

Generally, to reconcile the supplier's statement, adjust for any payments made on or before the reconciliation date. For the ledger account, add any invoices issued by the supplier on or before the reconciliation date, but not yet entered into the supplier's account.

Supplier statement reconciliation is an opportunity for accounts payable to spot any discrepancies before suppliers request for payment of unpaid invoices is processed and to make sure the invoice process is complete.

The key to identifying discrepancies is to determine which invoices or credit notes on the supplier statement that are not on the accounts payable ledger or vice versa.

Task 3b: How to raise a purchase order and purchase invoice

In the previous task, we saw that the first task in the accounts payable process was to raise a purchase order for the goods or services needed. Let's go ahead and do just that with the details of the requisition sent by email from the store manager.

Fig. 91

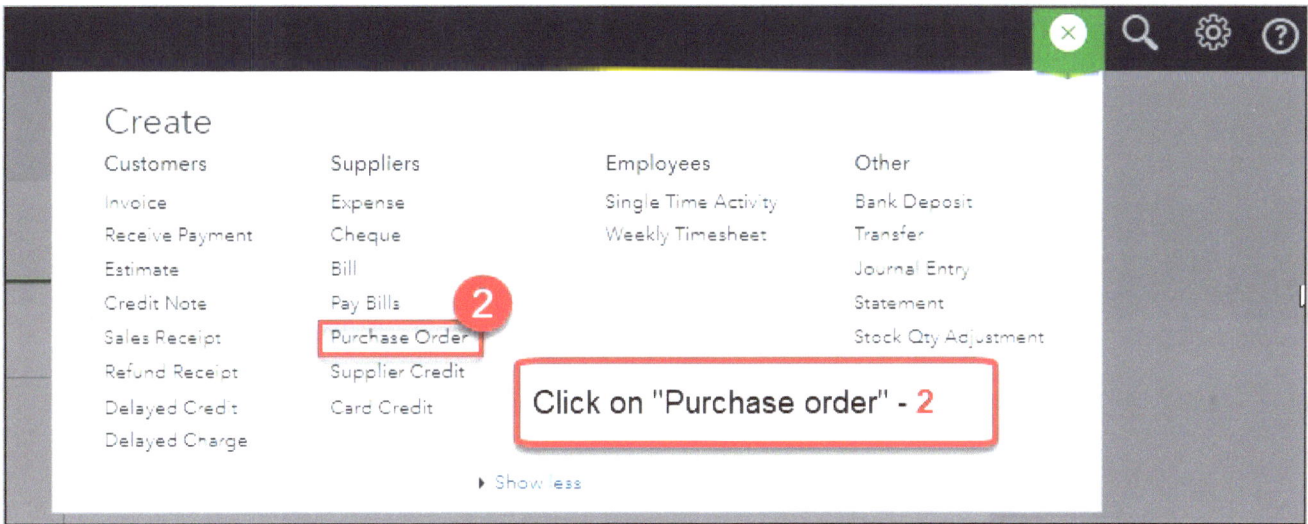

Fig. 92

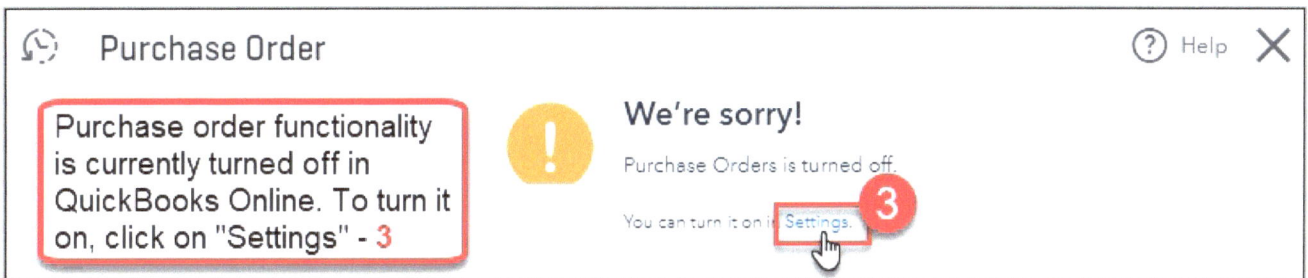

Fig. 93

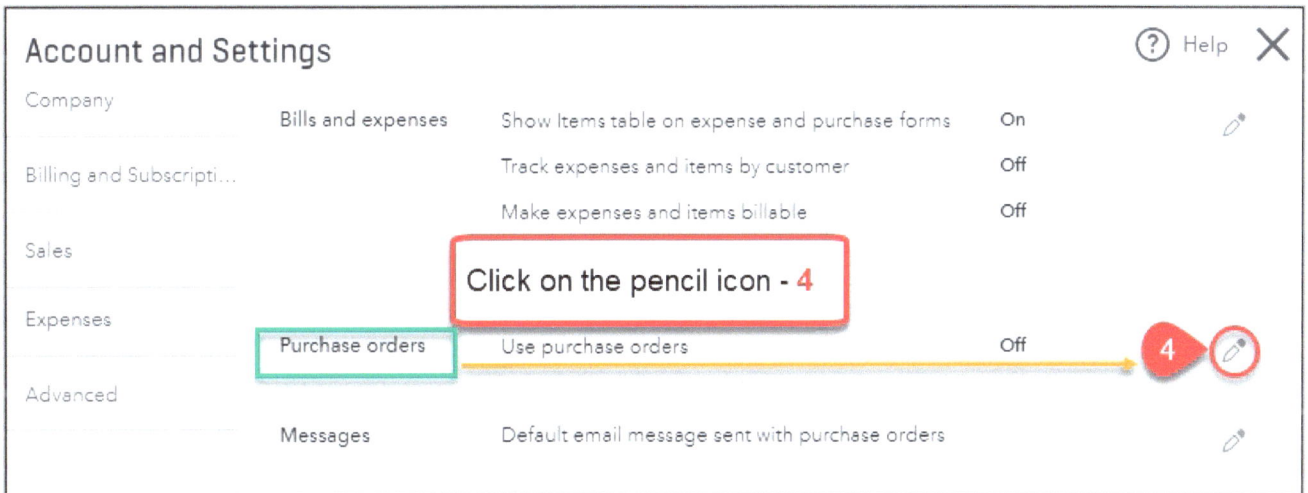

Fig. 94

This space is for notes

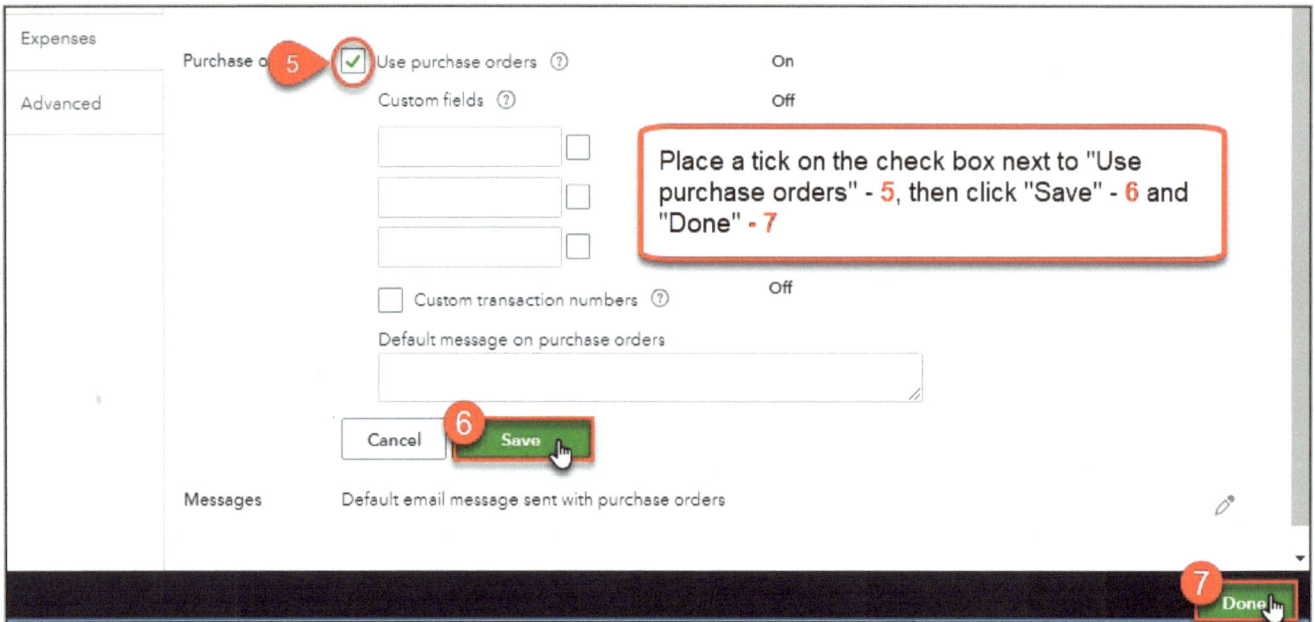

Fig. 95

You are now ready to create a purchase order.

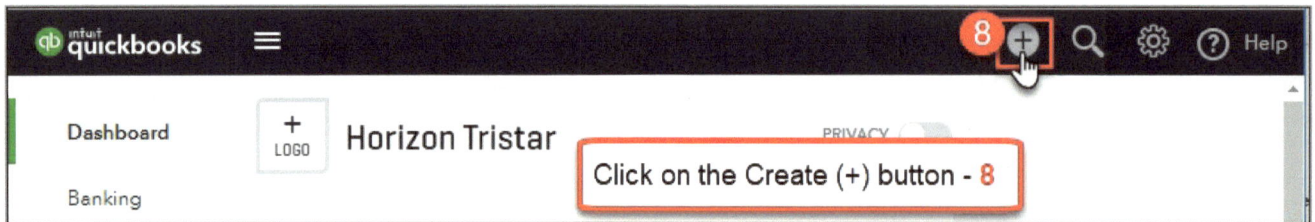

Fig. 96

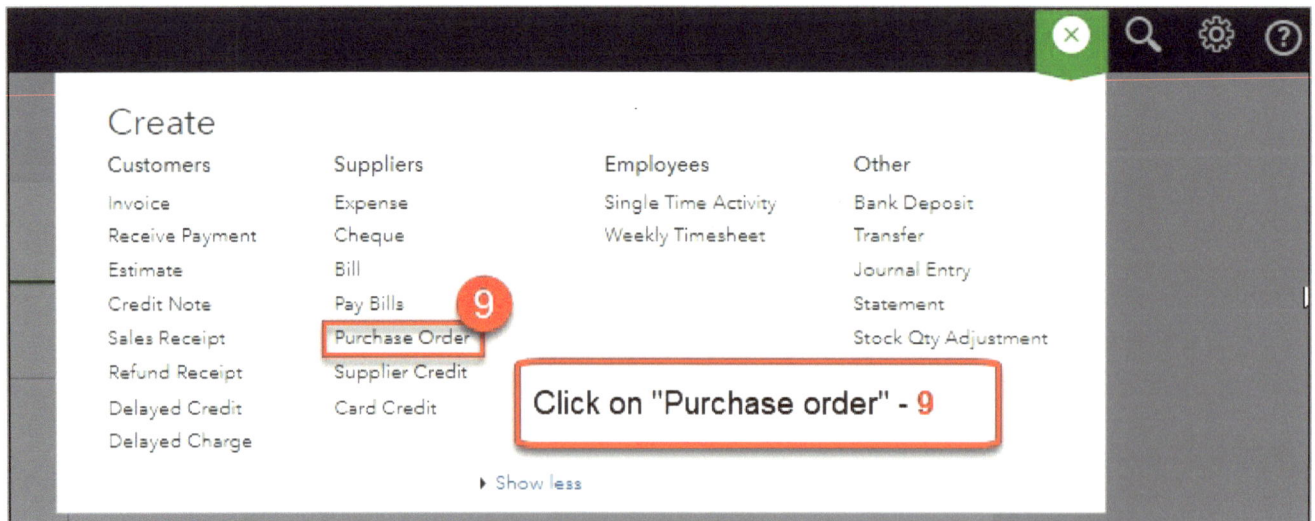

Fig. 97

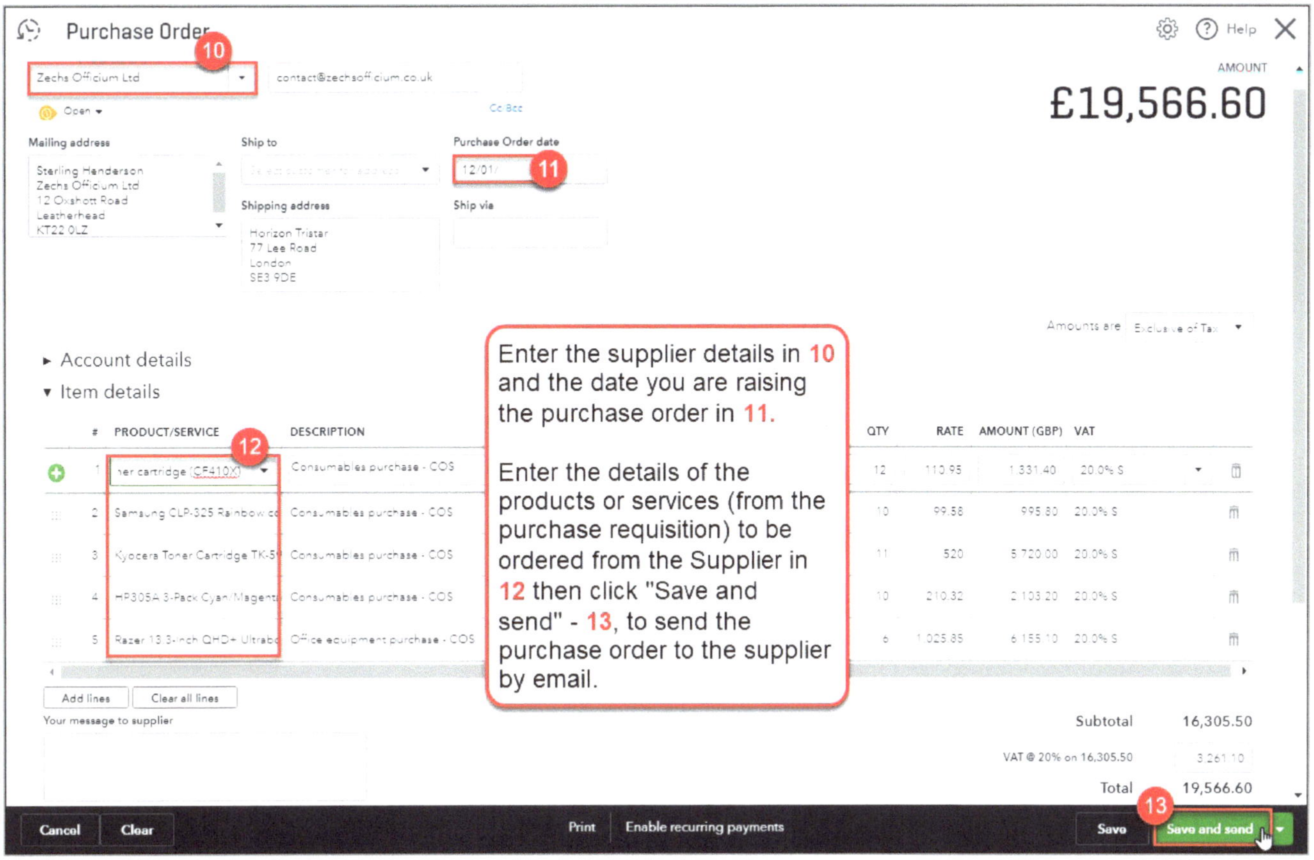

Fig. 98

This space is for notes

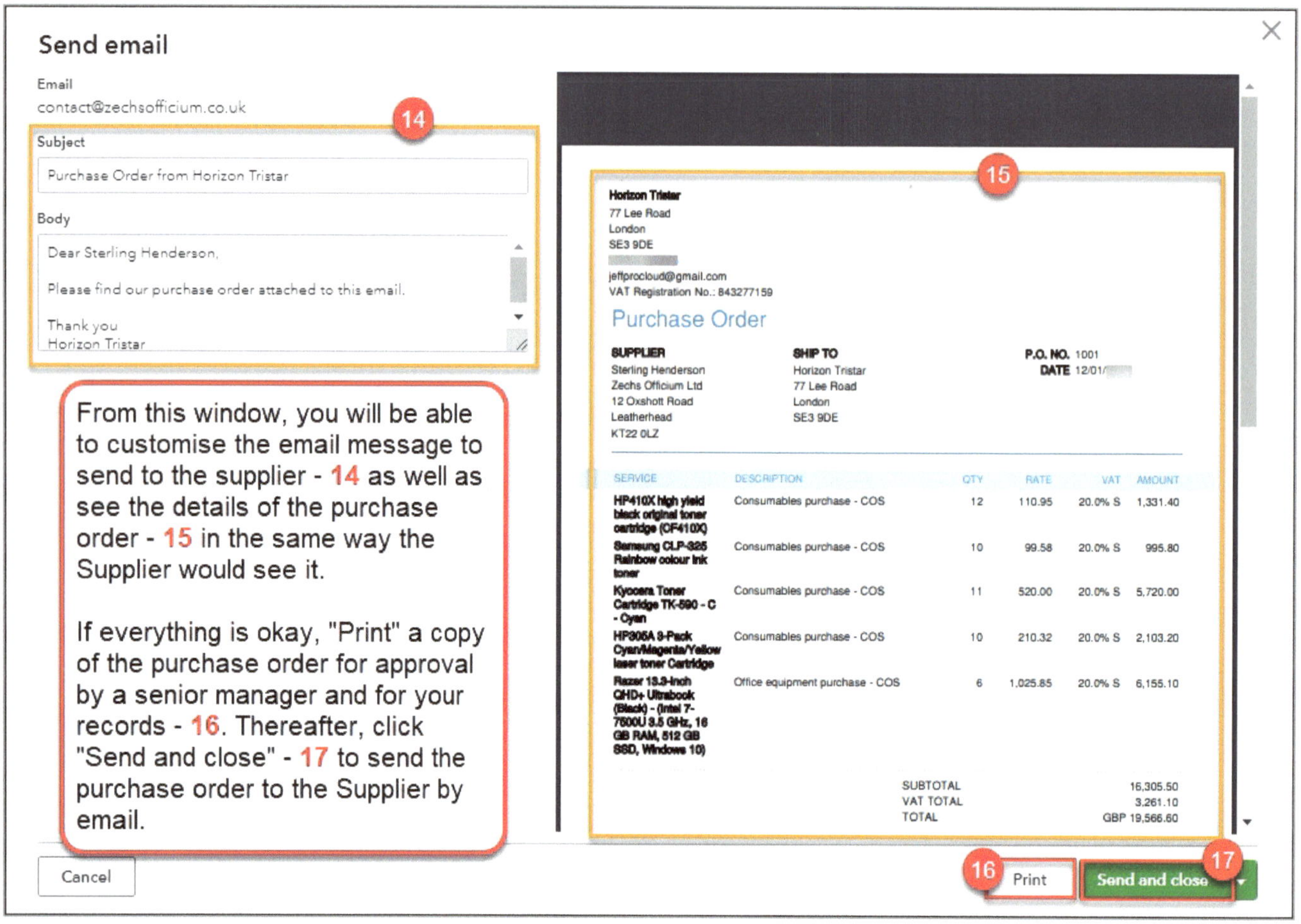

Send email

Email
contact@zechsofficium.co.uk

Subject
Purchase Order from Horizon Tristar

Body
Dear Sterling Henderson,

Please find our purchase order attached to this email.

Thank you
Horizon Tristar

From this window, you will be able to customise the email message to send to the supplier - **14** as well as see the details of the purchase order - **15** in the same way the Supplier would see it.

If everything is okay, "Print" a copy of the purchase order for approval by a senior manager and for your records - **16**. Thereafter, click "Send and close" - **17** to send the purchase order to the Supplier by email.

Fig. 99

It's now your turn.

There are still two more purchase orders to raise – one to Vandstone plc and the other to Joe Office Automation. **Follow steps 8 to 13 in figure 98 above** to raise those purchase orders using the details of the purchase requisition you received for Vandstone plc and Joe Office Automation.

Your final purchase order, ready to be sent to the Supplier (Vandstone Plc), should look like the figure 100.

This space is for notes

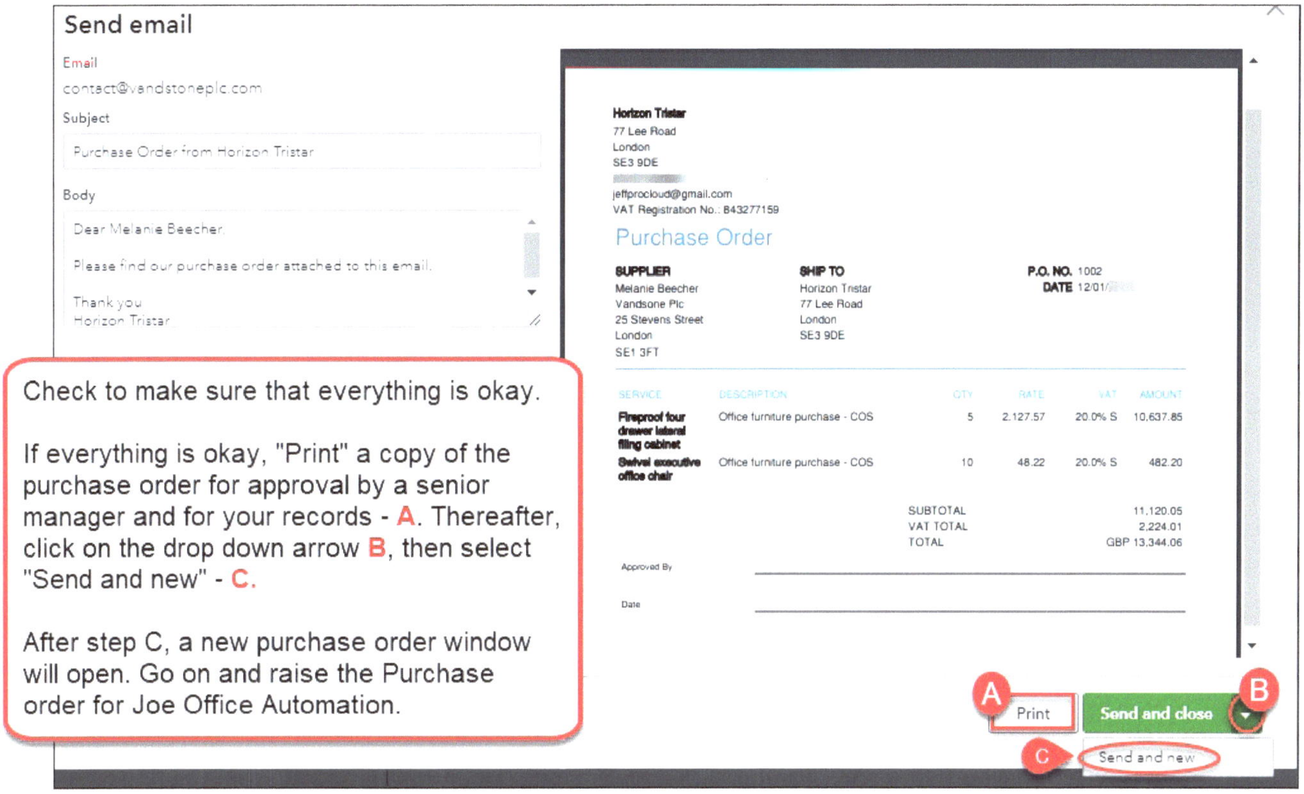

Check to make sure that everything is okay.

If everything is okay, "Print" a copy of the purchase order for approval by a senior manager and for your records - **A**. Thereafter, click on the drop down arrow **B**, then select "Send and new" - **C**.

After step C, a new purchase order window will open. Go on and raise the Purchase order for Joe Office Automation.

Fig. 100

From the new purchase order window that appears, enter the details from the purchase requisition for the product to be ordered from Joe Office Automation. The purchase order you raise, ready to be emailed to Joe Office Automation, should look similar to the figure below.

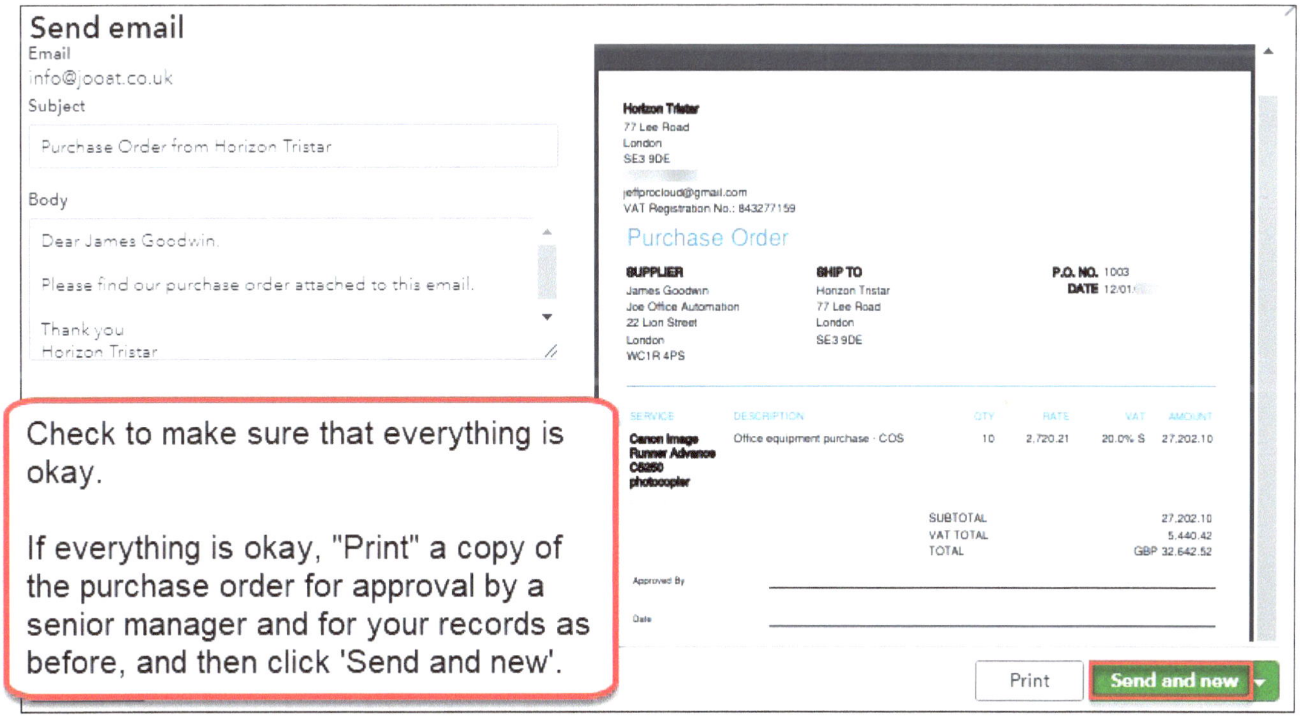

Check to make sure that everything is okay.

If everything is okay, "Print" a copy of the purchase order for approval by a senior manager and for your records as before, and then click 'Send and new'.

Fig. 101

Let's now check to make sure that we have raised all the purchase orders.

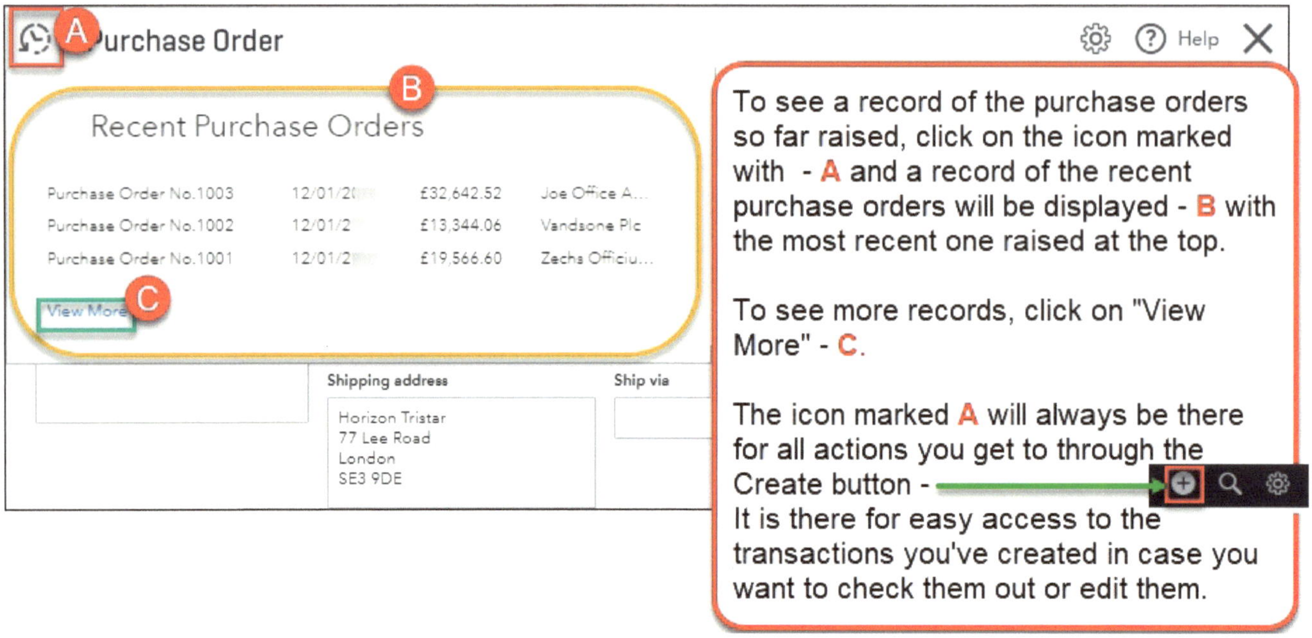

To see a record of the purchase orders so far raised, click on the icon marked with - **A** and a record of the recent purchase orders will be displayed - **B** with the most recent one raised at the top.

To see more records, click on "View More" - **C**.

The icon marked **A** will always be there for all actions you get to through the Create button -
It is there for easy access to the transactions you've created in case you want to check them out or edit them.

Fig. 102

What if you want to delete a purchase order you created in error, how do you go about doing it?

Let me show you.

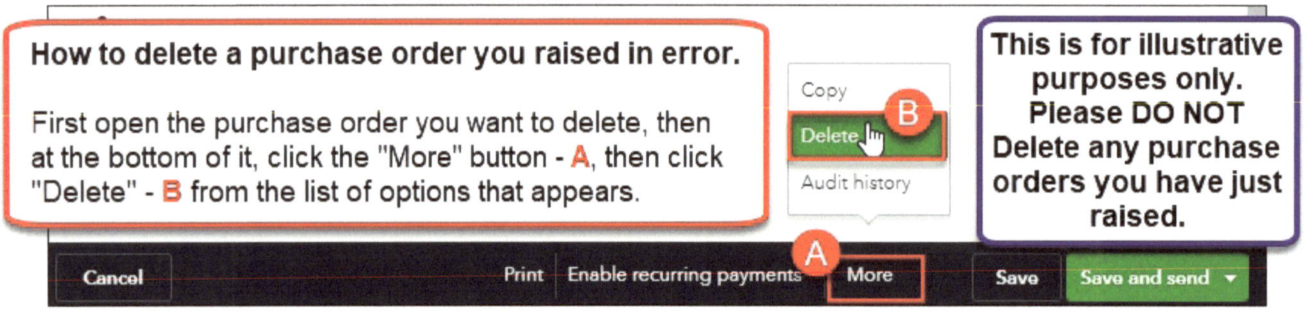

How to delete a purchase order you raised in error.

First open the purchase order you want to delete, then at the bottom of it, click the "More" button - **A**, then click "Delete" - **B** from the list of options that appears.

This is for illustrative purposes only. Please DO NOT Delete any purchase orders you have just raised.

Fig. 103

Zechs Officium Ltd, Vandstone plc and Joe Office Automation were delighted to receive "purchase orders" from Horizon Tristar Ltd and promptly delivered the products to Horizon Tristar on the 15th and 17th January.

What you need to do now is to post the invoices sent by those suppliers into QuickBooks Online.

This space is for notes

Task 3c: Processing Purchase invoices

There are two ways you can enter/process purchase invoices in QuickBooks Online.

Product Invoices

1st option is to:

Click on the create button - [icon], then select Bill from the options under supplier and then process the Supplier invoice by entering the details from the invoice received from the Supplier.

2nd option (the one we will use) is as shown below:

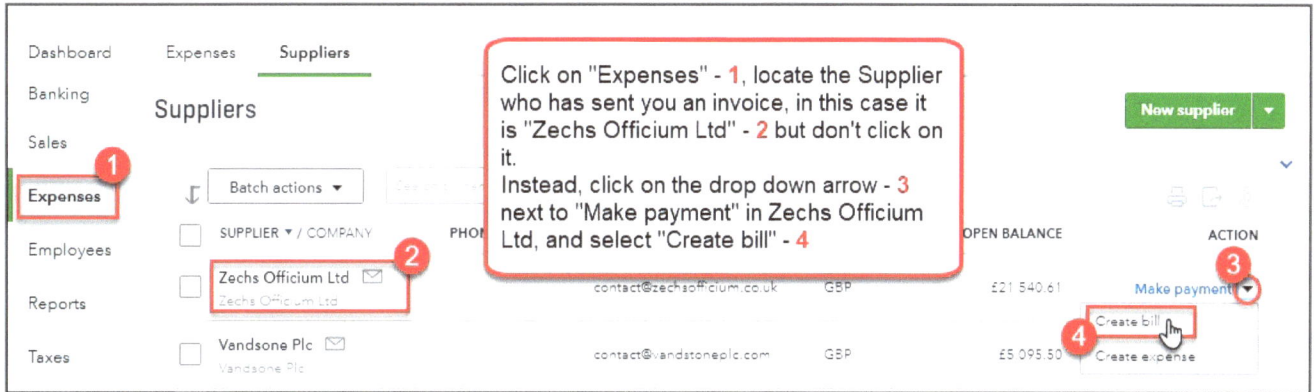

Fig. 104

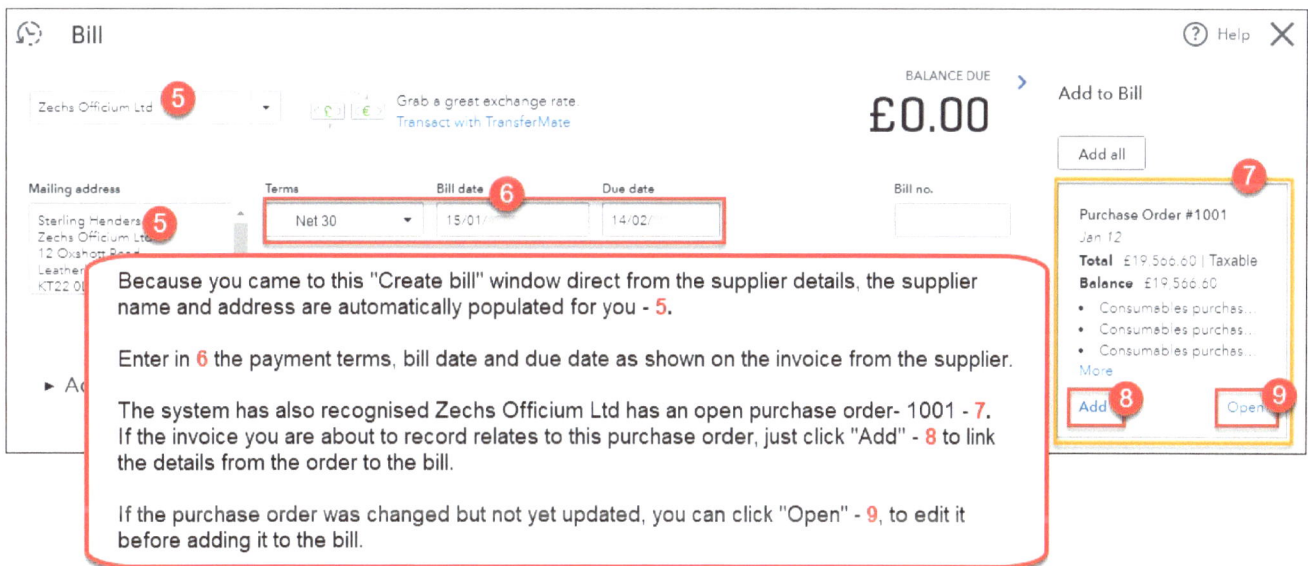

Fig. 105

> This space is for notes

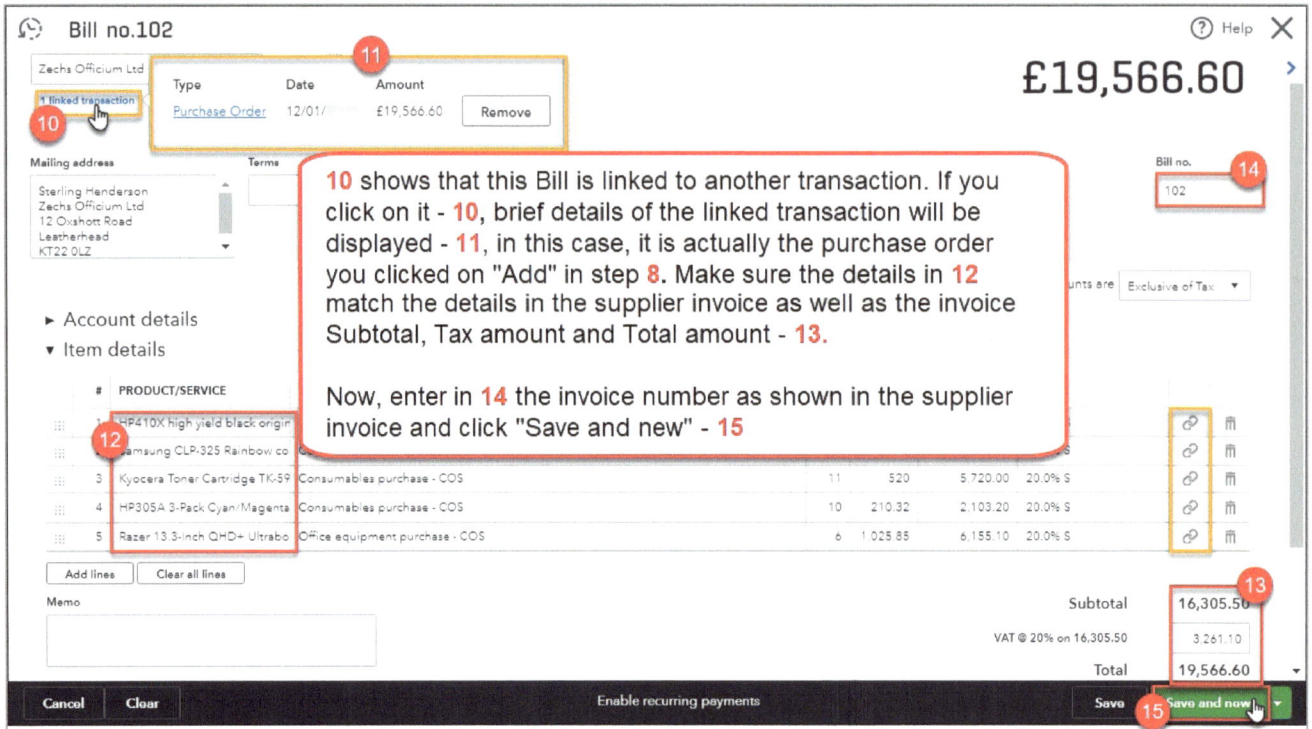

Fig. 106

Now it's your turn.

You have two more bills to process; one from Vandstone plc and the other from Joe Office Automation.

Here is what to do, from the new bill window that appears after step 13 in the figure above, **enter the supplier name – Vandstone plc** in the supplier name box. **Thereafter, follow steps 6 to 8 above** in figure 105 and your bill, ready to be posted, should look like what is shown in the figure below.

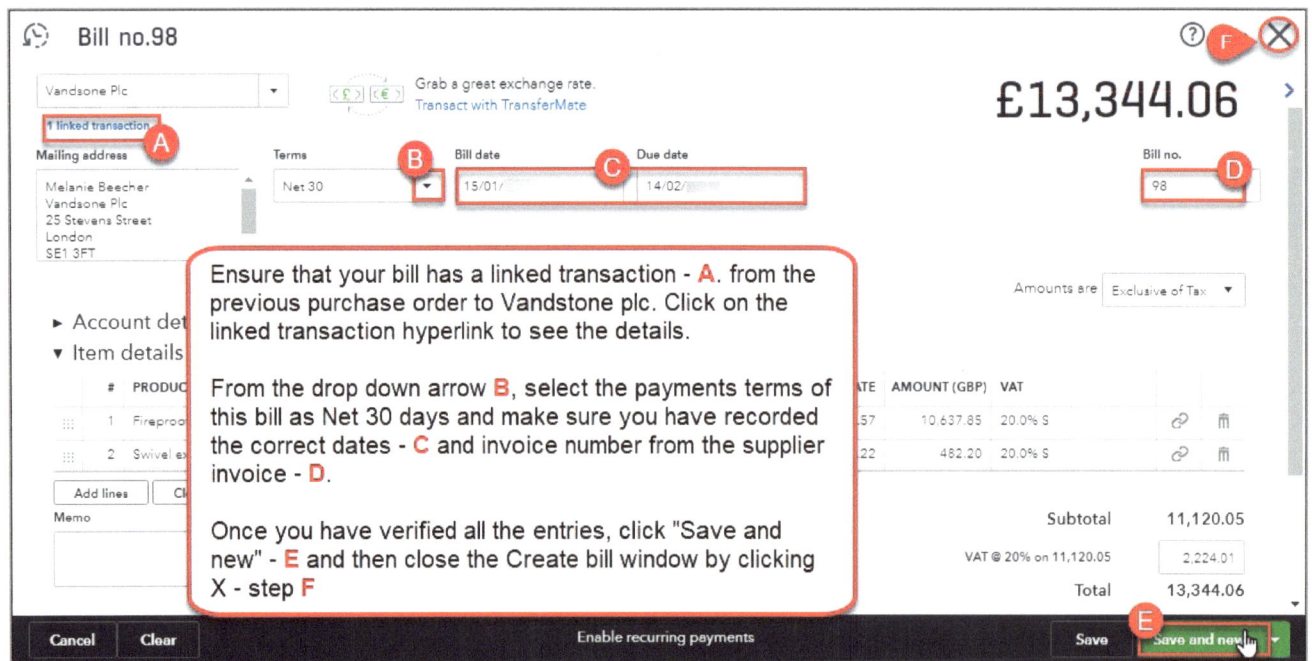

Fig. 107

Vandstone plc invoice is done.

Let's do the Joe office automation invoice together because it appears not all the products ordered from them were delivered – only seven of the ten items ordered were delivered, and as such we have to keep the purchase order open till all the items are delivered.

Let's do it.

We are going to process this invoice a bit differently, – from the purchase order window.

Click on the create button- [icon], then **select Purchase order** from the options under Supplier then follow the steps as illustrated in the figure below.

Fig. 108

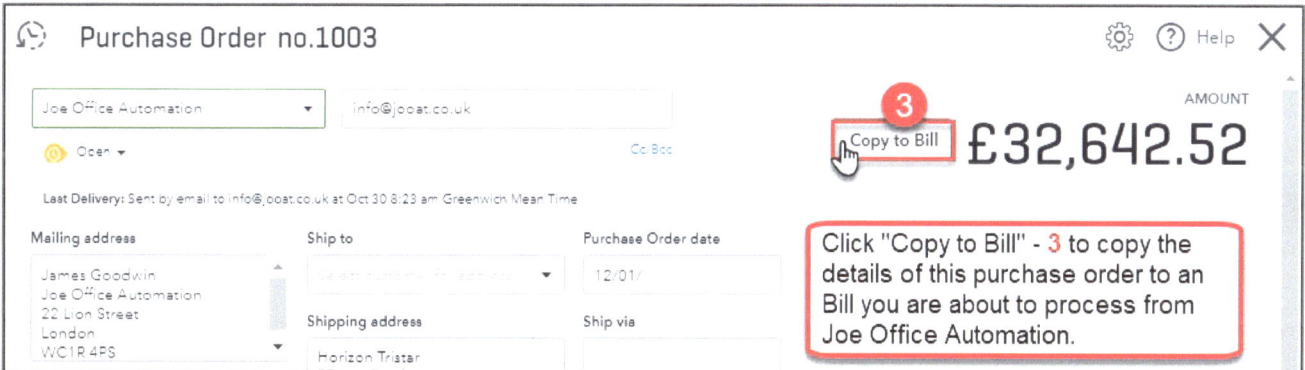

Fig. 109

This space is for notes

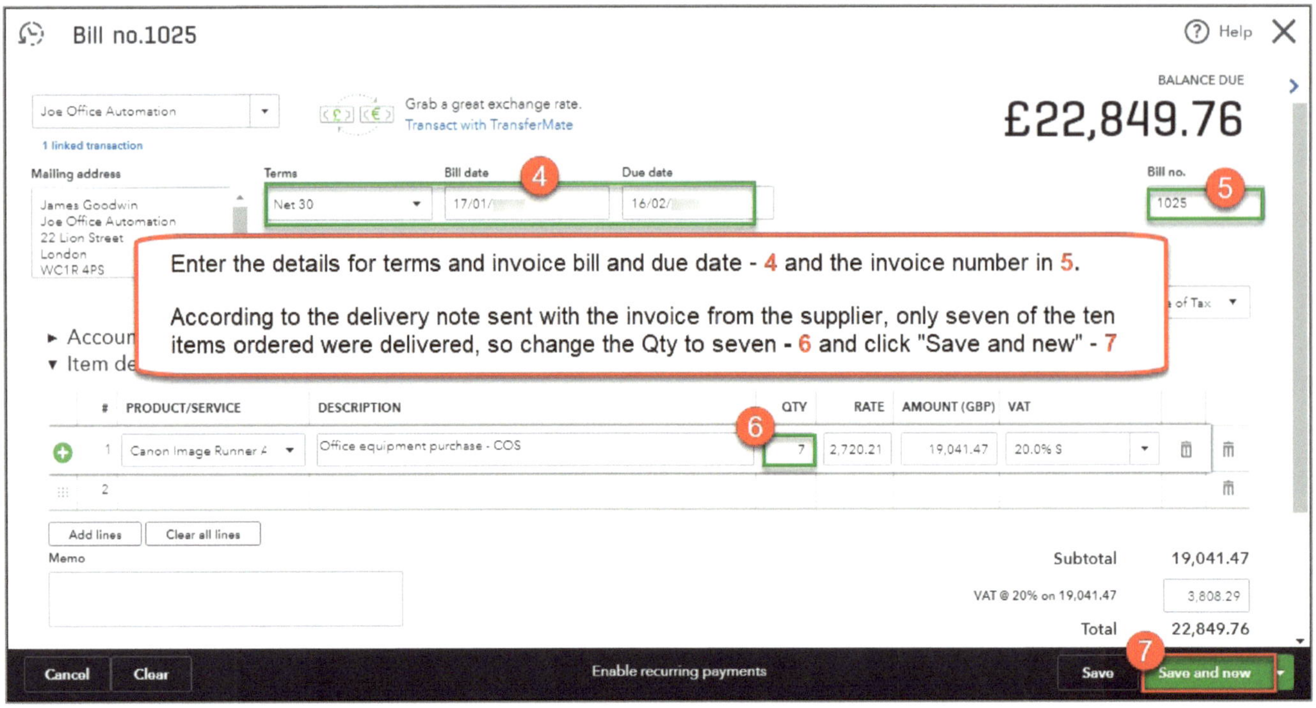

Fig. 110

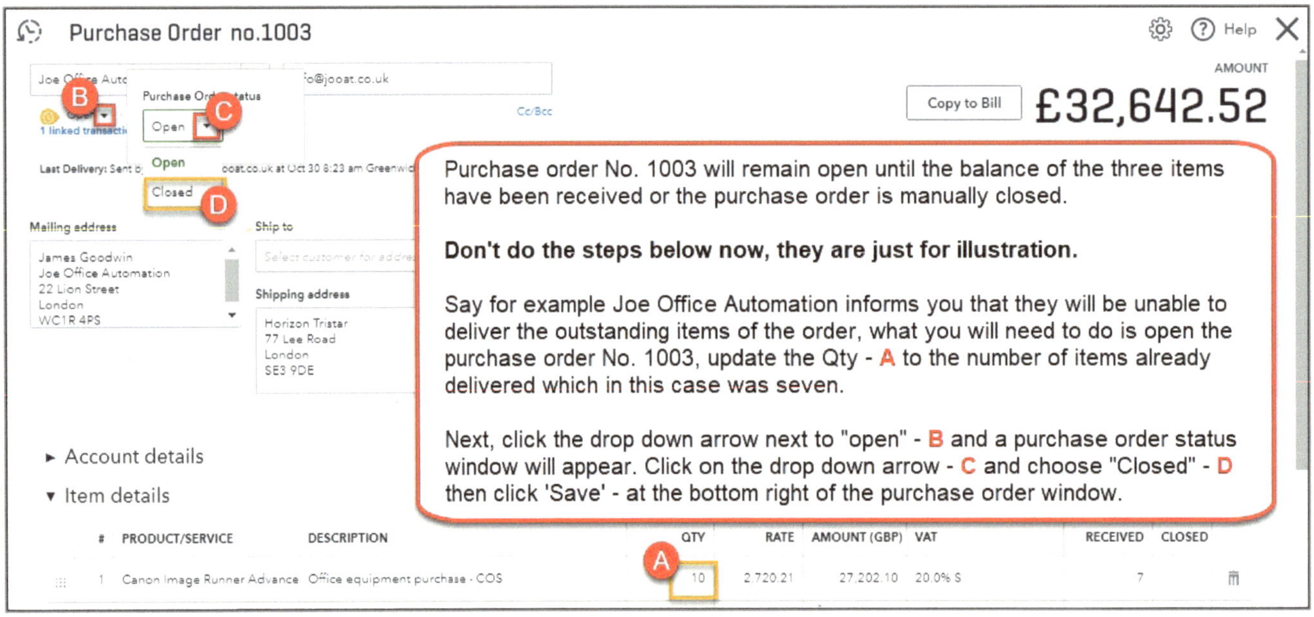

Fig. 111

Recording an advance payment made to a supplier

Horizon Tristar Ltd made a payment of £1,984.32 inclusive of Tax (VAT) to Bimpressive.com Ltd, a new supplier.

Here is how to record that payment in QuickBooks Online.

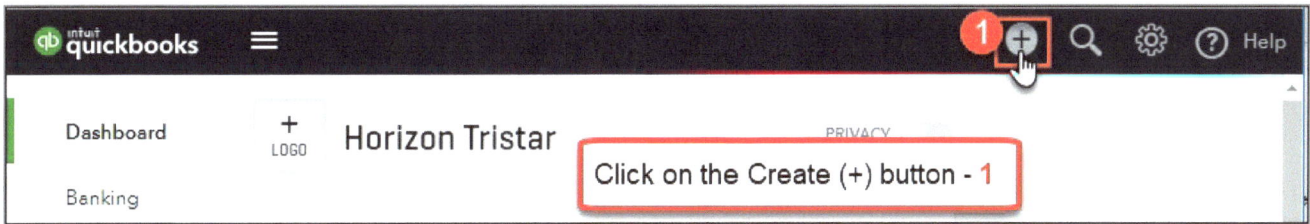

Fig. 112

Fig. 113

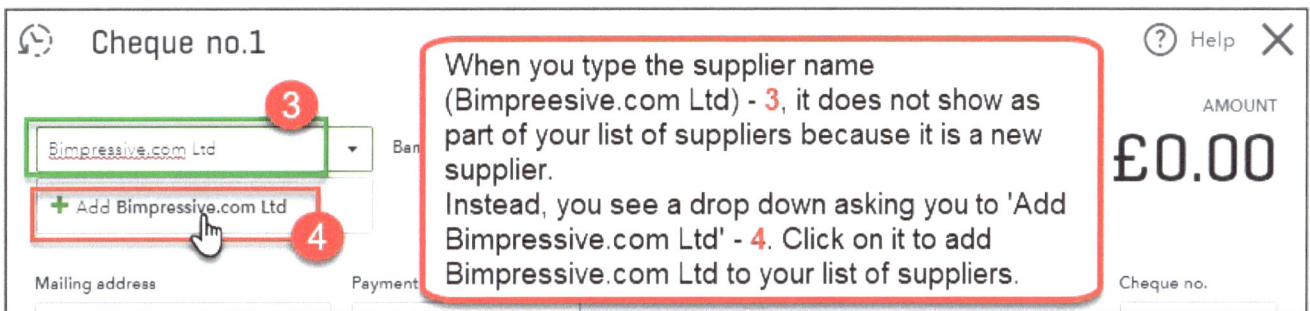

Fig. 114

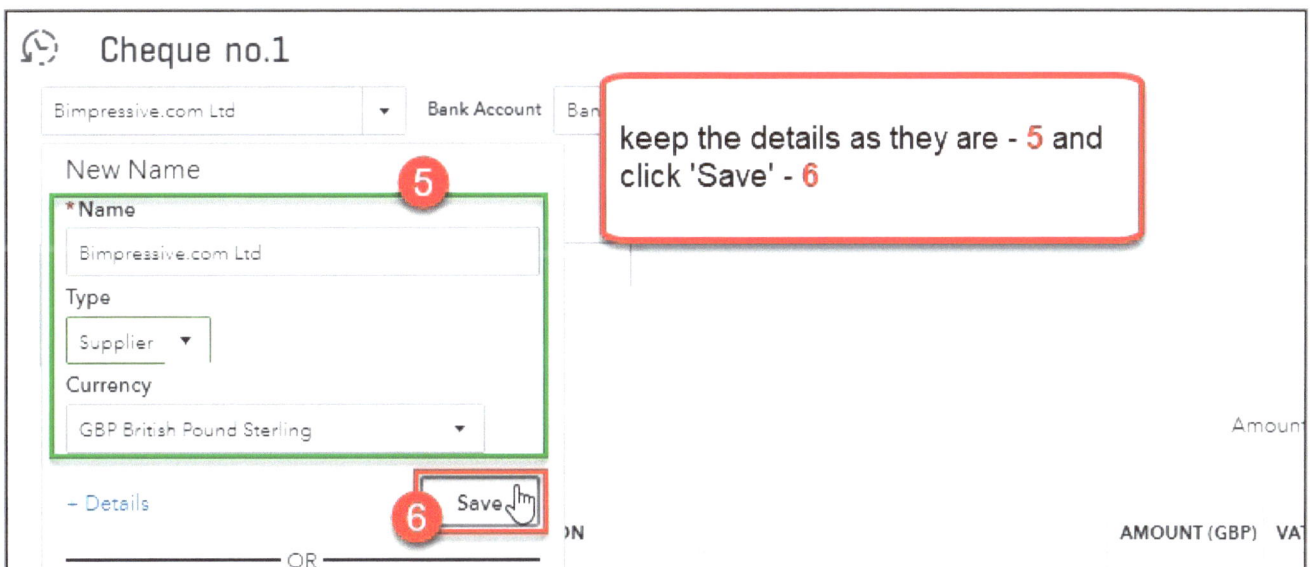

Fig. 115

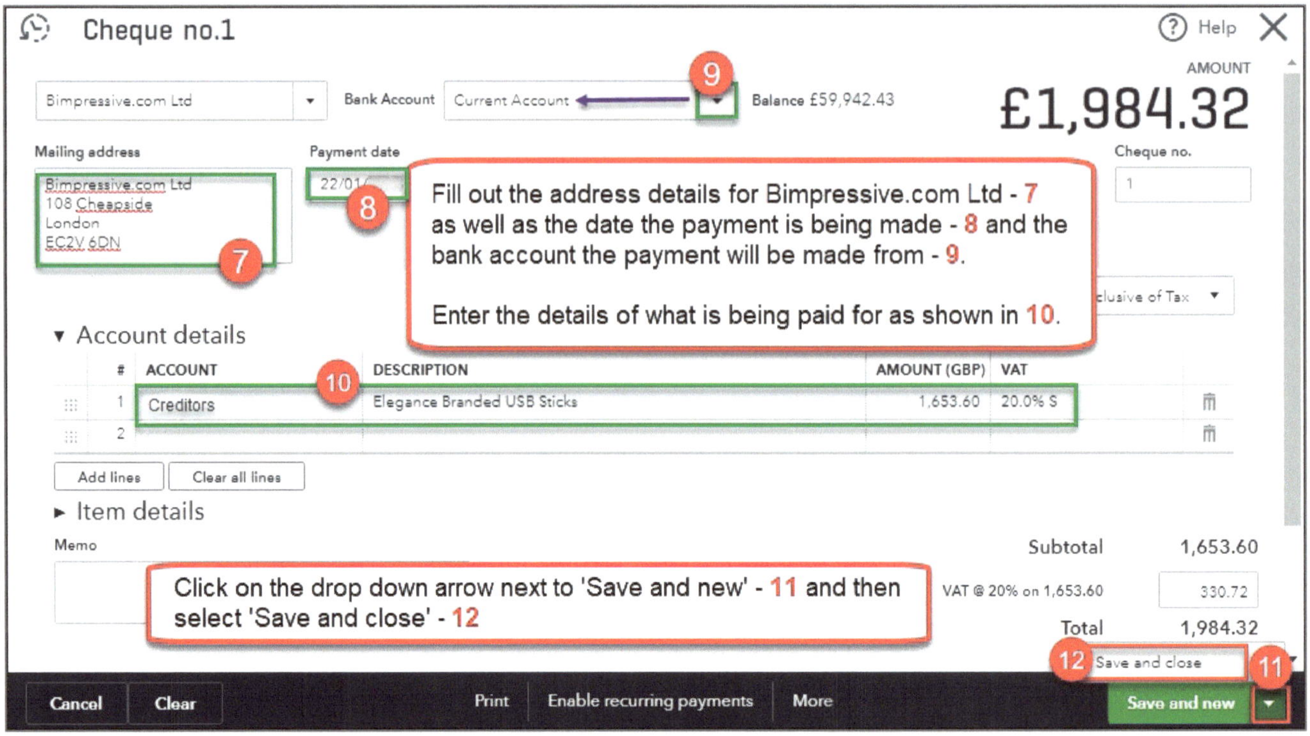

Fig. 116

Service Invoices

Processing supplier service invoices in QuickBooks Online is similar to processing supplier product invoices.

Click on the create button -  , **then select Bill** from the options under supplier and then process the Supplier invoice by entering the details from the invoice received from the supplier.

For **TD&A Certified Accountants Invoice**, enter TD&A Certified Accountants in the supplier name box and fill out the other details like the invoice number, terms, invoice date and enter the rest of the entries as shown in the figure below:

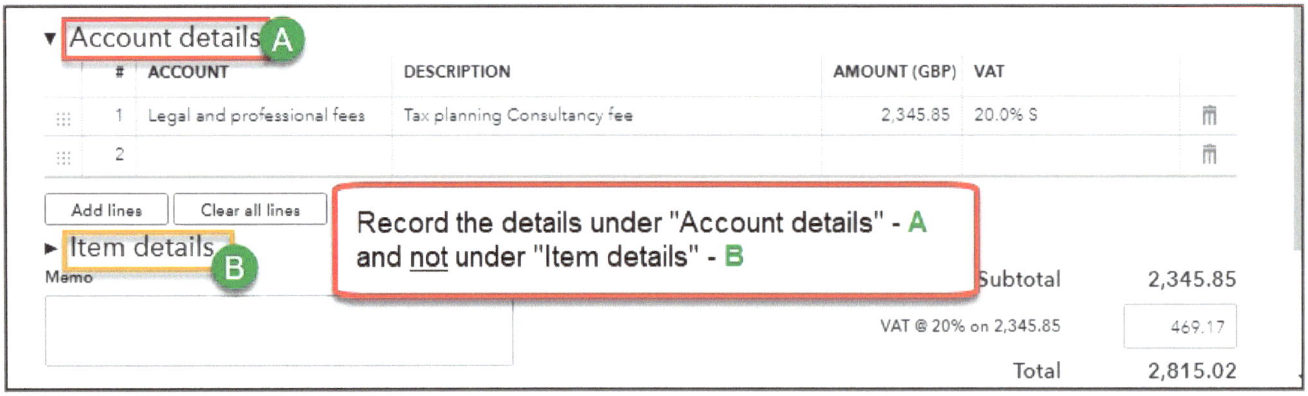

Fig. 117

For the **Office space Today invoice**, here is how the entry details should look like after you have entered the terms, invoice date and invoice number:

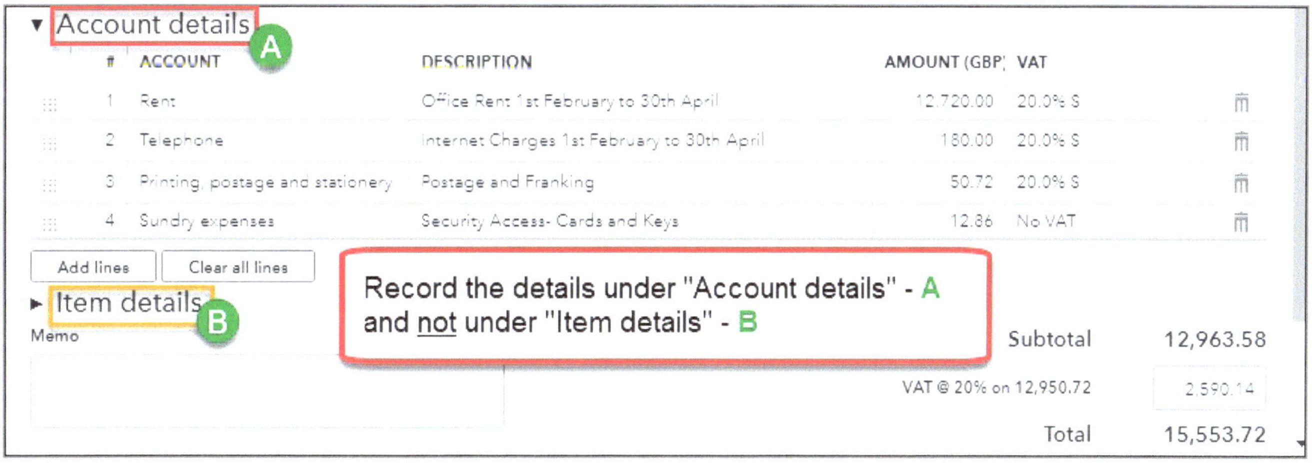

Fig. 118

For the **Spotless Clean invoice**, here is how the entry details should look like after you have entered the terms, invoice date and invoice number:

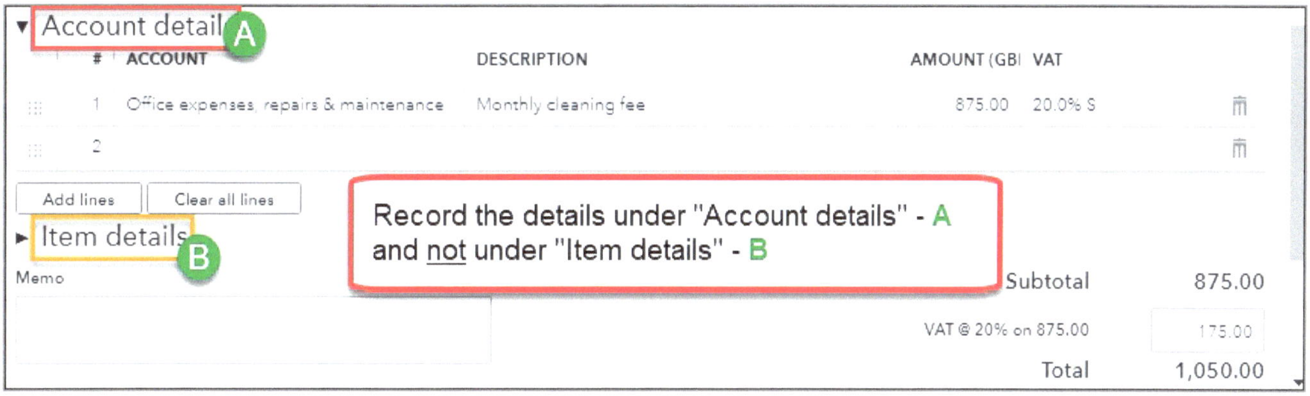

Fig. 119

For the **Bimpressive.com Ltd invoice**, here is how the entry details should look like after you have entered the terms, invoice date and invoice number:

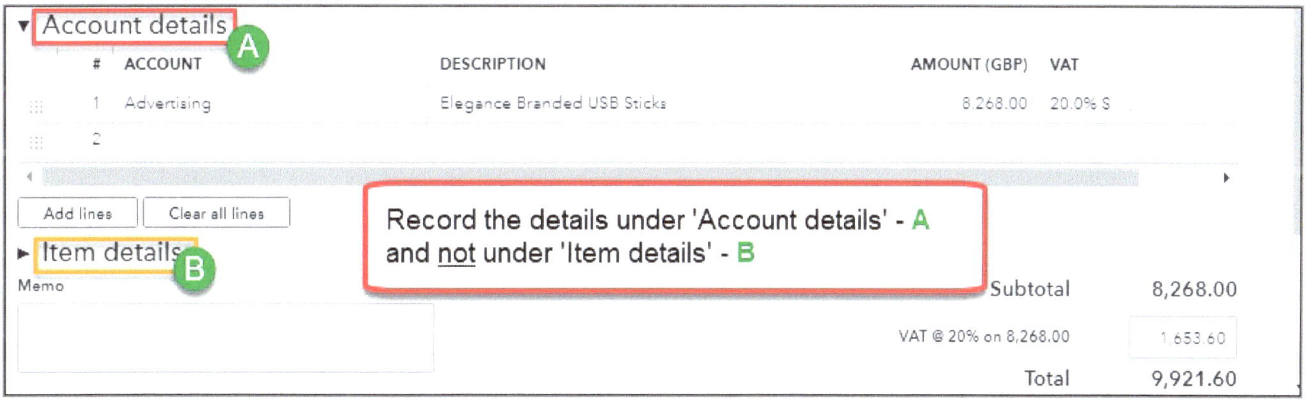

Fig. 120

Because the Bimpressive.com Ltd invoice was partly paid in advance, you now need to allocate that payment to the invoice you have just processed.

To do so, here is what you need to do.

Fig. 121

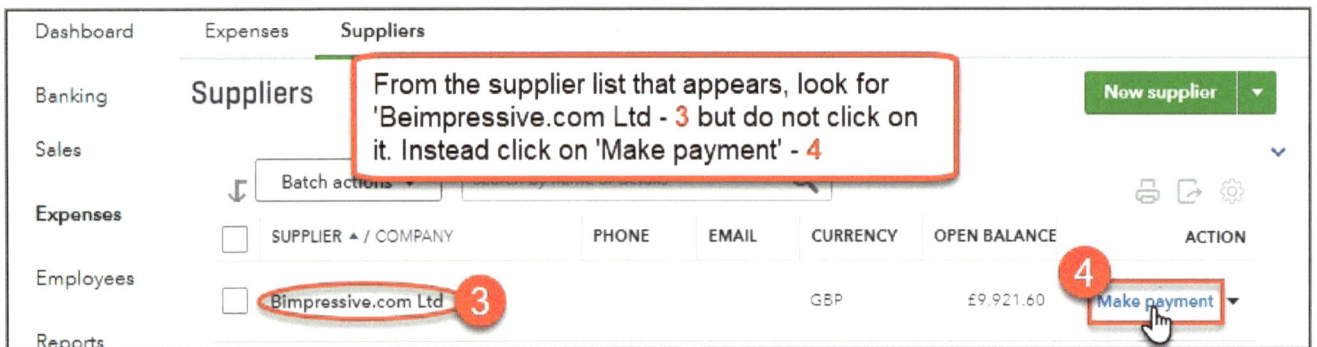

Fig. 122

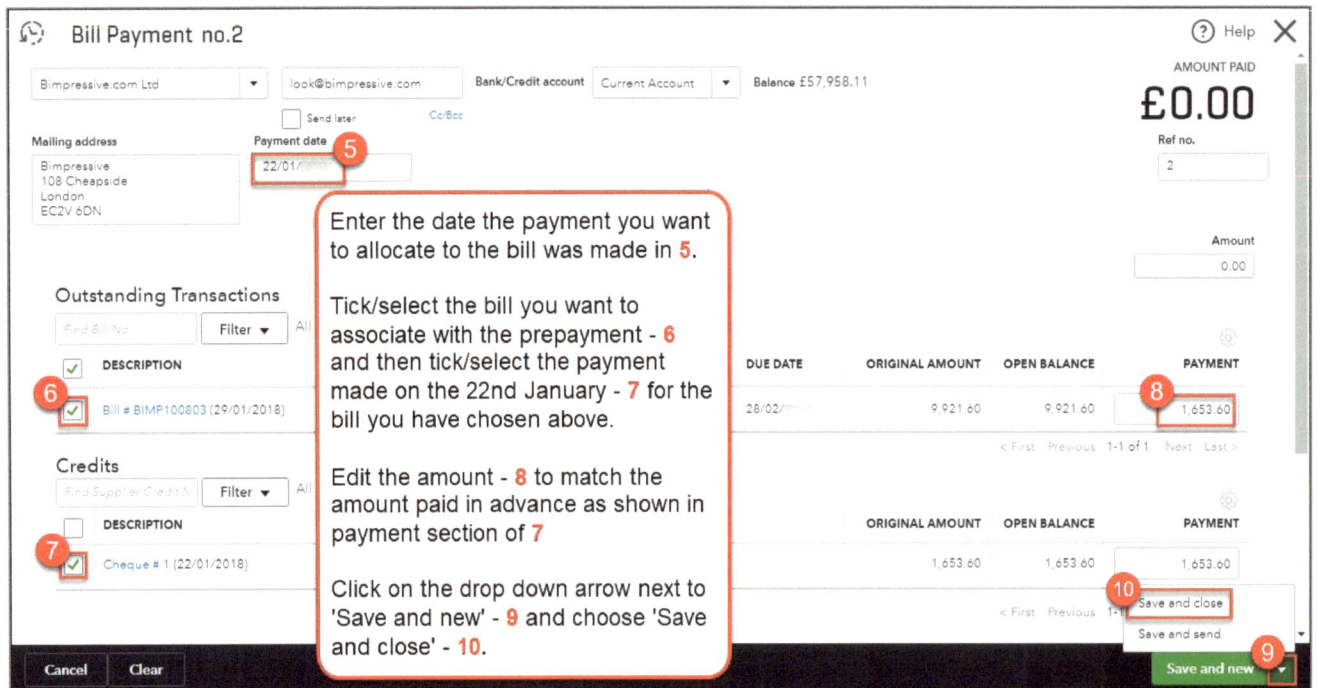

Fig. 123

Task 3d: How to process a purchase credit note

The store manager found out that two (2) of the HP305A 3 Pack Cyan/Magenta/Yellow original toner Cartridge (CF370AM) that were ordered from Zechs Officium Ltd and delivered on the 15th January were damaged. The supplier was informed, and he immediately issued a credit note and so you are now going to post that credit note into QuickBooks Online.

Here is how to do it.

Fig. 124

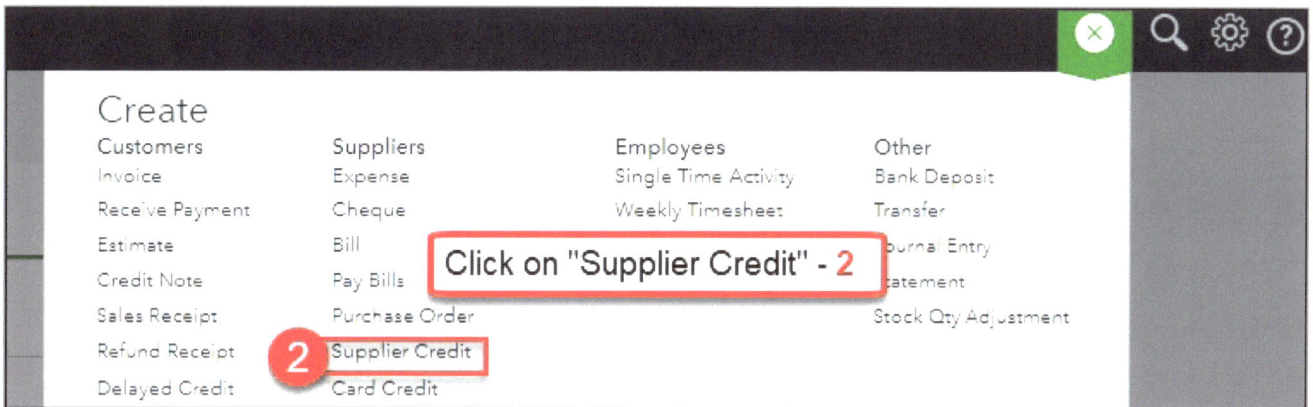

Fig. 125

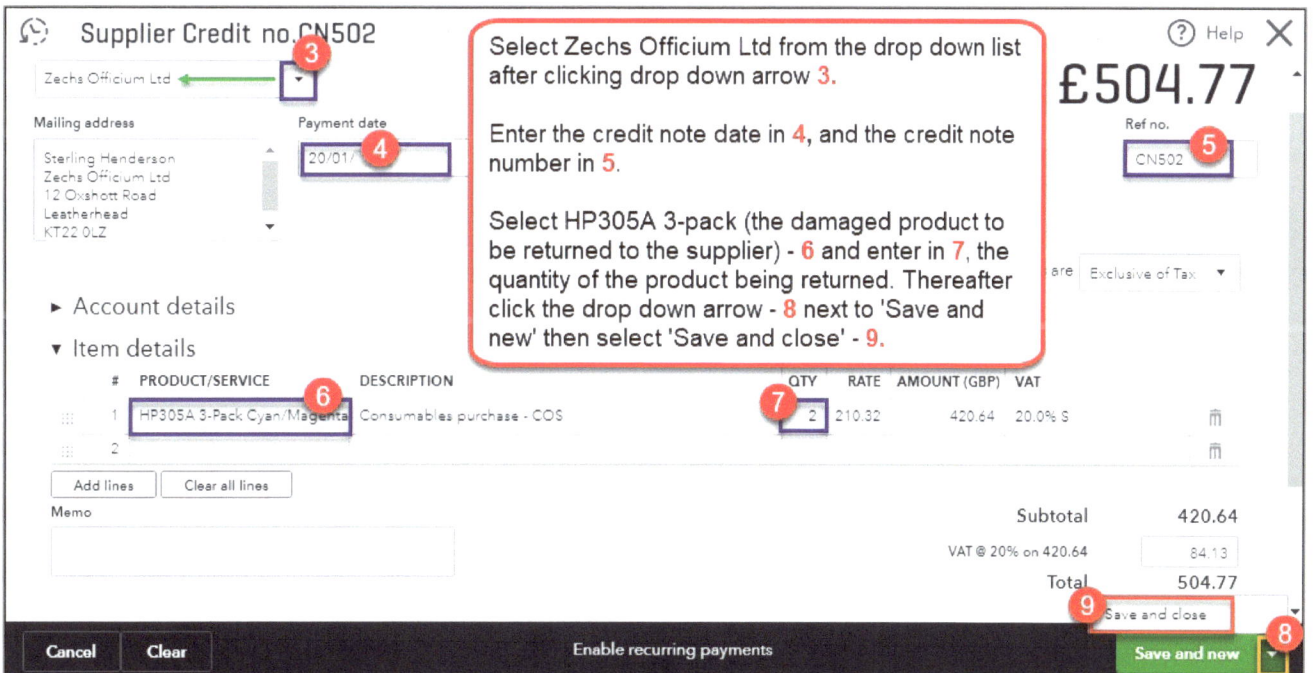

Fig. 126

Task 3e: How to record supplier payments & expense receipts

Overview of this task

There are three ways you can pay your suppliers:
1. Pay the outstanding invoice in full (full payment)
2. Pay part of the outstanding invoice (part payment)
3. Make a payment on account (payment made to reduce the overall outstanding on the account)

It is important to:
- Have a management policy on prompt payment of bills. Ensure that all staff are aware of it, especially but not only those in finance and purchasing.
- Agree on terms of payment at the start of all contracts.
- Monitor your payment system regularly for timely payment of invoices.
- Have a good system for clearing disputes quickly.
- Foster good relationships with suppliers by informing them of your payment procedures and who is responsible.

Key points to note when making payments are:

i. First check that there is enough money to make payment (perform a bank reconciliation)
ii. Get creditors ageing report
iii. Decide which suppliers to pay based on
iv. Credit terms with the supplier
v. Get approval from the manager
vi. Write the cheques or do BACS transfer
vii. Print remittance advice slip and send to the supplier

3e(i). Processing supplier payments

Here is how to make multiple payments at once – Batch payments or what is popularly known as payment runs.

Fig. 127

Fig. 128

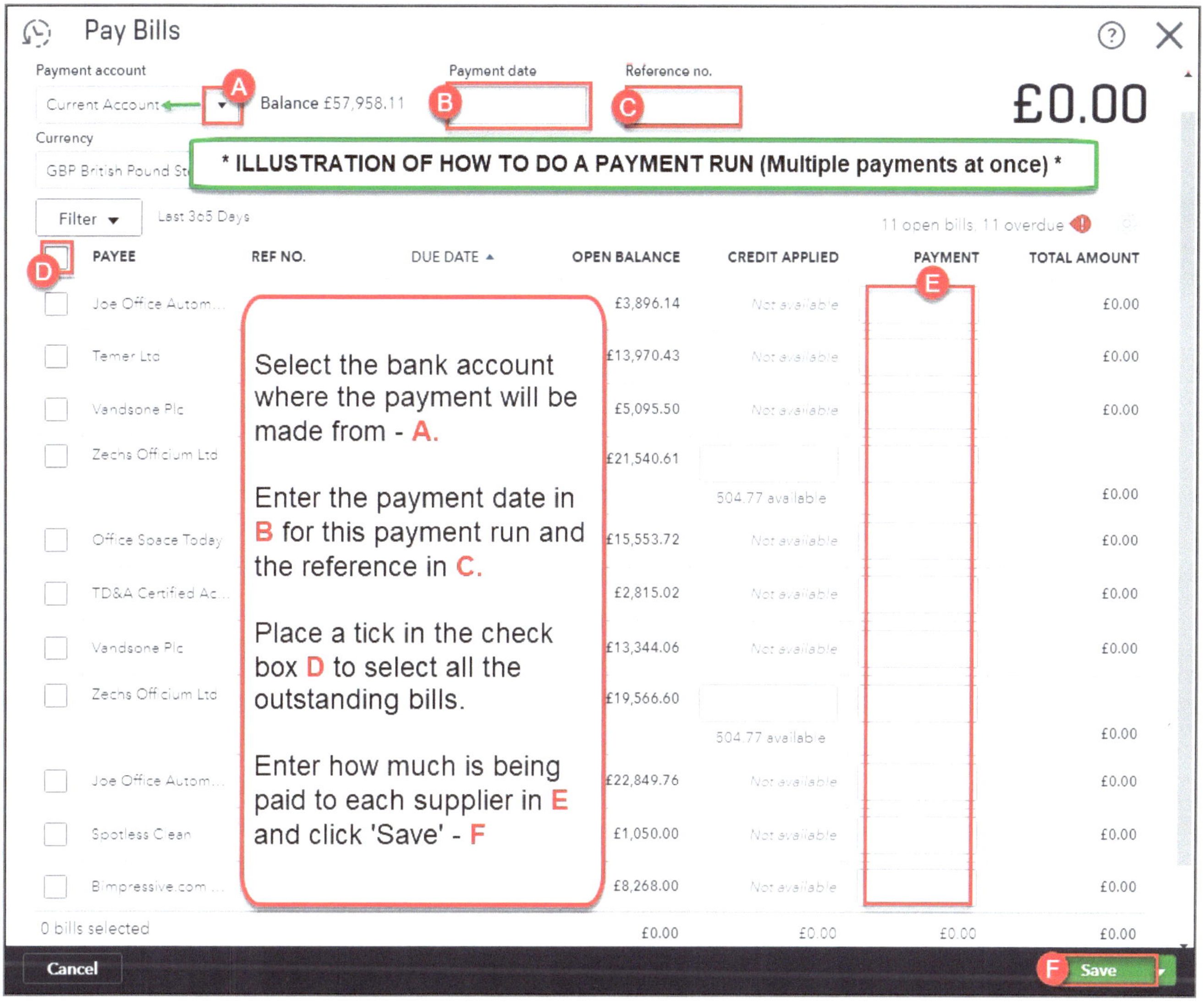

Fig. 129

Because the payments that Horizon Tristar Ltd is making to its suppliers are made on different dates, you can't do a payment run. Instead, you have to make payments one at a time.

This space is for notes

Now, from the Pay Bills window that is still open on your screen, record the payment that has been made to Temer Ltd.

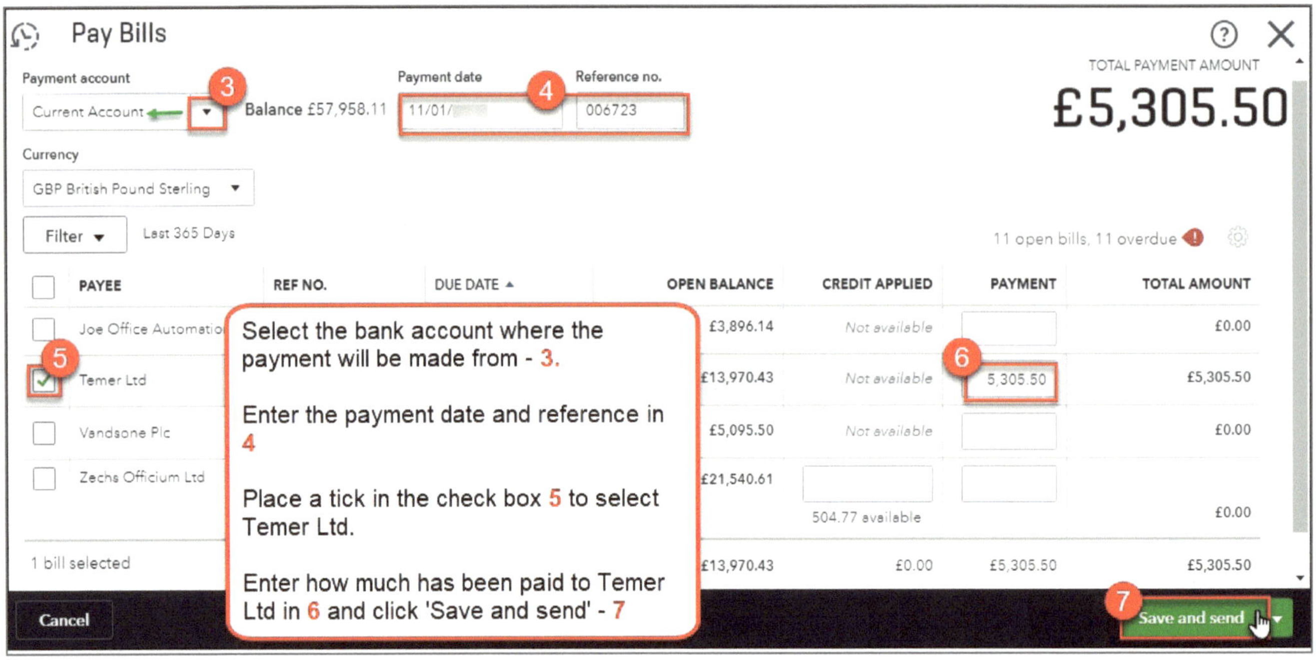

Fig. 130

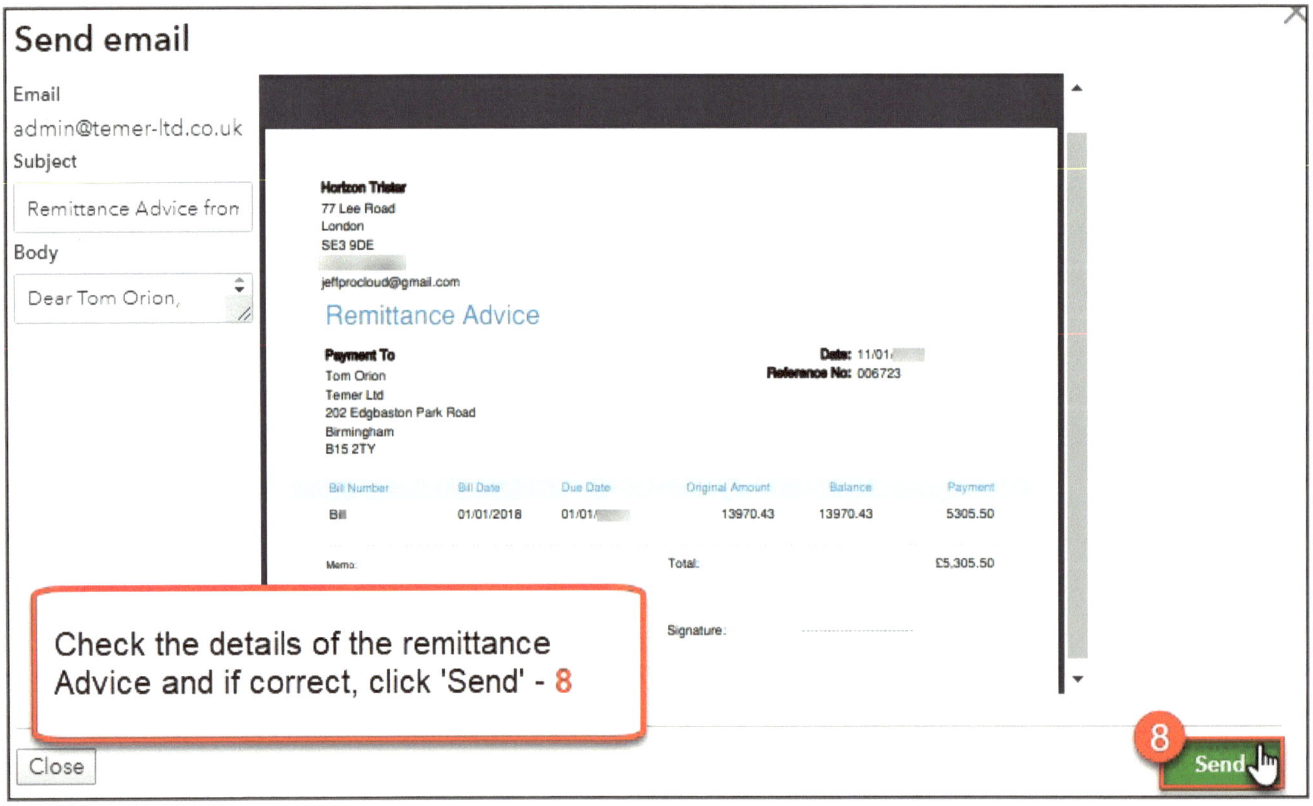

Fig. 131

From the Bill payment window still open on your computer screen, record payment to Joe Office Automation as illustrated in the figure below.

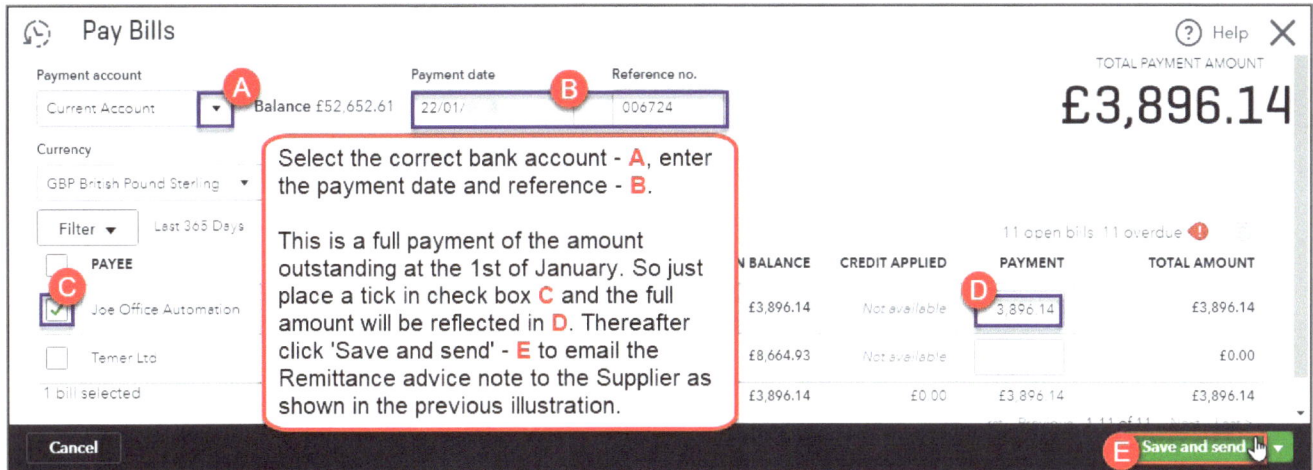

Pay Bills ⓘ Help ✕

TOTAL PAYMENT AMOUNT
£3,896.14

Payment account — **A** — Balance £52,652.61 — Payment date — **B** — 22/01/ — Reference no. 006724

Currency — GBP British Pound Sterling

Filter ▾ — Last 365 Days

11 open bills 11 overdue ⚠

C — PAYEE — Joe Office Automation — Temer Ltd

Select the correct bank account - **A**, enter the payment date and reference - **B**.

This is a full payment of the amount outstanding at the 1st of January. So just place a tick in check box **C** and the full amount will be reflected in **D**. Thereafter click 'Save and send' - **E** to email the Remittance advice note to the Supplier as shown in the previous illustration.

BALANCE — £3,896.14 — £8,664.93 — £3,896.14

CREDIT APPLIED — Not available — Not available — £0.00

PAYMENT — **D** — 3,896.14 — £3,896.14

TOTAL AMOUNT — £3,896.14 — £0.00 — £3,896.14

1 bill selected

Cancel — **E** — Save and send ▾

Fig.132

The next payment to Office Space today has been made by the Director – Terry Smith using his own funds, and as such, this transaction will need to be recorded via the Director Account and not the Current bank account.

Proceed by first setting up another Director account as a bank account, and this will be the account where all the Director transactions with Horizon Tristar will be recorded. There is already a Director account in the default chart of accounts in QuickBooks Online for limited companies. However, this account can not be used to pay supplier invoices (because it is a liability account) and hence why we need to set up a separate bank account and call it Director account. When the Director any transactions with the company like just happened with payment of the supplier invoice, use this account to record such transactions. I will give more details about Director account later.

Right, let me show you how to set up the Director 'bank' account and how to process the payment of the rent invoice by the Director – Terry Smith.

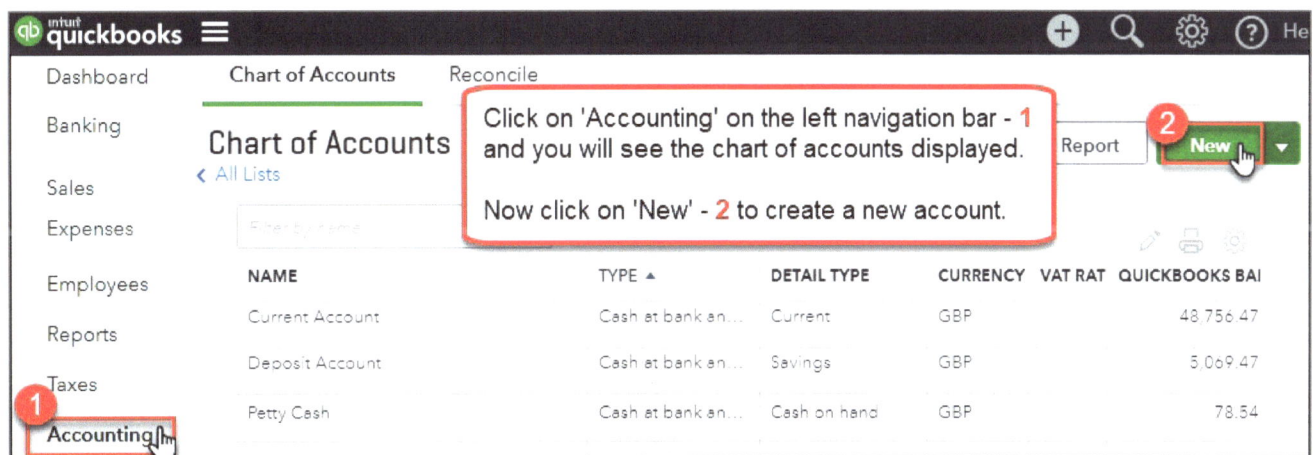

Dashboard — Chart of Accounts — Reconcile

Banking — **Chart of Accounts**

Sales — ‹ All Lists

Click on 'Accounting' on the left navigation bar - **1** and you will see the chart of accounts displayed.

Now click on 'New' - **2** to create a new account.

Report — **2** — New ▾

Expenses

Employees — NAME — TYPE ▲ — DETAIL TYPE — CURRENCY — VAT RAT — QUICKBOOKS BAI

Reports — Current Account — Cash at bank an... — Current — GBP — 48,756.47

Taxes — Deposit Account — Cash at bank an... — Savings — GBP — 5,069.47

1 Accounting — Petty Cash — Cash at bank an... — Cash on hand — GBP — 78.54

Fig. 133

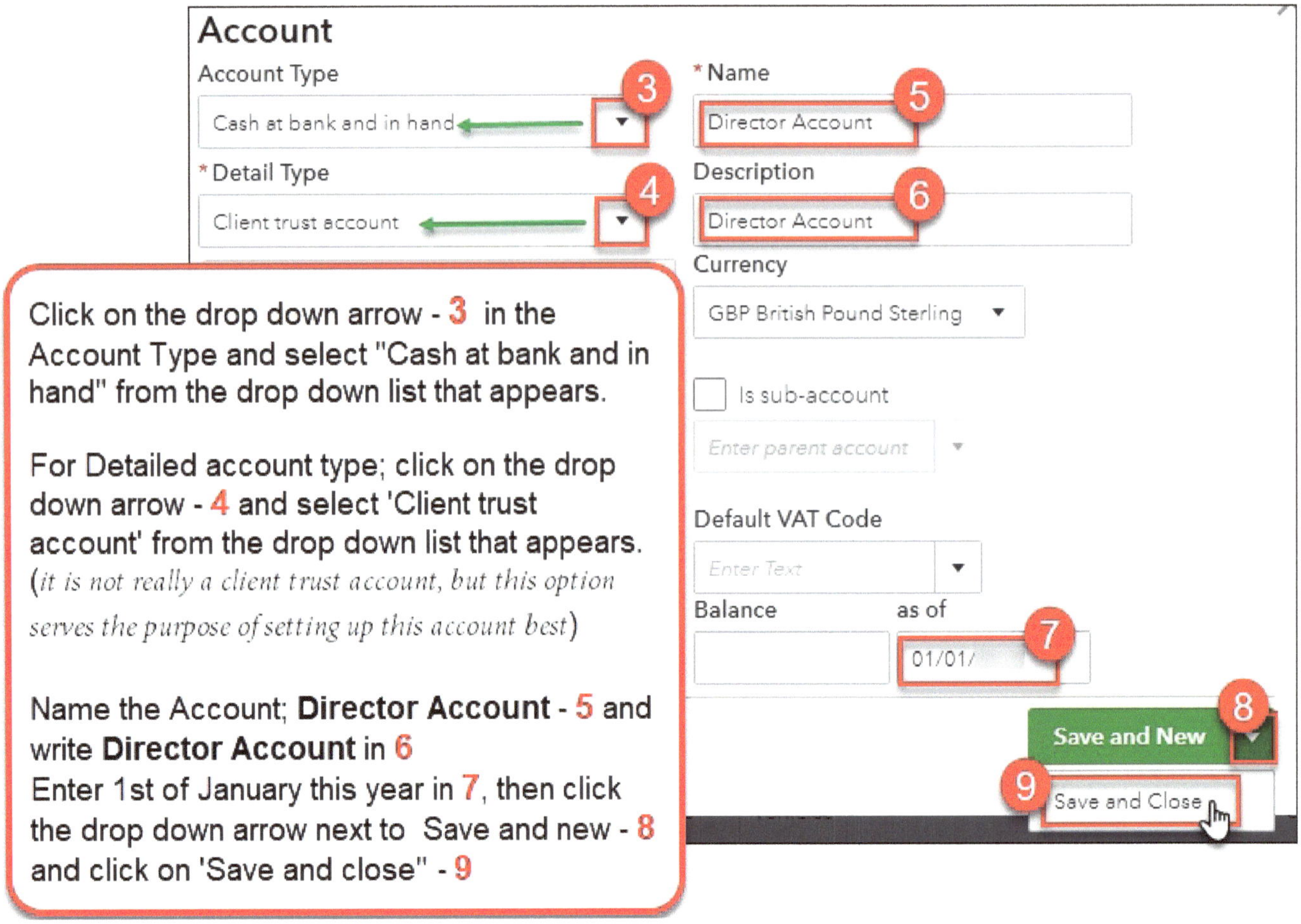

Account

Account Type

Cash at bank and in hand ← ▼ **(3)**

*Detail Type

Client trust account ← ▼ **(4)**

*Name

Director Account **(5)**

Description

Director Account **(6)**

Currency

GBP British Pound Sterling ▼

☐ Is sub-account

Enter parent account ▼

Default VAT Code

Enter Text ▼

Balance   **as of**

            01/01/ **(7)**

Save and New **(8)**

(9) Save and Close

Click on the drop down arrow - **3** in the Account Type and select "Cash at bank and in hand" from the drop down list that appears.

For Detailed account type; click on the drop down arrow - **4** and select 'Client trust account' from the drop down list that appears. *(it is not really a client trust account, but this option serves the purpose of setting up this account best)*

Name the Account; **Director Account** - **5** and write **Director Account** in **6**
Enter 1st of January this year in **7**, then click the drop down arrow next to Save and new - **8** and click on 'Save and close" - **9**

Fig. 134

Now you are ready to pay the invoice from Office space today using the Director account. Horray! Let's do it.

quickbooks ☰   ➕ **(1)** 🔍 ⚙ ❓ Help

Dashboard   + LOGO   **Horizon Tristar**   Click on the Create (+) button - **1**

Banking

Fig. 135

🔍 ⚙ ❓

Create

Click on 'Pay Bills' - **2**

Customers	Suppliers	Employees	Other
Invoice	Expense	Single Time Activity	Bank Deposit
Receive Payment	Cheque	Weekly Timesheet	Transfer
Estimate	Bill		Journal Entry
Credit Note	**(2)** Pay Bills		Statement
Sales Receipt	Purchase Order		Stock Qty Adjustment
Refund Receipt	Supplier Credit		

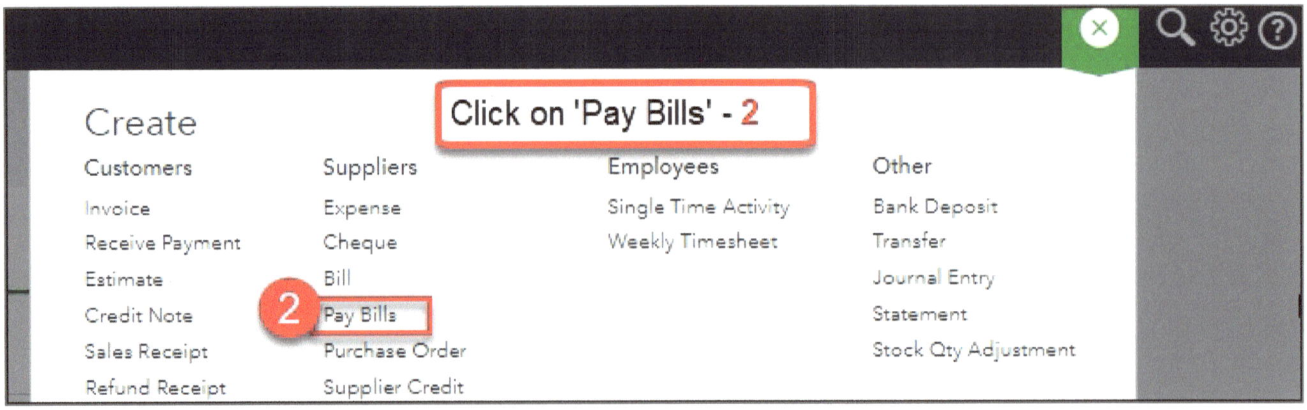

Fig. 136

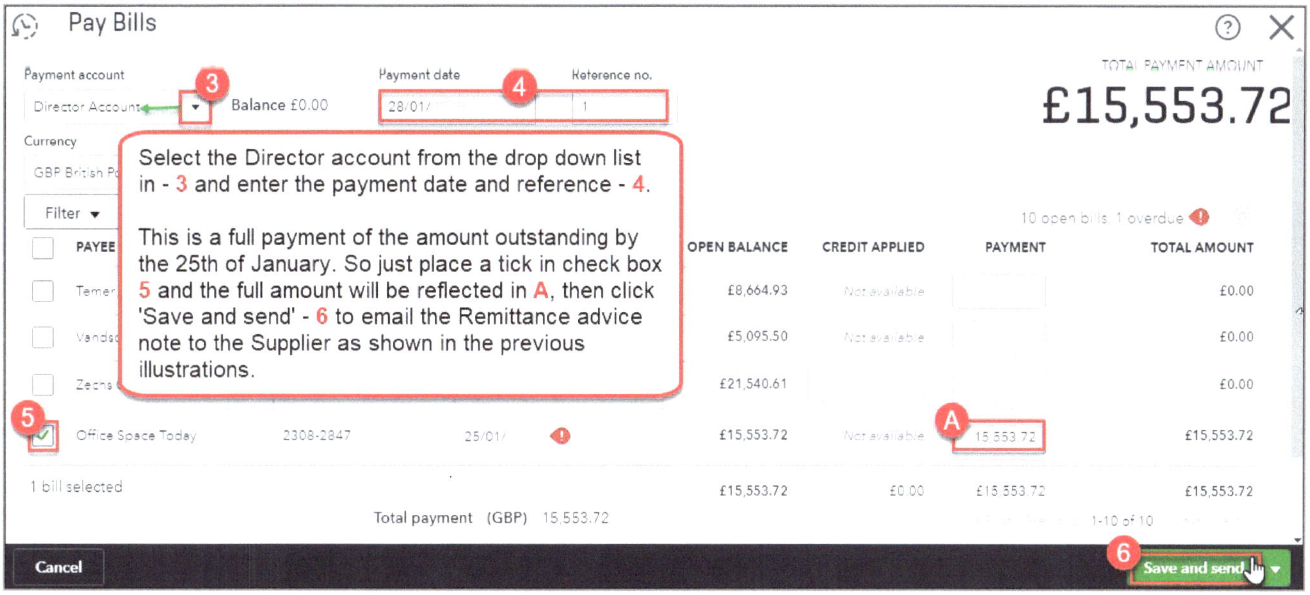

Fig. 137

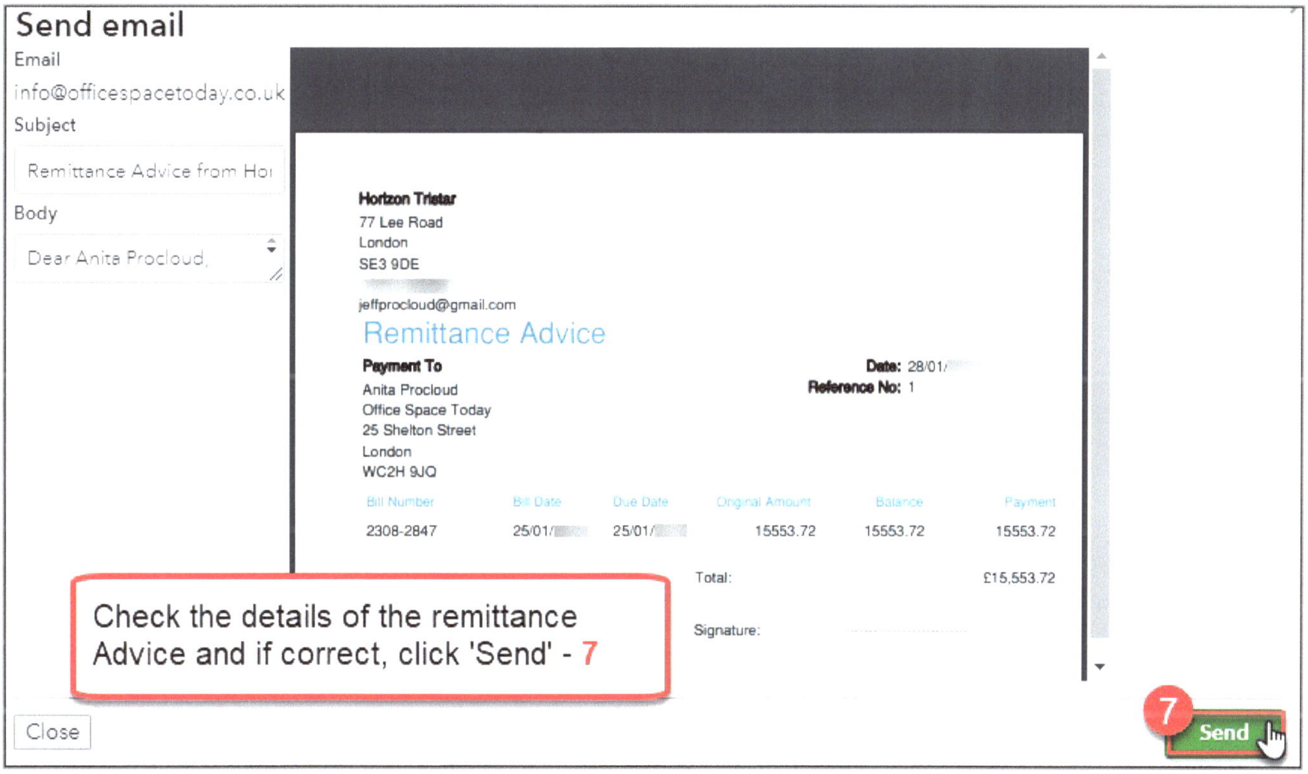

Fig. 138

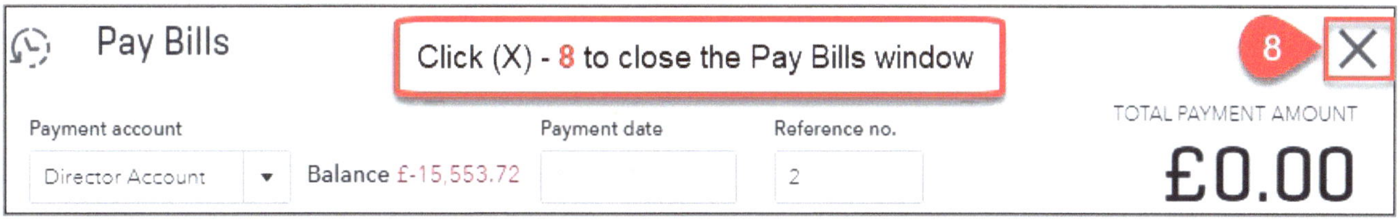

Fig. 139

Just one more thing to do. There is a balance in the default Director account that you now need to transfer to the Director bank account you have just created because this is now the Director account that will be used for all transactions between the Director and the business (Horizon Tristar Ltd).

To make the transfer, here is what you should do.

Fig. 140

Fig. 141

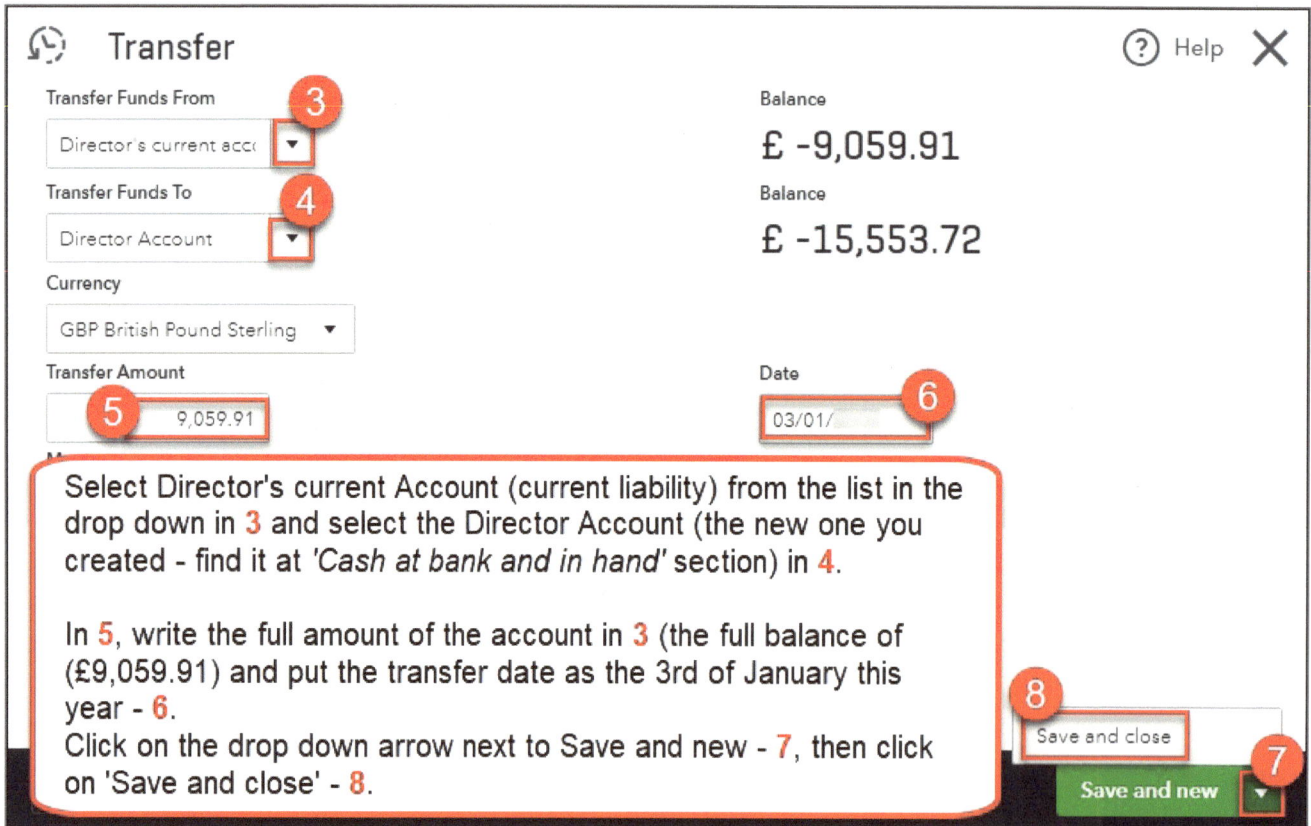

Fig. 142

If you now check the Director's current Account (Current liability), you will notice that the balance is 0.00 because you have moved all the amount that was in that account to the new Director account ('Bank account'). The previous debit balance in the Director's current account (the current liability account) meant that the Director – Terry Smith owed the company money – the £9,059.91.

However, when Terry Smith paid the rent invoice from Office Space Today Ltd using his own money, he in effect lent the company money – the £15,553.72.

The net position after these two transactions is that the company now owes Terry Smith £6,493.81 and if you check the Director account ('bank account') now, that is the amount you will see. Go on, check it out.

A brief overview of Director loan account

The Director current account (DCA) (also known simply as the Directors account) is a notional balance between a company and its Directors. It is not a real bank account and is not represented by real monies.

It records:

- Monies drawn by the director as salary or dividends (if not attributed to salary/dividend at the time of drawing), expenses etc.
- Other drawings by the director – e.g. personal bills paid by the company
- Net amounts of salary and dividend due
- Expense re-reimbursements due.

Task 3e(ii). Recording small expense receipts

First, begin by analysing all the receipts.

First receipt from Sainsbury's, the Wasabi receipts and the receipt from Boots have not been recorded yet due to insufficient analytical information: We know the date of the transaction and what was bought in each receipt, but we do not know whether these were business transactions or not. The best thing to do is to keep these receipts aside and not record them until all the analytical information is received.

The other Sainsbury's receipt is a transaction for the purchase of fuel (diesel) using the company credit card, the Clintons and Specsavers receipt are transactions using company debit card receipt.
These receipts have all the relevant analytical information for them to be recorded. We know the cards being used for payment, the Items bought, the date of the transactions.

To record these transactions into QuickBooks Online, here is what you should do:

Set up the company credit card account in QuickBooks Online because some of the expenses have been paid by Credit card and you don't have that set up yet in QuickBooks Online.

This space is for notes

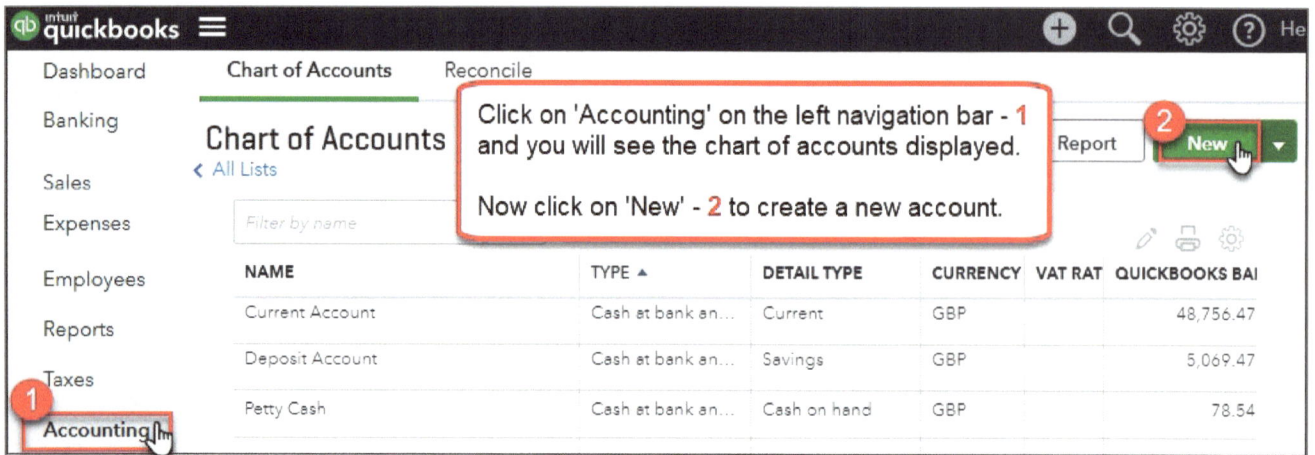

Fig. 143

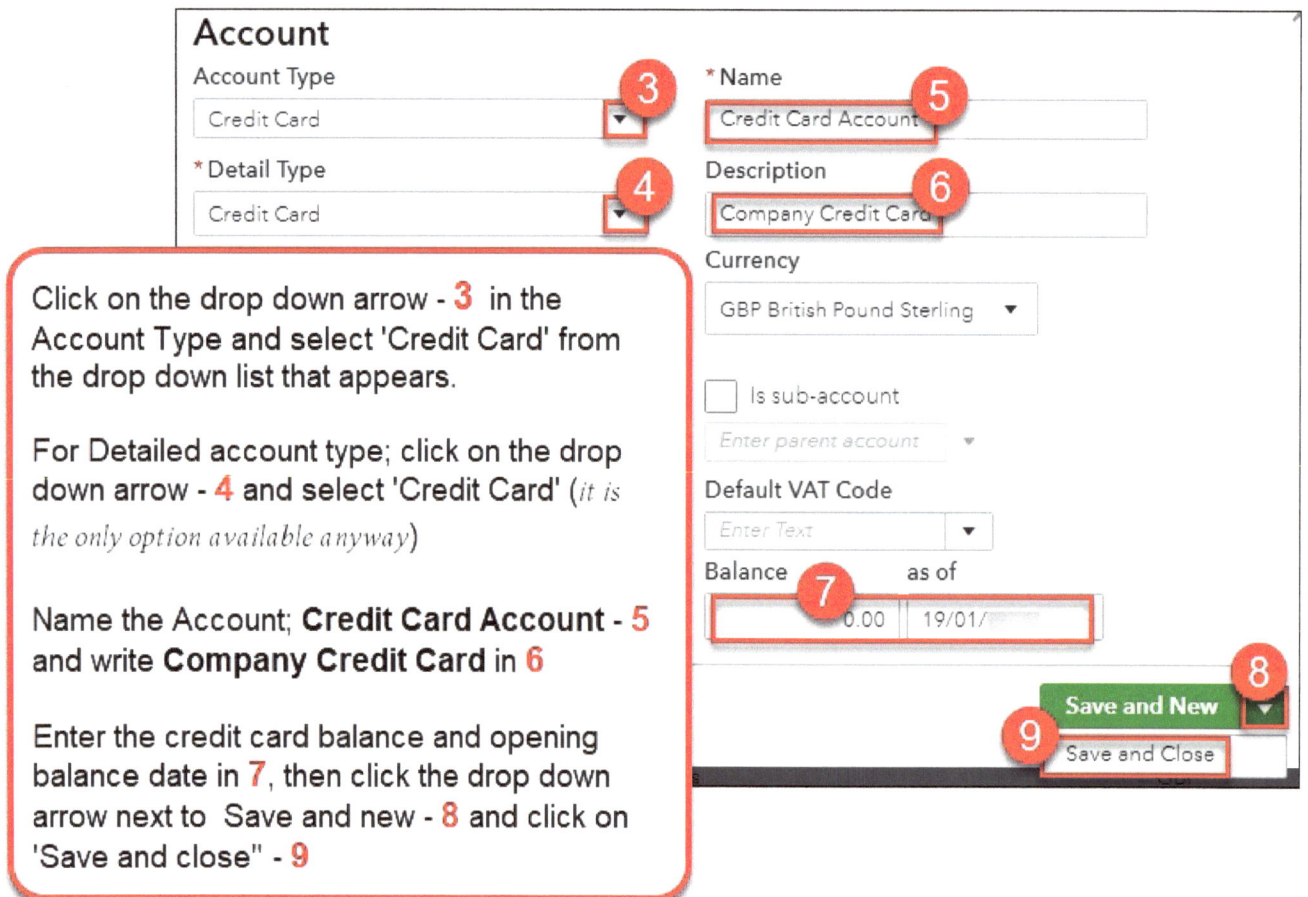

Click on the drop down arrow - 3 in the Account Type and select 'Credit Card' from the drop down list that appears.

For Detailed account type; click on the drop down arrow - 4 and select 'Credit Card' (*it is the only option available anyway*)

Name the Account; **Credit Card Account** - 5 and write **Company Credit Card** in 6

Enter the credit card balance and opening balance date in 7, then click the drop down arrow next to Save and new - 8 and click on 'Save and close" - 9

Fig. 144

Next,

Click on the Create (+) button - 1

Fig. 145

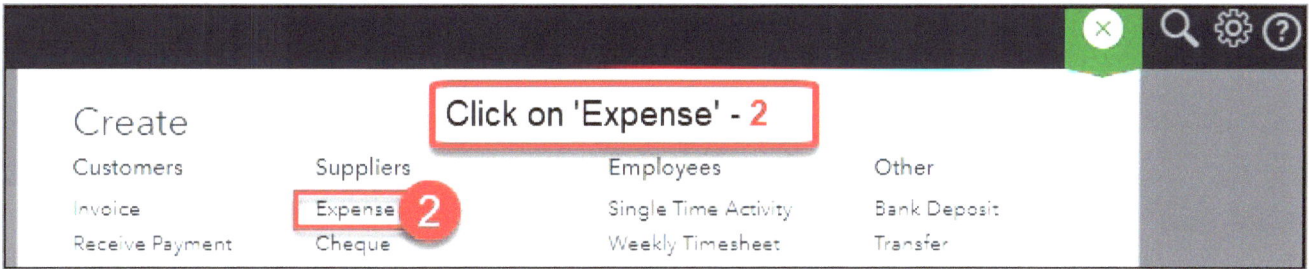

Fig. 146

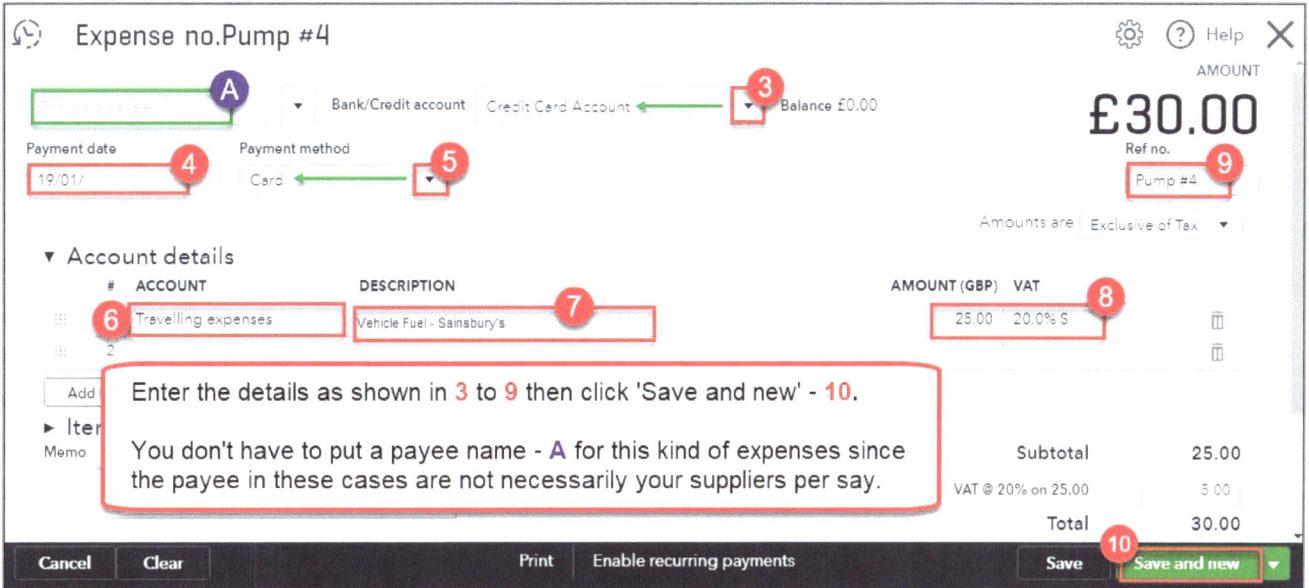

Fig. 147

For how to record the transaction from Clintons, see below.

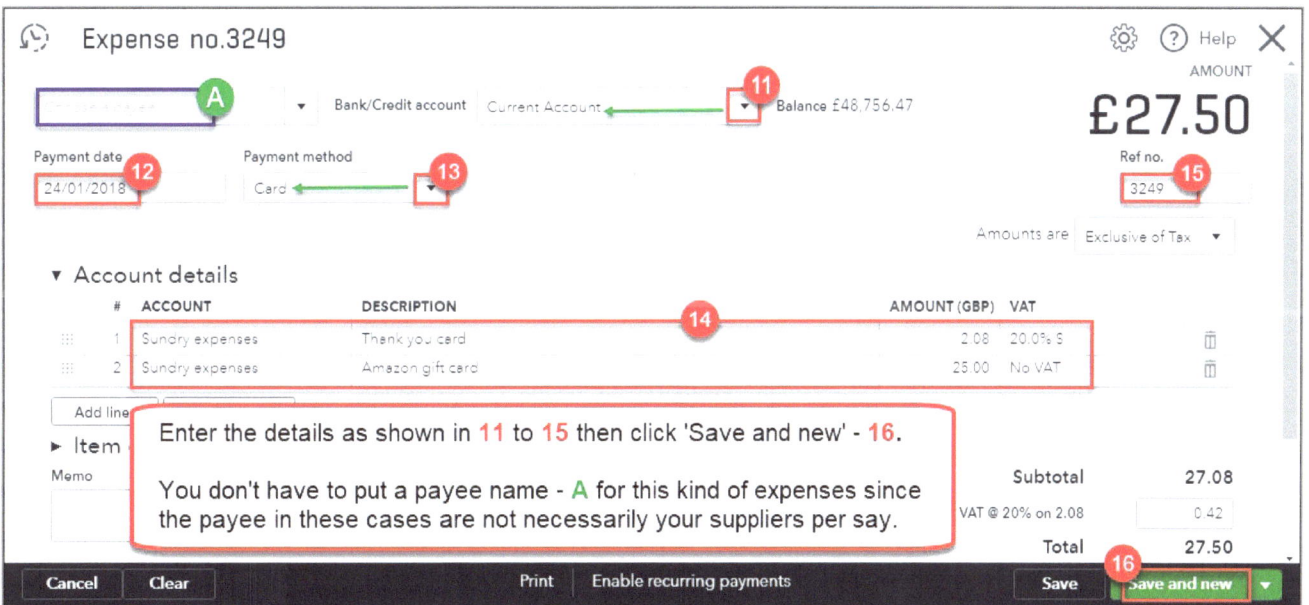

Fig. 148

And finally, the transaction from Specsavers is recorded as shown below.

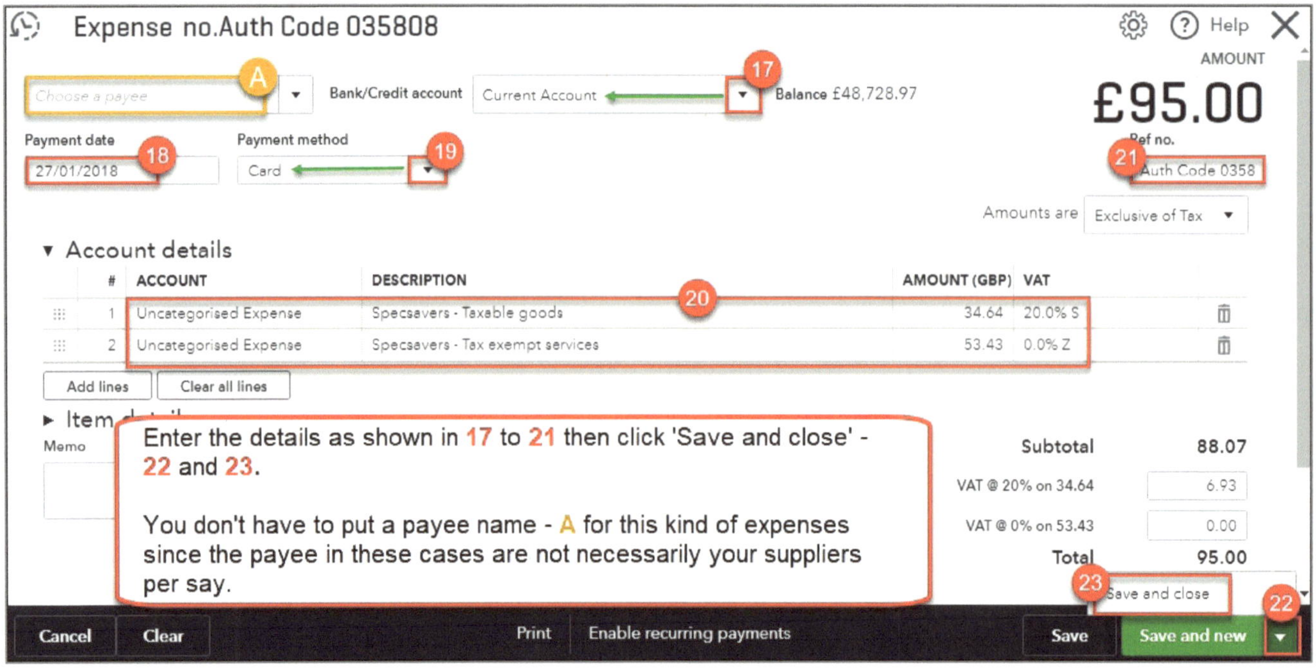

Fig. 149

Task 3f: Petty Cash management

The objective of the petty cash management is to ensure that control is kept over the petty cash tin and that all cash payments are recorded correctly and entered onto the accounting system.

Businesses generally keep small amounts of cash to meet small miscellaneous payments such as entertainment expenses and stationery costs. Such payments are generally handled by a petty cash imprest system whereby an amount of 'Float' is fixed (say £250). This is the maximum amount of cash that can be held at any time, and each time cash level runs low, the petty cash imprest is injected with cash by drawing a cheque.

When you give cash to an employee, have the person sign a slip of paper (Petty cash voucher) to keep a record of who, when and what the money was used for. The voucher should be authorised by the financial accountant or designated signatory.

For security reasons, the petty cash fund should be locked at all times when it is not in use. Access to petty cash tin is restricted and money cannot be taken out of it without approval.

Any money taken from the petty cash tin should be replaced with a petty cash voucher. At all times, the amounts on the Petty cash vouchers and the cash you have left in the tin/box should add up to the amounts you've float (which in the case of Horizon Tristar Ltd is £250).

Whenever a voucher is completed, it is good practice for the custodian to immediately update the petty cash book by adding the amount, type, and date of the expenditure and updating the running cash balance. For example, if you got some refreshments for the office, e.g. some sweets and you need to be reimbursed the amount you spent, you would need to fill out a petty cash voucher with the details of the purchase.

Petty cash tin illustrative picture.

Fig.

There was £178 transferred from the Current account to the petty cash account. To record that transaction, do the following.

Click on the Create (+) button - **1**

Fig. 150

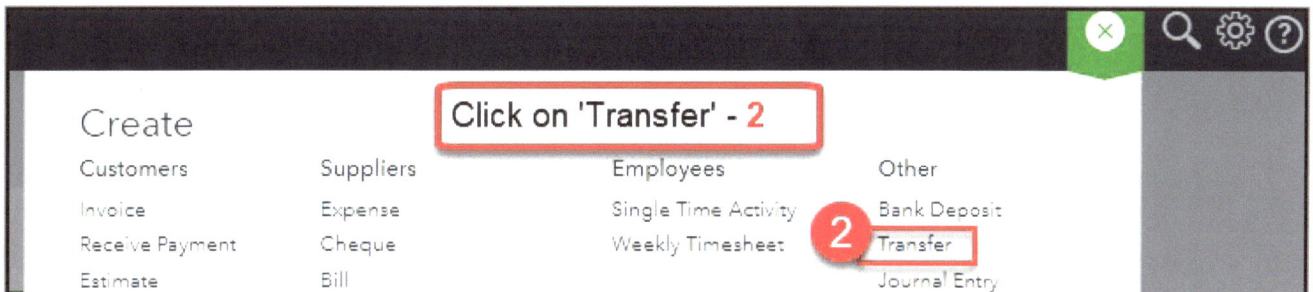

Click on 'Transfer' - **2**

Fig. 151

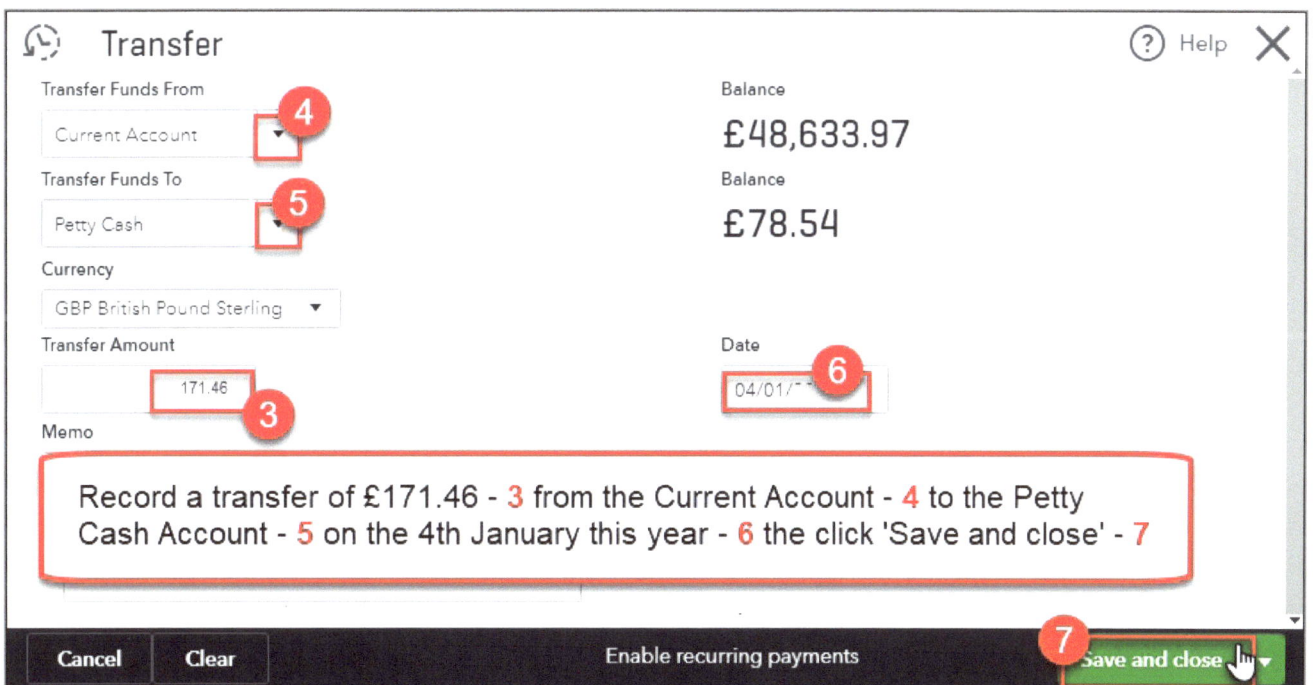

Record a transfer of £171.46 - **3** from the Current Account - **4** to the Petty Cash Account - **5** on the 4th January this year - **6** the click 'Save and close' - **7**

Fig. 152

Now it is time to record the transactions in the petty cash Vouchers.

Fig. 153

Fig. 154

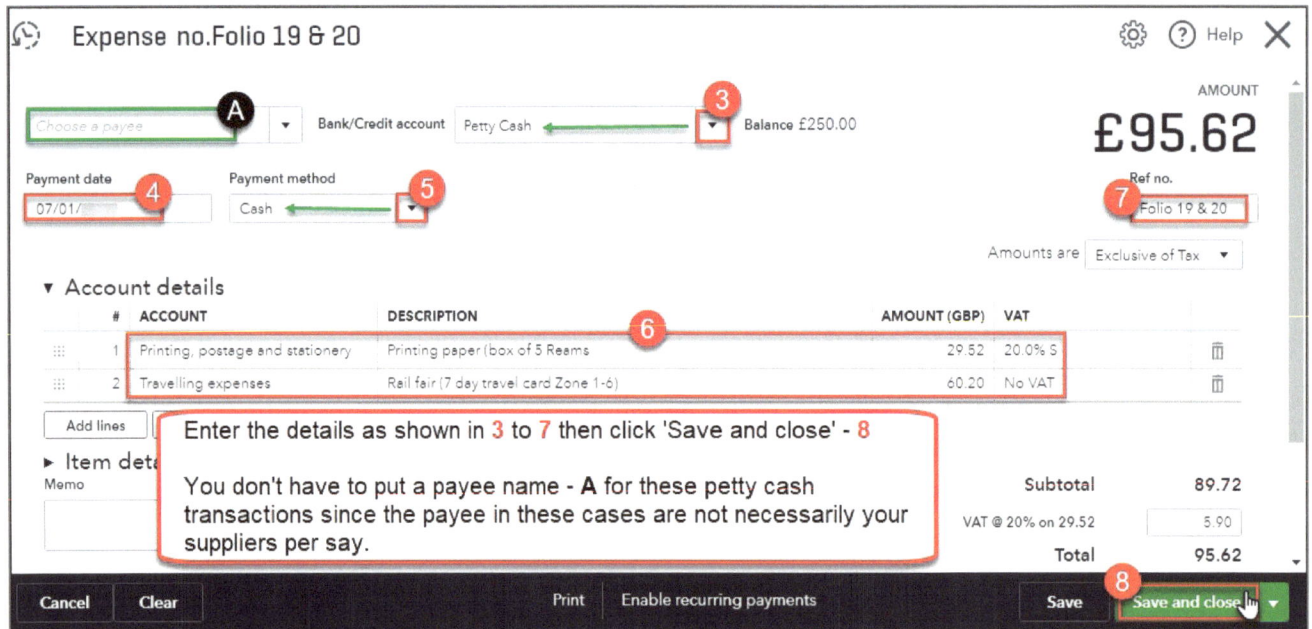

Fig. 155

Petty Cash

When you give cash to an employee, have them sign a slip of paper (Petty cash voucher) to keep a record of who, when and what the money was used for. The voucher should be authorised by the financial accountant or designated signatory.

TASK 4: DEALING WITH LEASES & RECURRING ENTRIES

Horizon Tristar Ltd purchased a BMW 3 series for £30,000 inclusive of 20% VAT on 2nd January this year for the Sales manager from BMW dealer 1. A cash deposit of £10,200 inclusive of VAT was paid and the balance is to be paid on finance: £654 gross (inclusive of finance cost -interest of £54) per month starting 1st of next month for 33 months.

So, step 1 is to record the deposit of £10,200 that was made by Horizon Tristar Ltd to BMW Dealer 1. Click on the plus button - 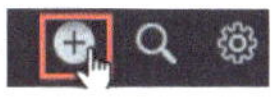 then select 'Cheque' under suppliers then fill out the details as follows.

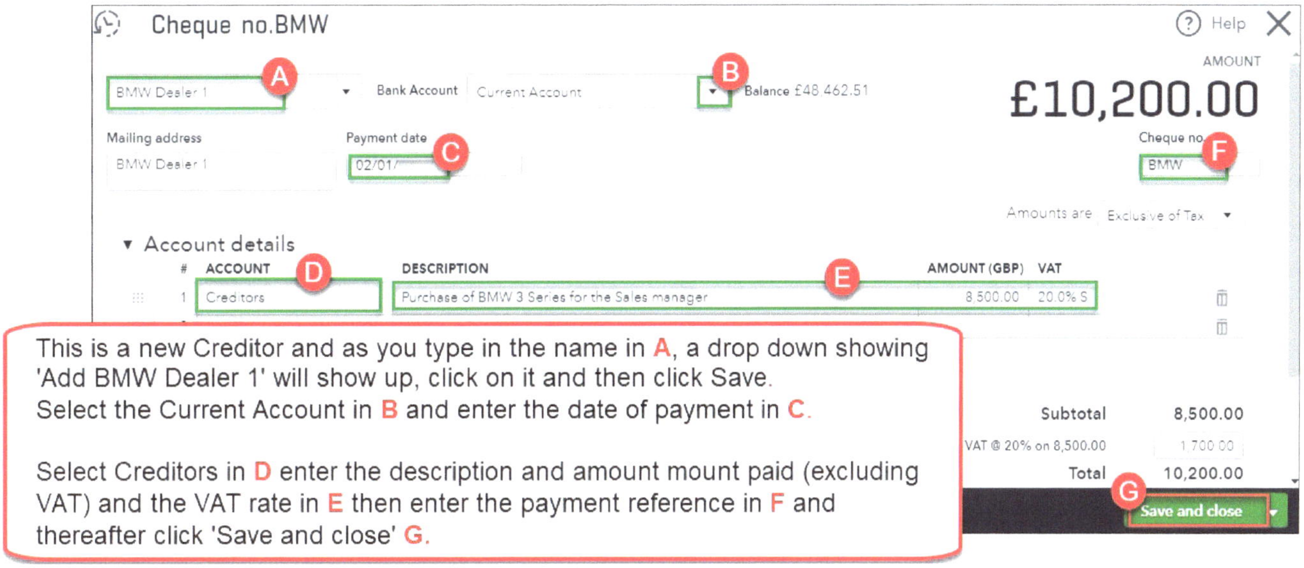
Cheque no.BMW
Help
BMW Dealer 1
Bank Account
Current Account
Balance £48,462.51
AMOUNT
£10,200.00
Mailing address
BMW Dealer 1
Payment date
02/01/
Cheque no.
BMW
Amounts are
Exclusive of Tax
Account details
ACCOUNT
DESCRIPTION
AMOUNT (GBP)
VAT
Creditors
Purchase of BMW 3 Series for the Sales manager
8,500.00
20.0% S
This is a new Creditor and as you type in the name in A, a drop down showing 'Add BMW Dealer 1' will show up, click on it and then click Save.
Select the Current Account in B and enter the date of payment in C.
Select Creditors in D enter the description and amount mount paid (excluding VAT) and the VAT rate in E then enter the payment reference in F and thereafter click 'Save and close' G.
Subtotal
8,500.00
VAT @ 20% on 8,500.00
1,700.00
Total
10,200.00
Save and close

Fig. 156

The next thing is to record the bill of £30,000 from BMW Dealer 1. Click on the plus button - 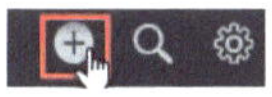 then select 'Bill' under suppliers then fill out the details as follows.

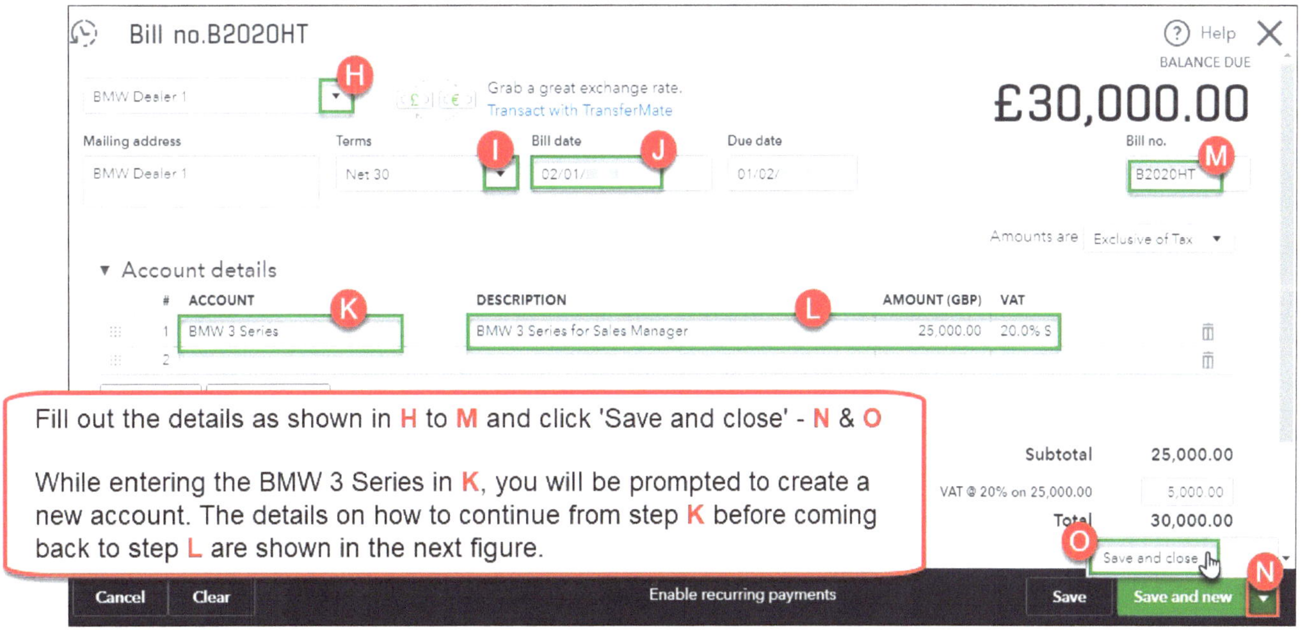
Bill no.B2020HT
Help
BALANCE DUE
BMW Dealer 1
Grab a great exchange rate.
Transact with TransferMate
£30,000.00
Mailing address
BMW Dealer 1
Terms
Net 30
Bill date
02/01/
Due date
01/02/
Bill no.
B2020HT
Amounts are
Exclusive of Tax
Account details
ACCOUNT
DESCRIPTION
AMOUNT (GBP)
VAT
BMW 3 Series
BMW 3 Series for Sales Manager
25,000.00
20.0% S
Fill out the details as shown in H to M and click 'Save and close' - N & O
While entering the BMW 3 Series in K, you will be prompted to create a new account. The details on how to continue from step K before coming back to step L are shown in the next figure.
Subtotal
25,000.00
VAT @ 20% on 25,000.00
5,000.00
Total
30,000.00
Save and close
Cancel
Clear
Enable recurring payments
Save
Save and new

Fig. 157

The next figure shows the details of how to finish step K in figure 157 in the previous page.

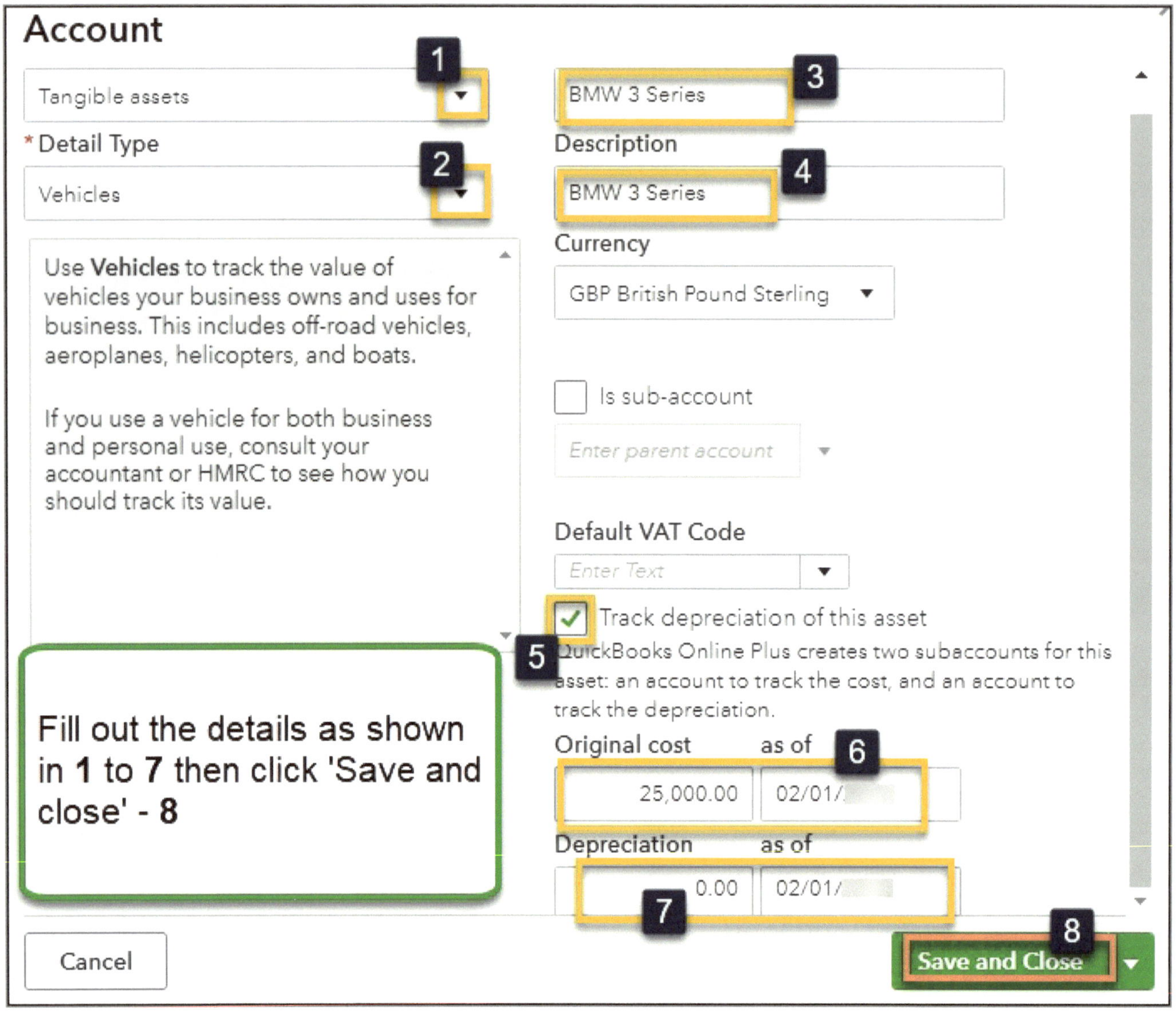

Fig. 158

Now, allocate the deposit payment of £10,200 made to BMW Dealer 1 to the invoice.

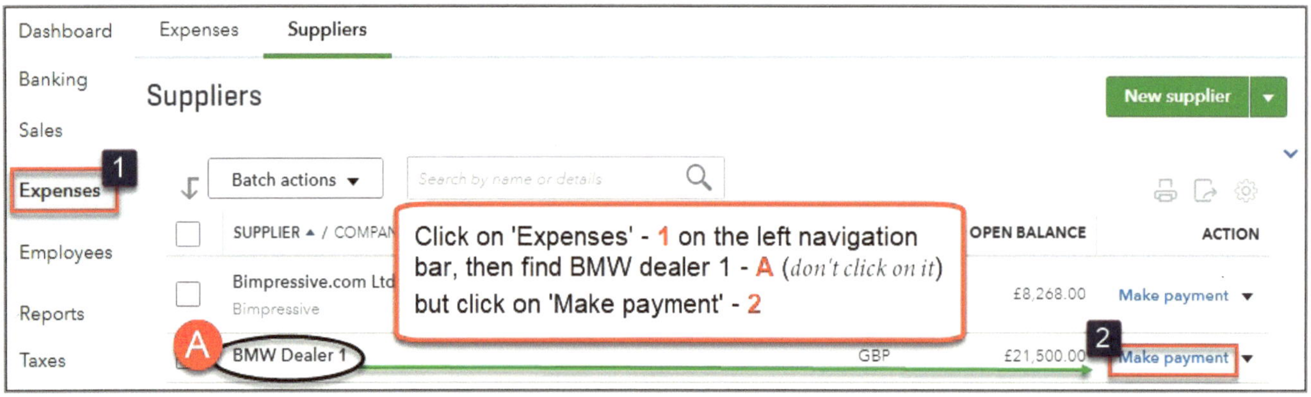

Fig. 159

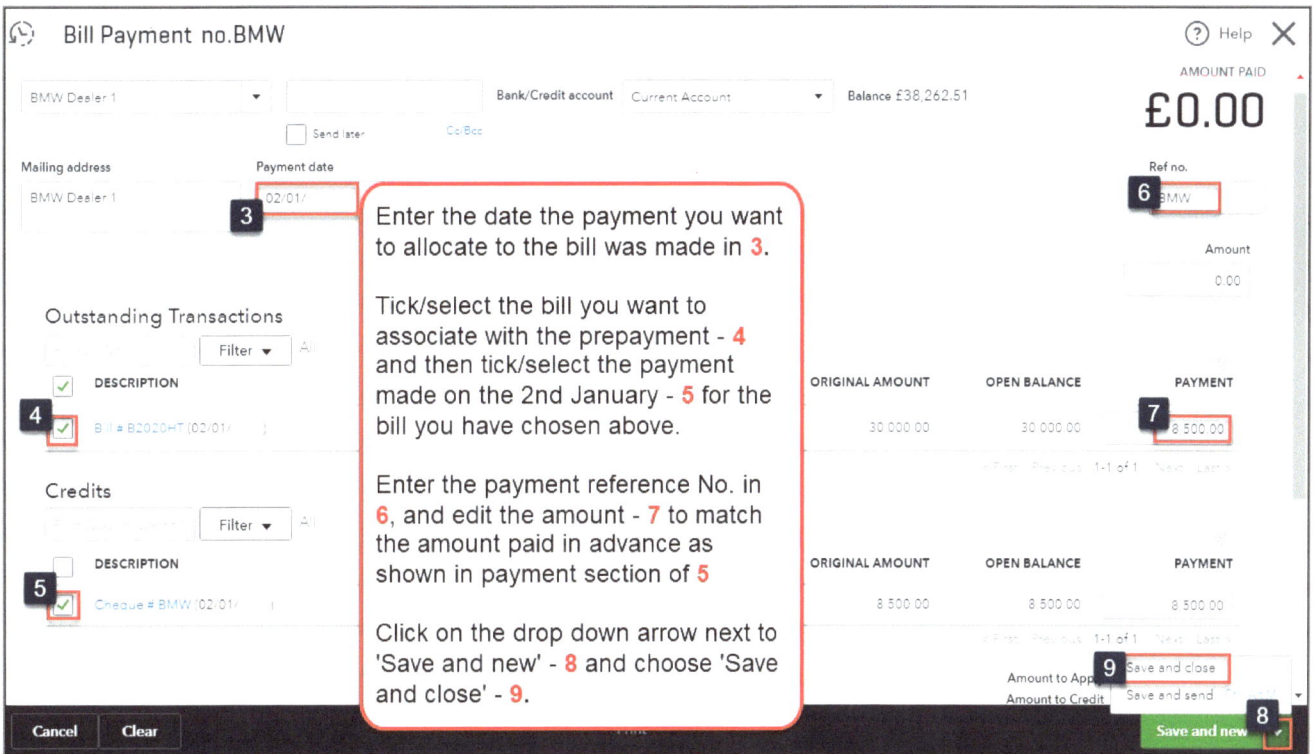

Fig. 160

How to set up and process standing orders and direct debits

In this task, you are required to set up recurring entry templates for the standing orders and direct debit mandates that have been set up in the bank. Refer to the updated list of the standing orders and direct debts you have been given to proceed.

Here is how to go about it.

Fig. 161

Fig. 162

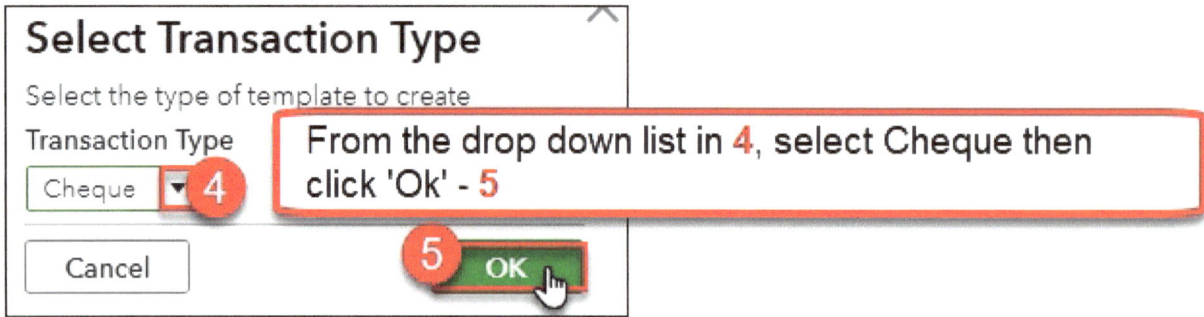

Select Transaction Type

Select the type of template to create

Transaction Type

Cheque ▼ **4**

From the drop down list in **4**, select Cheque then click 'Ok' - **5**

Cancel

5 OK

Fig. 163

For the hire purchase payment and interest recurring entry, here is how to set it up:

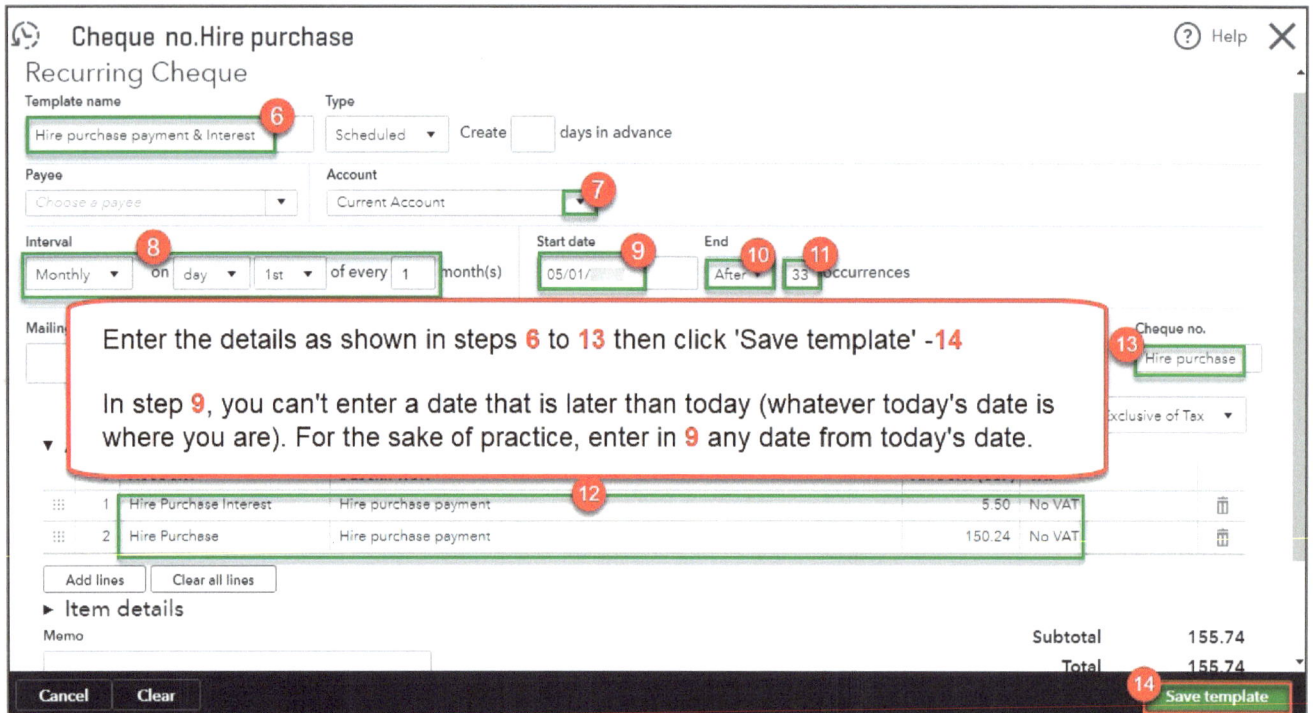

Cheque no.Hire purchase   ? Help ✕

Recurring Cheque

Template name   Type
6
Hire purchase payment & Interest   Scheduled ▼ Create ☐ days in advance

Payee   Account
Choose a payee ▼   Current Account ▼ **7**

Interval   Start date   End
8   **9**   **10** **11**
Monthly ▼ on day ▼ 1st ▼ of every 1 month(s) 05/01/   After ▼ 33 occurrences

Mailing   Cheque no.
                                                                    13 Hire purchase

Enter the details as shown in steps **6** to **13** then click 'Save template' -**14**

In step **9**, you can't enter a date that is later than today (whatever today's date is where you are). For the sake of practice, enter in **9** any date from today's date.

                                                                    Exclusive of Tax ▼

                                                        12

⫶ 1 Hire Purchase Interest   Hire purchase payment   5.50 No VAT   🗑
⫶ 2 Hire Purchase   Hire purchase payment   150.24 No VAT   🗑

Add lines   Clear all lines
▶ Item details
Memo   Subtotal   155.74
                                                Total   155.74
                                                                14
Cancel   Clear   Save template

Fig. 164

This space is for notes

It's now your turn. Go ahead and enter the recurring entry details for the Loan payment and interest.

When you are done, here is how it should look like just before you click 'Save template'

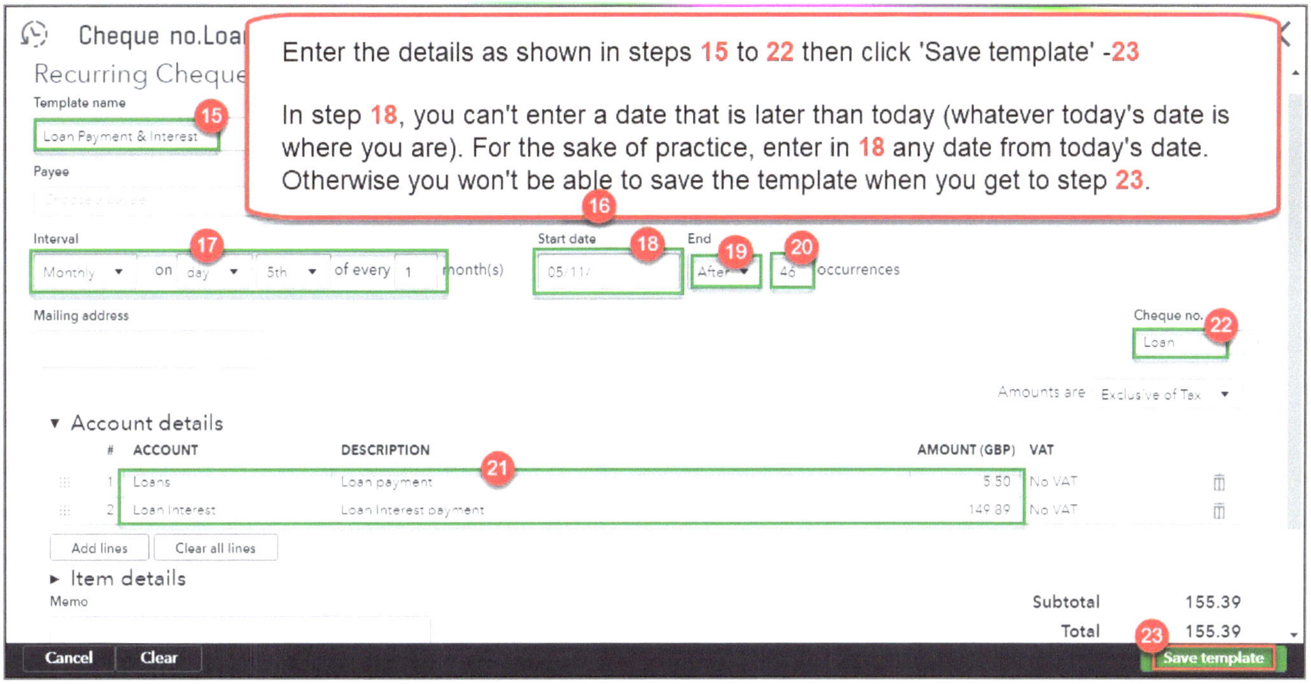

Fig. 165

And finally, here is how the recurring entry for the finance lease payments and interest should look like.

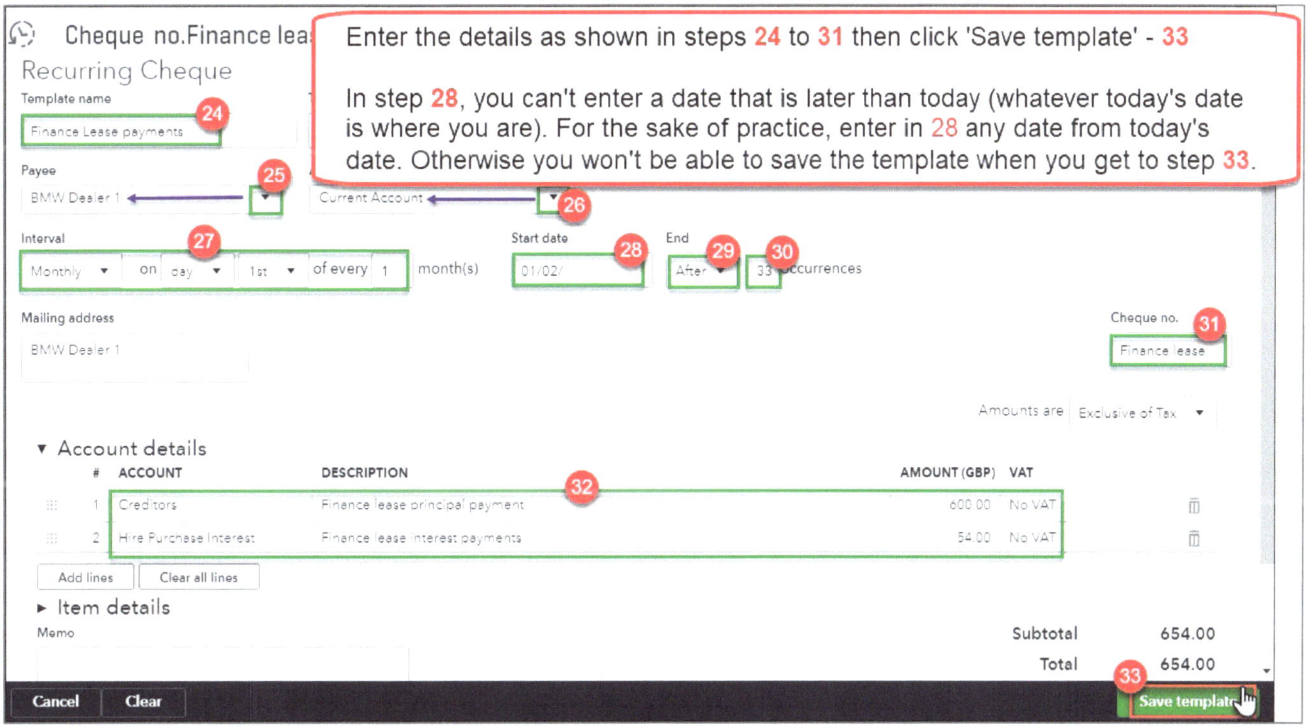

Fig. 166

Difference between a standing order & Direct Debit

"A **standing order** is a regular payment that you can set up to pay other people, organisations or transfer to your other bank accounts. You can amend or cancel the standing order as and when you like.

A **Direct Debit** can only be set up by the organisation to which you're making the payment. Normally, you sign a mandate that gives the company permission to take funds from your account in an agreed way – like a monthly gym membership or your mobile phone bill. It normally confirms who's receiving the payment, the account to be debited, the amount and the dates of the payment. You're protected under the Direct Debit Guarantee scheme so that any amount debited in error is refunded immediately".

Source: https://www.barclays.co.uk/help/payments/payment-information/difference-order-debits/

TASK 5: POSTING PAYROLL JOURNALS & DOING AD HOC ADMINISTRATIVE DUTIES

Posting payroll Journals

On the 31st January, the payroll was processed and below is the payroll report for you to post not the accounts using a payroll journal.

Employee Reference From : 1   Payment Period : All   Processing Date From : 06/01/▓

Employee Reference To : 9999999   Processing Date To : 05/02/▓

Process Date: 31/01/   Tax Week: 43   Tax Month: 10

E'ee Ref	Employee Name	Gross Pay pre Sacrifice	Gross Pay post Sacrifice	Taxable Gross	P.A.Y.E.	Employee NIC	Employer NIC	Employee Pension	Employer Pension*	Student Loan	SSP	SMP	SPP	SAP	ShPP	Net Pay
1	Z TOMILSON	2,333.33	2,333.33	2 333 33	274 80	198 24	227 98	0.00	0 00	0 00	0.00	0.00	0.00	0.00	0 00	1860 29
2	K PRICHARD	2,083.33	2,083.33	2 083 33	224 80	168 48	193 75	0.00	0 00	0 00	0.00	0.00	0.00	0.00	0 00	1690 05
3	A WILLIAMS	2,083.33	2,083.33	2 083 33	224.80	168 48	193 75	50.00	80 00	0 00	0.00	0.00	0.00	0.00	0 00	1640.05
4	J JONES	2,250 00	2,250.00	2 250 00	0 00	188 64	216 94	50.00	80 00	0 00	0.00	0.00	0.00	0.00	0 00	2011 36
5	C MCFARLANE	1,092 00	1,092.00	1 092 00	218 40	49 44	56 86	0.00	0 00	0 00	0.00	0.00	0.00	0.00	0 00	824 16
	Process Date Total	9,841.99	9,841.99	9,841.99	942 80	773 28	889 28	100.00	160 00	0 00	0.00	0 00	0.00	0.00	0 00	8025 91
	Report Total	9,841 99	9,841 99	9,841 99	942 80	773 28	889 28	100.00	160 00	0 00	0 00	0 00	0 00	0 00	0 00	8025 91

For salary sacrifice pension schemes this is the employer contribution including the amount sacrificed by the employee

Fig. 167

Here is what to do to post the payroll journal from the above payroll report.

Fig. 168

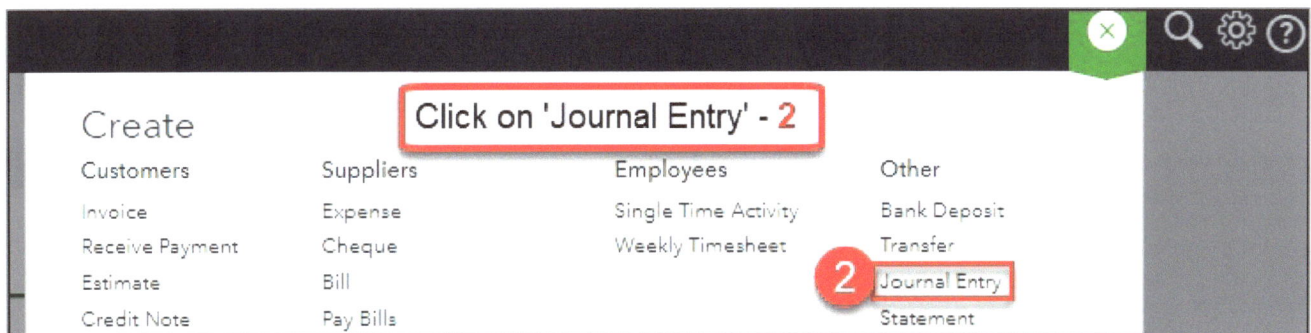

Fig.169

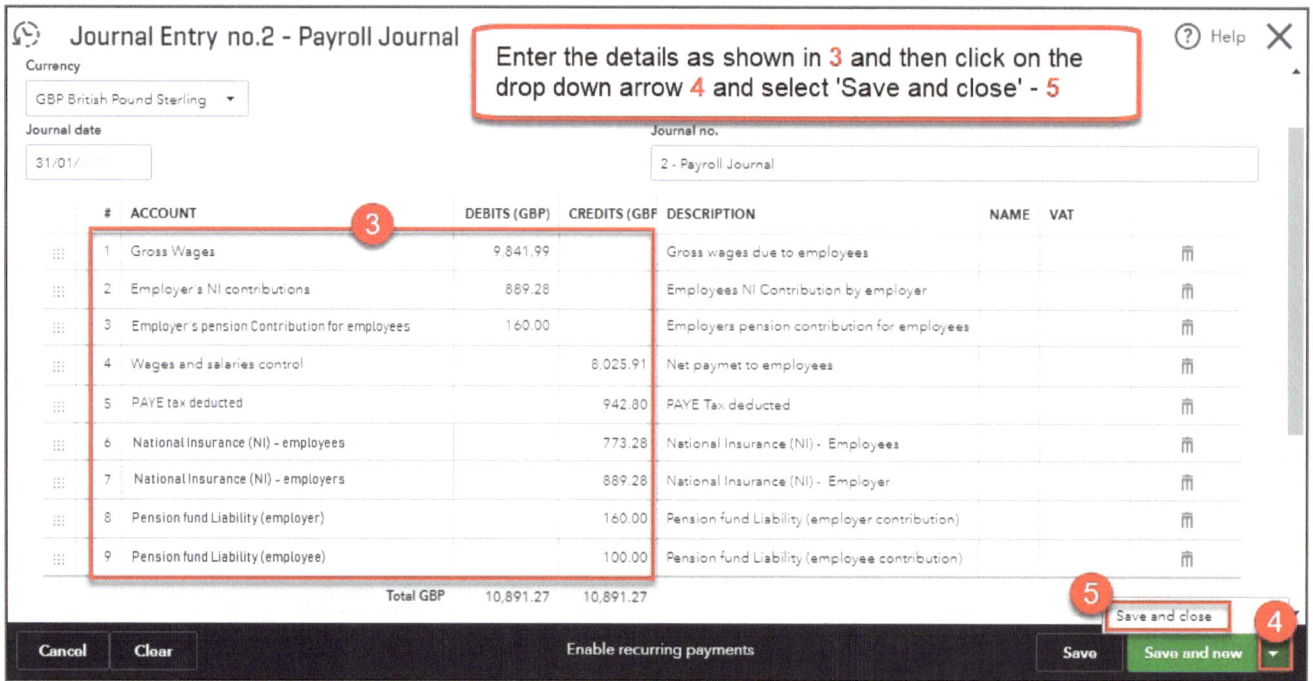

Fig. 170

Payroll Accounting Process

Payroll Accounting is the method of accounting for payroll. Payroll is the aggregate expenditure on wages and salaries incurred by a business in an accounting period. It can also refer to a listing of employees giving details of their pay.

Payroll includes the gross pay due to the employee and employer taxes. The gross pay is divided into net pay actually received by the employee and deductions made from the gross pay for employee taxes and other deductions such as pension contributions, healthcare contributions, and union subscriptions.

In payroll accounting it is important to distinguish between **employee** taxes which are deducted from the employees' gross pay and are therefore paid by the employee, and **employer** taxes which are in addition to the gross pay and paid by the employers.
Both payroll taxes are usually collected by the employer and paid over to the relevant tax authority.

Ad-hoc Administrative duties

Here are some common administrative duties that you will from time to time be called upon to do in your role as an Accounts payable/Purchase Ledger Clerk.
.
1. Sorting incoming post

The objective here is to make sure that incoming mail is dealt with in a secure and controlled way. Here is how to go about doing this duty;

    a. When mail is received, open envelopes addressed to the company

    b. Envelopes addressed to individual people within the company and marked as 'private and confidential' should be passed to them.

    c. Once mail is opened it should be date stamped and distributed to the relevant people.

d. If a courier arrives with a parcel, it should be checked for obvious damages and signed for.
e. The parcel should then be passed onto the relevant person.
f. If it is not addressed to anyone specific it should be opened and the contents checked to the delivery note attached to the parcel.
g. If the contents do not agree to the delivery note or are damaged in any way, contact the sender and advise them.
h. If the contents are as stated on the delivery note, the goods should be distributed, and the delivery note passed to the Financial Accountant.

2. Sorting out outgoing post

The objective here is to make sure that outgoing mail is dealt with in a secure and controlled way. Here is how to do it.

a. All outgoing mail should be put in envelopes and any enclosures checked to ensure that they are included.
b. Relevant information, such as PRIVATE AND CONFIDENTIAL, should be written clearly on the envelope.
c. The correct postage should be applied. Make sure that you have an up to date postage rate list.
d. All parcels should clearly show the receiver on the front and the sender (our company) on the back.
e. If you need to send a parcel by courier, ensure that the contents are securely wrapped.
f. Make sure that you know the value of the contents of the parcel and its approximate weight.
g. Contact the courier company and ask them to collect the parcel. Ask them for the cost of the service.
h. You will need to give the value and weight so that they can calculate the cost of the delivery.
i. Complete a purchase order form with the courier, parcel details and cost, and give this to the Financial Accountant.

3. Answering the customer telephone queries

The objective here is to ensure that all telephone answering is done in a consistent way, to always delight the customer. Here is how to do it:

a. Ensure that someone is always available to answer the telephone.
b. Keep a telephone message pad beside every telephone for taking messages.
c. Always keep an up to date list of people who are out of the office, in meetings or not taking calls.
d. When answering the telephone smile before you answer and use the script agreed by the team members.
e. Don't interrogate the caller, and if the person that they would like to speak to is unavailable, then see if you can help.
f. If a call needs returning, remind the person returning the call to make sure that it is returned.

This space is for notes

"And God saw the light, that it was good: and God divided the light from the darkness".

Genesis 1: 4 (KJV)

AFTERWORD

It was a real honour guiding you through this book to master how to do the Accounts Payable/Purchase Ledger Clerk's job role using QuickBooks Online and thanks for taking the time to follow through. I hope you able to understand and do every step of each task.

The Accounting profession is a very noble profession, and I am so humbled to be an accountant, and I hope you are too. You will need to keep updating and upgrading your skills because the world of accounting is continually undergoing technological change. The principles still stay the same but technology will warrants that you stay abreast of the developments on how your work is done with the latest technology.

I wish you a very fruitful and enjoyable career as an Accounts Payable/Purchase Ldeger Clerk and if our paths happen to cross somewhere on this planet, come over and say hi. That would be wonderful.

Thanks,

Sterling

"The greatest thing anyone can do for God and for man is to pray".

S. D. Gordon

ABOUT THE AUTHOR

Sterling Libs FCCA trained as a Chartered Accountant and has written several practical accounting books that have helped many accounting students and graduates in their accounting career journeys to getting accounting jobs. He studied and qualified for his professional accountancy career in London England and is now a Fellow of the Association of Chartered Certified Accountants. He currently lives and works in London, United Kindom.

Sterling is pragmatic, motivational and hard working. He has been very instrumental in training many accounting students, and graduates in gaining work-based practical accounting experience and many of his trainees have been able to get accounting jobs in the UK and abroad. His passion for practical accounting and training is profound, and he loves mentoring individuals to discover, develop and deploy their talents and gifts to make the world a better place for all.

He is passionate about inspiring confidence for work, and life in general, among all those he meets and interacts with.

STERLING
LIBS

www.ingramcontent.com/pod-product-compliance
Lightning Source LLC
Chambersburg PA
CBHW041454210326
41599CB00005B/248